COUNSELING
CRIMINAL
JUSTICE
OFFENDERS

COUNSELING CRIMINAL JUSTICE OFFENDERS

RUTH E. MASTERS

SAGE Publications
International Educational and Professional Publisher
Thousand Oaks   London   New Delhi

For information address:

 SAGE Publications, Inc.
2455 Teller Road
Thousand Oaks, California 91320
E-mail: order@sagepub.com

SAGE Publications Ltd.
6 Bonhill Street
London EC2A 4PU
United Kingdom

SAGE Publications India Pvt. Ltd.
M-32 Market
Greater Kailash I
New Delhi 110 048 India

Printed in the United States of America

Library of Congress Cataloging-in-Publication Data

Masters, Ruth E.
    Counseling criminal justice offenders / Ruth E. Masters.
        p.   cm.
    Includes bibliographical references and index.
    ISBN 0-8039-5532-4.   —   ISBN 0-8039-5533-2 (pbk.)
    1. Social work with criminals—United States.   2. Criminals—
Counseling of—United States.   3. Criminals—Rehabilitation—United
States.   I. Title.
HV7428.M3   1994
365'.66—dc20   94-5922

        97 98 99 00 01 10 9 8 7 6 5 4

Sage Production Editor: Astrid Virding

Contents

*This book is lovingly dedicated
to my husband, Skip, and my daughter, Taya.*

Preface

This book grew out of demands for teaching materials for a course in criminal justice counseling that I have been teaching to students at the California State University at Fresno since 1972. Most of the students who counsel offenders in criminal justice settings are not highly trained, skillful, licensed psychologists but are simply individuals to whom corrections has given a job. This book is intended for anyone who finds himself or herself counseling offenders on the front lines as a result of employment in the criminal justice system.

Over the years, a number of books have been published on the subject of correctional or criminal justice counseling. Each book has emphasized different aspects of counseling in criminal justice settings. Some emphasized modalities and treatment of the offender. Others emphasized effective counselor attitudes and therapeutic relating. Still others emphasized the counseling process, strategies, and intervention techniques. To date no book has given an adequate picture of offenders, their problems, and the problems criminal justice counselors face. To teach my course, I had to draw from different sources. And most of the sources tended to be too "theoretical," often stuffing the reader with abstractions and facts that had little to do with the reality of the criminal justice offender. I realized that there was a need for a practical text that would meet the unique needs of criminal justice students and better prepare them for interfacing and working with offenders.

Counseling Criminal Justice Offenders is designed to provide students and criminal justice workers with an understanding of (a) the criminal justice offender and his or her problems; (b) the counseling process, including laws criminal justice counselors must know; (c) proven modalities that have stood the test of time in American corrections; and (d) appropriate and effective counselor attitudes. The book takes the stand that empathy, caring, and the ability to listen well are critical for the criminal justice counselor.

Another objective of the text was to help students and criminal justice employees better interface with offenders. Counselees, including offenders, grow when people listen to them. The final objective was to develop a text with an understandable format that enhanced student learning and problem solving. Each chapter begins with "Chapter Highlights" and "Key Terms" and ends with matching exercises and discussion questions.

This book is divided into six chapters. Chapter 1 contains discussions about basic counseling concepts and important issues that counselors must grapple with. Chapter 2 contains discussions about the kinds of problems offenders tend to have. Chapter 3 deals with laws and legal considerations criminal justice counselors must keep in mind. Chapter 4 deals with the various and assorted counseling modalities used in the criminal justice field. Chapter 5 explains the counseling process and what counselors might expect to occur during counseling sessions. Last, Chapter 6 presents the findings of some of the counseling effectiveness research studies that have been done.

A few acknowledgments are appropriate. I am indebted to many people, especially the offender, for my own professional development in the field of criminal justice. I would like to extend special thanks and gratitude to John R. Payne, Lester Pincu, Robert Perez, James McCabe, Cliff Roberson, Eric Hickey, Holly Perez, and Harvey Wallace and to Rudolph Alexander and Denny C. Langston for reviewing the book.

Contributors

Lester Pincu
Department of Criminology
California State University, Fresno

Robert F. Perez
Department of Criminology
California State University, Fresno

Understanding Criminal Justice Counseling

CHAPTER HIGHLIGHTS

- Effective criminal justice counseling depends on an understanding of principles, concepts, and nomenclature.

- Criminal justice counseling can occur individually and in groups and with adults and juveniles.

- Criminal justice counseling happens at local, state, and federal levels and in private corrections agencies.

- At the heart of criminal justice counseling philosophy is the idea of protection of society.

- The concept of the protection of society in criminal justice counseling theory raises the issue of whether counselors in the criminal justice field can treat offenders.

- The terms *rehabilitation, treatment, cure,* and *client* have developed new meanings over the years for the criminal justice counselor.

- Today's criminal justice counseling rhetoric is more realistic than rhetoric of the past.

- Counseling supervision today involves surveillance of the offender.

- Today offenders take an active role in designing their counseling and treatment plans.

- The terms *counseling* and *therapy* are often used synonymously in criminal justice settings.

- There are enigmatic and meticulous distinctions between criminal justice counseling and therapy.

- Counselors in the criminal justice system play many roles.

- Many roles criminal justice counselors play have inherent dilemmas and conflicts that counselors must take into account.

- Burnout is a common problem for criminal justice counselors.

- Criminal justice counselors find themselves in ethical situations that do not have clear-cut rights and wrongs.

- Criminal justice counselors should avoid dual relationships with offenders, as they have the potential to impair the counseling relationship.

KEY TERMS

– **Criminal justice counseling**

– **Protection of society**

– **Criminal justice client**

– **Rehabilitation**

– **Treatment**

– **Medical model**

– **Supervision**

– **Communication**

– **Criminal justice therapy**

– **Closure**

– **Criminal justice counseling roles**

– **Transference**

– **Countertransference**

– **Burnout**

– **Offender self-determination**

– **Dual relationships**

– **Reintegration**

INTRODUCTION

Before an understanding of counseling in the criminal justice field can be found, we need to come to grips with some of the principles, truths, concepts, and nomenclature of criminal justice counseling. Criminal justice counseling takes place in a variety of modes and settings. Counseling can be offered on an individual basis or in a group. It occurs in prisons, probation agencies, parole agencies, diversion programs, group homes, halfway houses, prerelease facilities, and to some extent, U.S. jails. Counseling is available to adults and juveniles at the local, state, federal, and private levels (Bennett, Rosenbaum, & McCullough, 1978, pp. 13-14). To understand criminal justice counseling philosophy, we must have a knowledge of the concepts of protection of society, rhetoric, supervision, and communication as they relate to counseling. The counselor must also understand the meaning of the terms *counseling* and *therapy*. A discussion of selected roles a criminal justice counselor plays and the problems inherent within such roles creates awareness of the kinds of situations the counselor may encounter. Finally, the chapter ends with discussions of counselor burnout and ethical considerations the criminal justice counselor must face. In the following pages, the term *counselor* is used to refer to the criminal justice counselor and the term *offender* is used to refer to the counselee.

> **❝Society still demands, first and foremost, protection over treatment efforts on the part of counselors in the criminal justice system.❞**

PROTECTION OF SOCIETY

At the heart of criminal justice counseling philosophy is protection of society. *Protection of society* is a generic term that refers to protecting the community from the offender. From the beginning of American corrections, citizens, religionists, and the psychiatric profession alike demanded social conformity from offenders and that society be protected from criminals. This principle has remained intact and has not changed over the years. American society still demands, first and foremost, protection of society over treatment efforts on the part of counselors in the criminal justice system. This is what makes criminal justice counseling distinct from other types of counseling.

Counselors from all disciplines, including criminal justice, share similar knowledge, principles, procedures, and training. Educational counselors, psychiatrists, psychologists, marriage and family counselors, and others are not bound, in all situations, to put protection of society before individual treatment of their clients. In specific situations, laws force counselors not working in criminal justice settings to put protection of society ahead of client treatment and require counselors to breach counselor/client confidentiality by reporting what goes on in counseling. For example, in many states, such as California, law requires counselors to notify authorities and/or intended victims of clients who discuss intended harm to someone. Counselors are also required to break confidentiality and report situations in which the counselee is in danger of harming himself or herself. Crimes that counselors are required by law to report when they learn of them in therapy sessions are child neglect; emotional, sexual, and physical child abuse; and elder abuse. In addition, non-criminal justice counselors are not bound to report other crimes that they learn clients have committed before entering counseling, unless clients are using counseling to get away with the crime. Apart from such specific situations, the philosophy of counseling in general makes the client and his or her "wellness" the most important goals in the treatment process. This is not the case in criminal justice counseling. The most important goal in the treatment process becomes protection of society, and the client's treatment becomes a goal that must be pursued within this context. Any information that comes up in criminal justice counseling that the counselor deems important may be shared and reported. A rationale for this difference is that the offender as a result of conviction has lost rights that other citizens retain.

The trend beginning in the late 1970s of probation and parole officers carrying firearms is an illustration of the protection of society principle. The arming of probation and parole officers was initially defended to ensure the safety of criminal justice personnel not to protect others in the community. Today, however, many probation and parole officers when asked the purpose of their firearms respond that it helps them protect themselves and the community. The recent trend of probation and parole officers carrying firearms also raises several important questions about the viability of counseling under such conditions. Can counselors be armed and provide treatment? Can counselors with the power to lock a person up develop the trust necessary to successfully counsel offenders? Can counselors with power to determine an offender's freedom provide the environment necessary for offenders to feel free to open up and honestly share their problems? Can counselors accomplish the dual correctional demands of protection of society and treatment of the offender?

RHETORIC

The term *rhetoric* refers to the literary uses of language in prose or verse. All disciplines to some extent have unique uses of language. Most readers are familiar with criminal justice terms such as *joint, man, heat, bull,* and so forth. Criminal justice counseling also has its own terminology. The terms *rehabilitation, treatment, cure,* and *client* hold specific meanings for the criminal justice professional.

Rehabilitation

When I first began teaching criminal justice counseling courses in the early 1970s, I talked a lot about rehabilitating criminal justice clients. It was assumed that if students were taught the proper attitudes, skills, and ideas, they could become probation officers, parole officers, institutional counselors, and the like and change the behavior of offenders to whom they were assigned. Rehabilitation meant changing behavior. As soon as students were employed in the criminal justice system, reality set in. They learned quickly that the acquisition of excellent counseling attitudes, skills, and ideas was not enough to change the offender's behavior, attitudes, and values.

Over time, the term *rehabilitation* in the criminal justice field has taken on more realistic meanings. A useful definition of rehabilitation is "the result of any planned intervention that reduces an offender's further criminal activity, whether that reduction is mediated by personality, behavior, abilities, attitudes, values, or other factors" (Sechrest, White, & Brown, 1979, p. 4). Change that is derived from maturation or intimidation is excluded from the definition.

Today rehabilitation has come to refer to casework intervention strategies that counselors employ to help offenders achieve law-abiding behavior. Offenders are seen as responsible for their own behavior and choices within the alternatives available to them. The counselor's role is to expand the range of alternatives for the client. The counselor helps the offender adjust to society by casework interventions and strategies that expand the offender's alternatives.

Rehabilitation, in the sense that offenders change behaviors, attitudes, and values, does occasionally take place in criminal justice settings. Today it is assumed that the counselor is not solely responsible for such change (Peoples, 1975). It is the offender himself or herself who is responsible. It is my opinion that for rehabilitation to occur several factors must be present. First, the offender must be in excruciating pain. This pain can be either physical or emotional. Second, the offender must be at his or her rock bottom. The concept of rock bottom is subjective and can be defined only by the person going through the experience. Sometimes it appears that offenders who loose jobs, family, financial stability, status in the community, and so forth have hit their bottom many times. Why then do they continue to engage in criminal activity? An explanation is that they have not yet hit their rock bottom, the point at which the offender says, "I have nowhere else to go." The student should recognize that there

> **❝No counselor can rehabilitate an offender, unless the offender wants to be rehabilitated.❞**

are people who seem to have a limitless bottom, and these people never change. This is a reality that must be faced by every professional working in the criminal justice system. Last, for rehabilitation to occur, the offender must be motivated to change. If a person is not motivated to change even though the person has hit rock bottom and is in horrendous pain, change will not occur. It is in the area of motivation that counselors can be empowering to offenders. The term *rehabilitation* is frequently used by criminal justice counselors today, but it is recognized that no counselor can rehabilitate an offender, unless the offender wants to be rehabilitated.

A popular goal in modern criminal justice counseling that is related to rehabilitation is reintegration. Reintegration refers to helping the offender readjust and fit into the community. Many criminal justice practitioners have come to believe the idea of changing an offender is difficult and/or impossible. A more manageable goal for the counselor is to help the offender smoothly adjust to society. It is believed that if the offender is helped to reintegrate, then the offender will be less likely to recidivate and the community/society is best served.

Treatment

The concept of treatment in the criminal justice setting parallels the development of the medical model of treatment during the 19th century (Lehman, 1975). The medical model provided a framework for identifying, diagnosing, and treating offenders (Lester & Braswell, 1987). Medical model concepts were developed as a result of working with medical illnesses, and then they were applied to behavioral and mental problems. The model saw criminality as an illness similar to a physical disease. Offenders were viewed as sick, and the criminal justice system's job was to treat them, make them better, and return them to society as law-abiding citizens. The counselor studied the offender, attempted to make an accurate diagnosis, and developed a treatment plan. Face-to-face interaction with counselors, education, vocational training, and religious instruction were considered treatment. Today, with hindsight, we know that most offenders are not sick in the medical sense of the word and counseling, education, vocational training, and/or religious instruction do not ensure law-abiding behavior. Counselors frequently use the term *treatment,* and it normally refers to the application of programs offered to offenders.

Cure

In the not too distant past it was assumed that the corrections component of the criminal justice system would treat and ultimately cure offenders—in other words, prevent the offender from recidivating. The term *corrections* means "to fix and/or cure" and has its roots in the medical model. Just as an antibiotic can cure infection, correctional programs were thought of as curing criminality. According to Satir (1967), cure occurred when the person developed new values and attitudes. Today most of us recognize that criminality is not a disease. We understand the problems inherent in such logic, and criminal justice counselors shy away from the use of the term *cure.* Such a term misleads us into thinking offenders can be cured, if only we could find the correct medication. Our experience has shown us that if programs could cure, then recidivism would be a thing of the past.

Client

Offenders have been known as clients, counselees, offenders, parolees, probationers, cons, ex-cons, felons, criminals, charges, patients, and so forth. The term *patient* is not used in most criminal justice settings today. *Patient* is a term that had its roots in the medical model. During the 1950s and 1960s, it became popular to call offenders "clients." Today it is popular for counselors to refer to their charges as offenders, residents, inmates, parolees, probationers, and sometimes clients, depending on the setting of counseling. How correctional counselors refer to offenders relates to the politics and ideology of the criminal justice system at any given point in time. For the purposes of this book, I have chosen to use the generic terms *offender* and *counselee* to refer to the person being counseled.

SUPERVISION

The meaning of criminal justice counseling supervision has changed over the years. In the past, counseling supervision meant to not work with or treat the offender. Counselors assumed reactive stances and provided little more than surveillance, which is frequently considered a police responsibility. Counselors took no initiative to help offenders solve their problems. Offenders were left to their own devices to work difficulties out.

Today, the concept of supervision has changed in theory, but economic and political realities have created situations in which counselors are again forced to do little more than surveillance and policing. Counselors are taught in colleges, universities, and agencies to work with, treat, and be proactive advocates for offenders, but burgeoning caseloads and lack of counseling personnel have prevented counselors from doing these things. Counselors in criminal justice fields often feel frustrated because they are unable to work with offenders from a treatment standpoint. Counselors today want to be proactive in spotting potential problems with offenders, assist in the offender's adjustment to society and reintegration process, and facilitate the offender's development of a law-abiding lifestyle. The gap between what counselors are taught to do and what they can do frequently leads to disillusionment, stress, and burnout.

COMMUNICATION

In the past, criminal justice counseling did not involve dialogue with offenders. Monologue or one-way communication was the rule. The counselor told the offender what to do and the offender did it or suffered the consequences. The counseling relationship was not reciprocal or collaborative in that the offender was not allowed to take an active role in his or her counseling plan.

Today, dialogue, two-way communication, collaboration, and reciprocity between the offender and counselor are the norm. Most counselors want to participate in the offender's correction by being proactive and anticipating offenders' needs. Today's criminal justice counseling philosophy assumes that the offender is an active participant in his or her counseling plan. It is also assumed that offenders must be self-determining of their futures. Without offender involvement in counseling plans, counseling goals are rarely accomplished. Offenders today are given choices and alternatives from which to choose as opposed to the past when counselors told offenders what to do, how to do it, and when to do it. Current criminal justice counseling philosophy holds that society's protection is most likely to occur if the counselor through the use of counseling strategies assists the offender in his or her personal growth and satisfaction (Peoples, 1975). Table 1.1 summarizes some of the changes that have occurred in criminal justice counseling.

COUNSELING VERSUS THERAPY

The terms *counseling* and *therapy* are at times used interchangeably by counselors. There is a very fine line between the two, and the result of both is to assist the offender in behavior, attitude, and value change, positive mental health, problem solving, personal effectiveness, and responsible decision making (Hatcher, 1978). To complicate the problem of distinguishing between the two processes, there are job opportunities for both counselors and therapists in the criminal justice system that frequently sound the same. It becomes a futile exercise to try to separate the two processes, and some authors are of the opinion that we are spinning our wheels if we try to define them (Lester &

TABLE 1.1. Comparison of Past and Present Criminal Justice Counseling Principles

Past	Present
Protection of society	Protection of society
Unrealistic rhetoric	Realistic rhetoric
Autocratic supervision	Supervision allows for offender self-determination
One-way communication	Reciprocal communication
Reactive counselor	Proactive counselor

Braswell, 1987). Nonetheless, the following discussion attempts to illuminate how the terms are sometimes used by criminal justice professionals.

Counseling and therapy can differ in the approach taken with offenders. Counseling is mostly present oriented in that it deals with current issues and situations that impact the offender. It is concerned with immediate problem resolution, crisis intervention, and here-and-now reality concerns. On the other hand, therapy is more likely to be concerned with the offender's past, present, and future issues. Therapy takes into account all realms of the offender's life. As a result, therapists frequently spend a great deal of time examining childhood events. Criminal justice therapists are also more likely to emphasize long-term attitude, behavior, and value changes as well as immediate problem resolution.

Counseling is often of shorter duration than criminal justice therapy. Immediate problems generally can be resolved within a specific time frame, whereas, attitudes, values, and behaviors often take many years and perhaps a lifetime to change. The current determinate sentencing trend works against long-term therapy in criminal justice settings.

Therapists tend to work with offenders on a frequent, ongoing basis. Counselors want to see offenders regularly, but due to large caseloads and time constraints, they generally settle for "putting out fires."

Counselors often do not get to see closure—the end or conclusion of the therapeutic process. Probation and/or parole are often terminated before counselors are finished with offenders. Therapists are more likely to experience closure with clients because they work with them frequently, longer, and deal with a broader range of issues than counselors.

TABLE 1.2. Comparison of Criminal Justice Therapy and Counseling

Therapy	Counseling
Past, present, and future oriented	Mainly present oriented
Duration is long term	Duration shorter
Closure likely	Closure unlikely
Specialists	Generalists

Criminal justice therapists tend to be specialists, often trained in one or two major modalities. Counselors tend to be generalists and are more likely to use any modality or therapeutic technique that works and is in keeping with the counselor's philosophy. Criminal justice counselors have a wide range of general knowledge but are masters of none. They reach into their grab bag of therapeutic techniques and attempt to find one that works with offenders. If they are lucky, through the process of elimination, they will eventually find something that works. Table 1.2 compares some features of therapy and counseling.

ROLES CRIMINAL JUSTICE COUNSELORS PLAY

Criminal justice counselors are players of many roles. In the course of a day the counselor may be called on to play myriad emotionally taxing roles with offenders. Each of the roles a counselor may need to play can influence the counseling relationship in dramatic and subtle ways. The more positively the counselor handles the stresses and strains the roles produce, the more effectively he or she will deal with offenders and the less likely he or she will be to experience counselor burnout.

The following list of roles criminal justice counselors play is not exhaustive but representative.

1. Cop/police officer
2. Friend
3. Confidant
4. Adviser
5. Teacher

6. Moral guider
7. Parent/nurturer
8. Change agent
9. Crisis intervener
10. Role model
11. Consultant
12. Social influencer
13. Resource broker/advocate
14. Problem manager

Each of the identified roles poses certain inherent dilemmas for counselors. It is important for counselors to be aware of such dilemmas so that they can be better prepared for dealing with problems that emerge in the counseling relationship.

Cop

It is the role of cop or police officer that separates criminal justice counseling from all other types of counseling. As a result of this, criminal justice counseling has been referred to as coercive counseling. Usually, the counselor carries a badge that enables him or her to arrest and incarcerate offenders. The counselor may carry handcuffs, leg and body chains, electronic surveillance bracelets, and even firearms. As mentioned earlier in this chapter, some authorities are of the opinion that effective counseling relationships cannot be developed under such conditions. A rationale for their position is that offenders normally do not come to the counselor voluntarily. Another rationale is that offenders will be reluctant to be honest with counselors if they know that honesty may lead to arrest and loss of freedom, and as a result, we can only go so far in helping offenders. Offenders will feel free to open up to counselors about superficial problems that have nothing to do with criminality but will not open up to counselors about problems directly related to criminality, because the offenders are afraid of reprisal. Trust is considered a key to effective counseling. Many authorities are of the belief that as long as the counselor plays the cop role, trust and effective counseling cannot exist.

Friend

The friend role can cause difficulties for the criminal justice counselor. Good friends sometimes share qualities of a good counselor and/or therapist. Both friends and counselors can be good listeners who provide for talk and release of feelings. Both can be supportive, concerned, warm, involved, genuine, caring, sympathetic, and empathetic, and both can relieve feelings of isolation and hopelessness that often accompany depression and anxiety. Nevertheless, there are major distinctions between the role of counselor and friend. Counseling and friendship differ with respect to objectivity, privacy, training, and undivided attention.

Objectivity

Criminal justice counselors must always remain objective, or fair decision making about an offender can be jeopardized. The counselor's job is to help the offender grow by analyzing, challenging, and revealing where the offender's vision is skewed. Counselors need to be impartial observers who can identify and point out patterns in offenders' lives. Friends are not impartial observers, because we generally choose friends who are like us and see things the way we do. In addition, friends accept us despite our faults and frequently take our sides whether we are right or wrong. We also temper differences that arise in a friendship so as to retain the comfort of friendship. We seek comfort, vindication, esteem, and support from friends, not analysis. Therefore, it is not easy to challenge a friend's viewpoint. It should also be noted that we are more likely to play the role of friend with offenders who are similar to us than with offenders who are different from us. When we find ourselves playing the friendship role with an offender, our ability to make impartial, objective decisions about him or her is threatened. If it is necessary to remove an offender from society, such a decision can become excessively painful and difficult for the counselor. Sometimes offenders realize that if counselors become their friends, they may have greater power over the decisions that are made about them. Friendships are also relationships with strong emotional components. When a counselor becomes emotionally involved with offenders, objectivity is impossible.

Privacy

Privacy and confidentiality with a counselor are guaranteed and, in most states, are protected by law (see Chapter 3 for a discussion of laws related to criminal justice counseling). In criminal justice counseling, the concept of privacy is somewhat different from the concept of privacy in non-criminal justice counseling and therapy. Because criminal justice counselors frequently have law enforcement powers, they tend to share information learned in counseling sessions with other criminal justice professionals, only if the information can prevent law violations and protect the community. Privacy is rarely ensured with friends, for human nature mitigates against it. Friends who share touchy problems with friends and ask for privacy often find themselves disappointed. Friends feel for suffering friends. This frequently creates a need on the part of the friend to share the problem with others.

Training

Friends are usually good at attacking symptoms, not causes. Generally, friends can get you through low periods, but few friends are equipped by education and/or experience to attack underlying causes of problems. Even if a friend is a trained professional, emotional involvement makes him or her the worst person to help. A subjective person is usually too close to a situation and hence not helpful. An emotionally involved friend often expects too much too soon. Emotional involvement is one reason why counselors and therapists do not work with their own family members and why surgeons do not operate on family members.

Undivided Attention

In a counseling relationship, the offender is ensured of the counselor's undivided attention. It is the counselor's job to listen, help, and give. The relationship is not reciprocal. In private counseling, the client frequently purchases the right to seek as much help as is needed. There are few corresponding obligations on the part of counselees. On the other hand, friendships are reciprocal relationships. Friends must get as well as give. To repeat, counseling and therapy relationships are not reciprocal. The counselor's job is to give to the offender, and the offender's job is to take from the counselor. If the counselor gets anything from the relationship, it is in the knowledge that he or she has done everything possible to help the offender. Counseling relationships are not personal friendships. Friendships are reciprocal. Both parties give and take at times.

Confidant

The definition of a confidant is one to whom secrets are confided. Counselors and therapists working in private sectors and non-criminal justice settings frequently become confidants for their counselees. For counselees, the sharing of sometimes shameful secrets becomes therapeutic, especially when the counselor accepts the person unconditionally and without reprisal. In the criminal justice setting, the confidant role is much more difficult for the counselor. For example, if a parolee has a parole condition of no drinking and confides to his or her parole agent that he or she drank a glass of champagne at a friend's wedding reception, the parole agent must take action. The action taken could be as little as a reprimand, depending on the circumstances.

Adviser

In the adviser role, the counselor gives advice to offenders. This role has its difficulties in that counselors are taught that advice giving is a poor way of responding to offenders (Egan, 1990). A rationale for the avoidance of advice giving by counselors is that offenders seldom listen and do what counselors tell them to do. Furthermore, offenders frequently get defensive and angry when they are told something they do not want to hear. Advice giving can also be presented with a preachy, self-righteous, omnipotent attitude on the part of the counselor. This can be a turn-off for the counselee. Last, mainstream counseling theory assumes that no human being, not even a trained counselor, can know for sure what is best for another person.

If we look to the *American College Dictionary* (1970, p. 276) for the meaning of the word *counsel,* several meanings are established. One meaning is "advice, opinion or instruction given in directing the judgment or conduct of another," and another is "to urge the doing or adoption of." In reality, I believe it is impossible for any counselor to abstain totally from any form of advice giving. Advice giving may be subtle, covert, and veiled, but it forms the basis of the modalities counselors use to counsel offenders and, as a result, is always present.

There are differences between advice giving with the impact of a strong command and advice giving with the impact of a possibility to be considered. The former is likely to be coercive and the latter is not; therefore, the offender is more apt to listen to the latter.

Teacher

Sometimes criminal justice counselors assume the role of teacher. In the teacher role, the counselor instructs and provides the offender with information. An example would be the counselor helping an offender prepare for a job interview. Sometimes counselors have to instruct offenders in how to fill out job applications and how to dress properly. A problem with this role is that sometimes counselors do not have the expertise that an offender might need.

Moral Guider

The role of the moral guider can present the criminal justice counselor with difficult problems. Ideally, counselors must not bring their morals and values to the counseling relationship, and forcing offenders to accept the counselor's values is considered a taboo. In reality, however, counselors can never totally leave their values behind. Values may be well controlled in counseling sessions but are still operative. Most criminal justice counselors see offenders whose values approximate their own or, in the counseling process, change to approximate their own as better adjusted than offenders whose values are not similar to the counselor's. An example of how the criminal justice counselor can be thrust into the role of moral guider is the case of Sandy, a parolee on my caseload a number of years ago.

Sandy, a young recently paroled woman with a heroin problem, contacted me by telephone. From the sound of her voice, she was upset and in a state of crisis. She wanted to meet with me as soon as possible. As I talked with her, I learned that she was frightened by the feelings she was having for another woman. During our conversation she kept repeating that while she was incarcerated she had never considered engaging in homosexual activities. She had a young child and had always been attracted to men. She kept asking me what she should do.

She wanted to know if it was morally right for her to pursue the relationship. As a counselor, how would you counsel Sandy? What values relative to the situation would you bring to the counseling relationship? Could you avoid imposing your moral attitudes on the parolee?

Parent/Nurturer

Criminal justice counselors, whether counseling juveniles or adults, often find themselves in the role of a parent or nurturer. Offenders who are hurting want care, concern, rapport, and support from counselors. In the parent role, being nice is not always in the best interest of offenders. Sometimes good parents must be tough, firm, and set limits. As a result, this can be perceived by offenders as authoritarian and can result in problems such as rebellion.

Another problem that can emerge in the parent role is transference, the unconscious identification of the counselor by the offender with someone in the offender's past. Freud was the first to identify transference in psychoanalysis. Transference is a complex phenomenon that involves the offender projecting onto the counselor strong early childhood feelings, attitudes, and behaviors that are really meant for mother, father, and/or parental surrogates. The strong feelings operate just below the surface and can emerge in myriad indirect forms (Shulman, 1979). Transference relationships are usually intense, and the offender relates and reacts to the counselor as if the counselor were a mother, father, and/or parental surrogate. The offender confuses the counselor's identity with the identity of past figures, usually significant authority figures. Whenever an offender unconsciously reenacts in his or her relationship with a counselor feelings, attitudes, behaviors, wishes, and/or experiences involving the offender's parents or some other significant authority figure from the past, transference occurs. The closer the relationship between the offender and counselor, the more likely transference.

A sign that transference is occurring between the offender and counselor is an emotional overreaction on either party's part. Countertransference, a transferential reaction toward an offender by a counselor, can also occur. Transference in counseling relationships should always be dealt with honestly and counselors should strive not to get caught up in it. Normally, the objects of transference are close authority figures, and criminal justice counselors are prime targets. Finally, counselors must be aware of and watch for transference in counseling because it could possibly lead to ethical problems for the counselor, for example, sexual involvement with offenders.

Change Agent

The change agent role assumes that the criminal justice counselor is in an excellent position to assist the offender in making the necessary life changes that will prevent recidivism. One of the major problems with this role is that sometimes no matter what counselors do for offenders, they continue to break the law. This can lead to frustration and disappointment on the counselor's part.

Crisis Intervener

A great deal of the criminal justice counselor's time is spent in the crisis intervener role. In fact, as criminal justice budget problems worsen, caseloads increase, and agency policies become reactive as opposed to proactive, many counselors will be forced to do primarily crisis work. As a crisis intervener, the counselor is dealing with offenders' intense emotional reactions and inabilities to cope. When offenders are in crisis, they are not always rational, coherent, and/or able to communicate and function. Dealing with people in this state takes a lot of energy and is emotionally taxing. It can also be dangerous, because the counselor cannot predict what the offender might do. There are specific ways to handle and counsel a person in crisis (see Chapter 4 for a discussion of the crisis intervention modality.)

Role Model

Criminal justice counselors sometimes find themselves as role models. Being a role model can be precarious for the counselor. As long as the counselor lives up to the images, expectations, and fantasies of the offender, then this role provides the counselor with a great deal of social influence and power over the offender. I have seen offenders so taken with counselors that they might imitate hairstyles, clothing, makeup, language style, and so forth. It makes no difference whether the offender is a juvenile, adult, male, or female. Being a role model gives the counselor power and leverage over the offender. The offender identifies with and tries to please the counselor. In a sense, the counselor becomes a demigod or superior person and is put on a pedestal in the eyes of the offender. The counselor is perceived as a person without human frailties and who always handles life's problems in a positive manner. If the counselor fails to meet the offender's expectations, then the power, influence, and leverage immediately disappears. Once the counselor falls from grace in the offender's eyes, normally trust disappears, and the relationship cannot be repaired. The counselor's credibility is lost. It is important for the counselor not to put himself or herself into positions in which his or her status as a role model could be compromised.

Consultant

The counselor when playing the consultant role listens, observes, collects data, reports observations, teaches, trains, coaches, provides support, challenges, advises, offers suggestions, and advocates (Egan, 1990). Counselors provide specialized information and explain, confer, consider, and deliberate with offenders. The counselor helps the offender sort out problems and figure out effective strategies to solve problems. The rest is left up to the offender. The counselor, in this role, does not take responsibility for the offender's decisions. One danger of this role is that it is easy for the counselor to get caught up in advice giving, and if the offender takes the counselor's advice and things do not work out, the counselor is blamed. Another danger of this role is that the counselor may be perceived by the offender as too detached, detail oriented, objective, and uncaring.

Social Influencer

As a social influencer, the criminal justice counselor has power to influence the offender. The counselor is viewed by the offender as an authority and someone who can convince the offender of the error of his or her ways. Note that the counselor is not put on a pedestal like a role model, but is seen as someone whose opinion is significant and is taken into account by the offender. In the social influencer role, the criminal justice counselor is expected to establish a power base and then use the power base to influence offenders to do whatever is necessary to lead law-abiding lives. Establishing a power base is not a simple matter. Much depends on the offender and how he or she views the counselor. If the counselor is viewed as credible, trustworthy, competent, and attractive, then the counselor may be a social influencer (Egan, 1990).

Resource Broker/Advocate

As a resource broker/advocate the criminal justice counselor identifies and locates community resources that might be helpful to offenders. Then the counselor puts the offender in contact with the community resources that best meet his or her needs. If the offender needs mental health services, educational counseling, vocational counseling, and so forth beyond the scope of the counselor's expertise, a referral to the appropriate community resource is made. As a resource broker, the counselor might depend on the community's resources for the major part of the offender's treatment plan. A problem that might emerge when the counselor plays the resource broker/advocate role is that the offender might feel that the counselor is pawning him or her off to others. As a result, the offender may never develop trust and intimacy, which are necessary for the counselor to deal with other problems the offender may have.

Problem Manager

The goal of the criminal justice counselor in the problem manager role is to assist offenders in more effectively managing problems that prevent them from living happy, productive, and law-abiding lives. The counselor in this role teaches the offender a problem-solving process that can be used whenever problems present themselves. Sometimes, counselors playing this role begin to believe that every problem can be solved. It is not always possible or desirable to eliminate all problems and conflict. Such a belief can lead to frustration and burnout because there are some life situations that have built-in, unresolvable conflicts, for example, a chronically ill relative or an unmarried mother.

CRIMINAL JUSTICE COUNSELING AND BURNOUT

Burnout is commonplace in the helping professions. A conservative estimate would be that between 65% and 75% of those working in the helping professions will experience burnout within the first 3 to 5 years of employment; however, it can be experienced at any point and many times in a career. Burnout can be defined as a psychoemotional state or condition characterized by a cynical, hardened, calloused, or numbed attitude toward the counselor's work. Burnout can also affect the counselor physically. Physical symptoms can manifest themselves in mild fatigue or they can be severe. Some manifestations of counselor burnout are listed below.

> **❝Between 65% and 75% of those working in the helping professions will experience burnout within the first 3 to 5 years of employment.❞**

1. Loss of objectivity toward offender.
2. Belief the offender will never change due to ineffectualness of past criminal justice interventions.
3. Belief that the counselor's professional and personal life will not improve or be any different in the future.
4. Belief that the criminal justice system does not work.
5. Feeling of futility by not being able to find meaningful approaches to the offender.
6. Telling offenders one thing and doing something entirely different, for example, not following through with offenders.
7. Manipulation of offenders.
8. Hiding behind bureaucracy's walls instead of actively working with offenders.
9. Interpreting rules and regulations in such a way that the counselor establishes a role for himself or herself that leaves no leeway in establishing a meaningful relationship with offenders.

10. Detached noninvolvement.

11. Verbalizing interest or stating a desire to help an offender when the counselor is really saying no.

12. Using excuses or methods to avoid the responsibility of telling the offender what the counselor is willing or unwilling to do.

13. Using counseling time to pass pleasantries rather than for the business of counseling.

14. Calling in sick when the counselor is not; taking long weekends (not working on Fridays and Mondays).

15. Slacking off; not working up to potential with offenders and agency.

16. Engaging in self-destructive behaviors such as drinking alcohol more frequently, perhaps while working.

Burnout can be prevented by first becoming aware of it and its symptoms. The counselor can also deal with burnout by identifying what makes him or her grow as a human being. People who continue to grow generally cope better with the realities of their professions and are less likely to become overwhelmed with the negative aspects. The prescription for growth is different for each counselor. For some continuing education is the answer. For others the answer may be in exercise, travel, therapy, socializing with friends, or a combination of activities.

ETHICAL CONSIDERATIONS IN CRIMINAL JUSTICE COUNSELING

The counselor must be aware of moral and ethical obligations to offenders and to criminal justice organizations. Situations without clear-cut rights and wrongs often present themselves to counselors in criminal justice settings. Ethics are codified by national organizations such as the American Psychological Association, American Association for Counseling and Development, and the American Association for Marriage and Family Therapists. It is important for the counselor to feel that his or her conduct and actions are appropriate and in keeping with the standards of his or her profession. Criminal justice counselors must have integrity, scruples, and high standards and must be beyond reproach. There are many opportunities when working with offenders for counselors to taint themselves. As a general rule, true professionalism dictates that the counselor's relationships be restricted to professional services he or she provides offenders. Counseling literature warns counselors to avoid entering dual relationships with counselees, for any dual relationship has the potential of impairing the counselor's judgment or increasing the risk of offender or counselor exploitation (Vinson, 1989). There are probably dual relationships that will not result in problems; however, most are risky. The following sections identify some types of dual relationships criminal justice counselors should avoid at all costs. Awareness of ethical considerations is an important start in keeping counselors honorable. A discussion of the counselor's legal obligations to offenders, organizations, and society can be found in Chapter 3.

Confidentiality

Confidentiality is an ethical term dealing with the offender's right to privacy and differs from the legal term *privileged communication,* which deals with the offender's right to discuss things and not have the information reported in court. Confidentiality of information is considered a basic principle of any counseling relationship. It is considered a building block to trust, and without trust counseling can not take place. It is essential that the counselor not share what is heard in counseling sessions unnecessarily; however, the counselor might learn important information that he or she is obligated to report to appropriate authorities (see "Protection of Society," earlier in this chapter). Furthermore, law or agency policy might dictate that certain information be reported (see Chapter 3). The counselor should always maintain confidentiality, when appropriate. It is the counselor's obligation to let the offender know the limits of confidentiality at the time of the first contact, that is, what circumstances would constitute an exception to confidentiality (Monahan, 1980). Sometimes counselors will share information learned in counseling with professionals and colleagues; however, the counselor should never share information unless there is a compelling reason to do so. The counselor should not make unrealistic promises of unqualified confidentiality to establish the climate for good offender relationships. Such practices will destroy relationships when the counselor has to break confidentiality because of the law or agency policy.

Needless to say, sharing information learned in counseling with the offender's family members, employers, and friends is considered equivalent to spreading gossip and is a breach of ethics in the criminal justice, medicine, and mental health fields. Sharing information learned in counseling with inappropriate sources may also result in physical danger for the offender. The basic principle of "do nothing to harm the counselee" is important for the counselor to keep in mind at all times (Ivey, 1991).

Gratuities

Theoretically, the acceptance of gratuities of any sort is considered unethical conduct on the part of the criminal justice counselor. The acceptance of gratuities, no matter how small, binds the counselor to the offender in a different way. Most of the time, the counselor is flattered that an offender thinks enough of him or her to give a gift. The offering of a gift to the counselor can change how the counselor feels about the offender. The acceptance of the gift can change how the counselor acts toward the offender. Once the counselor accepts the gift, a feeling of indebtedness is likely to occur. In short, the acceptance of gratuities makes it hard for counselors to remain objective when important decisions must be made about the offender. Consider the following true story that happened to me while I working as a parole agent.

I was working with a 19-year-old female heroin addict. She was from an upper-middle-class background. The mother was deeply distressed about her daughter's addiction and subsequent criminal involvement. The mother wanted to help her daughter and was an excellent source of information for me. Whenever the mother felt frustrated dealing with her daughter, she would contact me for help. We had many conversations. As the Christmas season approached, the mother felt so filled with gratitude that I had helped her daughter, she made a special trip to present me with homemade baked goods, a nice bottle of wine, and an expensive bottle of perfume. As she presented them to me, she was overcome with tears. I thanked her and told her that I couldn't accept her gifts. She was insistent and refused to take the gifts back. I took the gifts to my supervisor and told him what happened. He suggested that not accepting them might alienate a valuable collateral contact. It is human nature to give back to people who are helpful. Should the counselor reject all attempts offenders make to thank them? Where should the line be drawn? Another story comes to mind in which an inmate offered his prison counselor a fully paid vacation to Mexico in a private jet.

Giving Money and Objects to Offenders

Another problematic situation can arise when the counselor loans money or objects to offenders. The rule should be "Don't loan it unless you are prepared to loose it," and be sure you can honestly loan it unconditionally. If the counselor has expectations of the offender (i.e., to be paid back by a certain date) and if the expectations are not met, the counseling relationship is in jeopardy in that the counselor's feelings can spill over into decisions made about the offender. The loaning of money and objects to friends creates major stresses on relationships in the best of circumstances. The criminal justice counseling relationship where the counselor has tremendous power and authority over the offender can become contaminated quickly. The counselor should exercise great caution in loaning money or objects to offenders.

Entering Business
Relationships With Offenders

Entering a business relationship with an offender can lead to problems, because it creates a dual relationship that may impair the counselor and/or offender's judgment in such a way that the counseling relationship becomes compromised to the point that counseling cannot proceed. Sometimes offenders are employed in a position from which they can offer their counselors goods and services at a reduced price or for free. This situation can be tempting and, on the face, may seem harmless; however, it must be avoided for it contaminates the primary, professional relationship between the counselor and the offender. If the counselor accepts goods and/or services from the offender, the offender then expects leniency from the counselor. Criminal justice agency policy normally prohibits formal and informal business relationships, and such conduct could lead to termination of employment.

Taking Offenders Home

Most people enter helping professions to be of service and help to others in need. When a counselor can resolve problems for offenders, he or she feels good. I have known adult and juvenile parole and probation officers who have given offenders their telephone numbers and have even taken offenders home with them. Taking offenders home creates a dual relationship in which the altruistic, friendly act made by the counselor ends in problems that affect the counseling relationship. The counselor should always check agency policy in regard to sharing telephone numbers and addresses with offenders. In private counseling, it is frequently considered appropriate and necessary to give telephone numbers to offenders in case of crisis. In the criminal justice field, however, the counselor might deal with extremely disturbed and dangerous people. Knowing home telephone numbers and addresses may put the counselor and his or her family at risk. The following story was related to me by a female parole agent.

> A female parole agent had a female parolee who was in transition and did not have a place to stay for 2 days. The parole agent liked the parolee, so after exhausting other residential possibilities she invited the parolee to spend the 2 days in her home. The parolee was an ideal guest; however, a week later the parole agent's house was burglarized. The parole agent could not shake the feeling that the parolee was involved in the burglary; however, there was no evidence to prove it. Could the parole agent make objective decisions regarding the parolee when, in her heart, she felt the parolee was involved in the burglary of her residence?

Giving Favors for Favors

The practice of giving favors for favors (another example of a dual relationship) in criminal justice counseling is not only unethical but can be illegal. Such behavior is bribery and is abuse of the counselor's position as a public servant. These actions totally discredit the counselor and render him or her useless. Such actions also have far reaching effects in that they discredit the criminal justice system as a whole. This practice results in the offender seeing the system and workers within it as corrupt. It is the counselor's responsibility to report any miscarriages of justice observed in the criminal justice system. It is important for offenders to view criminal justice counselors as exemplars who lead honest, law-abiding lives. The law enforcement role of the criminal justice counselor sometimes tempts the counselor to give favors for important information. This practice sullies the counseling process and draws into question the counselor's motives. Therefore, it must be avoided.

Abuse of Power

Criminal justice counselors have a great deal of power over offenders and must not misuse the power vested in them by the state. They have power over the offender's freedom. Their recommendations can result in incarceration or freedom in the community for the offender. They also have power in that they possess intimate psychological information about the offender and sometimes confidential details of an offense. Counselors can cause great difficulty, trauma, and perhaps great physical harm or death for offenders and their families if they were to innocently slip or deliberately share information with the wrong people (Trester, 1981). This type of abuse of power is abominable. Another more subtle type of abuse of power is when the counselor imposes his or her own values and belief systems on the offender (Monahan, 1980). All offenders should be treated fairly, justly, and humanely by the criminal justice counselor.

Sexual Attractions and Romantic Relationships

Sexual attractions between criminal justice counselors and offenders occur. The counseling relationship involves trust, opening up, and sharing of emotions. A bond develops between offender and counselor in effective counseling relationships. The counselor's professional warmth can be misunderstood by offenders, causing attractions and crushes. Counselors must gear their warmth to the offender's needs and not to their own needs (Egan, 1990). They need to learn to care genuinely and on appropriate grounds about offenders.

Sexual or romantic relationships with offenders are examples of dual relationships that are unethical and strictly forbidden. In such relationships, objectivity is always lost. It is the counselor who is held accountable for the development of romantic relationships, for it is the counselor who is the professional and takes advantage of the offender's vulnerability. Whenever such relationships are discovered in criminal justice settings, they normally lead to termination of the counselor.

Counselors may develop attractions for offenders, but must refrain from entering sexual or romantic relationships with offenders. Acting on such attractions is considered a violation of the trust relationship and professional ethics. Counselors who experience such attractions must put them into perspective and deal with them professionally.

Use of "High-Risk/High-Gain" Counseling Techniques

It is a highly questionable practice to use counseling techniques that are based on deceit and manipulation of offenders. Also, counseling techniques that involve sarcasm and asocial responses should be used with extreme care. The counselor should be aware that such techniques are used but can backfire in an instant. Consider the high-risk/high-gain examples two probation officers shared with me.

One probation officer dealt with a young woman who attempted several suicides. He was beside himself because the youngster kept threatening to slash her wrists. He felt that she wanted attention, had no intention of committing suicide, and decided to tell her during a counseling session that if she did it again she should do it right. He was extremely uneasy until the next session with the young woman. She did not attempt suicide again. The probation officer was lucky, for this technique could have easily backfired.

The other probation officer was in the mountains trying to apprehend a delusional, paranoid offender. She took another officer with her as backup. The offender was spotted on a dangerous, mountain trail. The probation officer caught up with the offender who was walking rapidly. The probationer kept looking to his rear and stated that the group of people behind wanted to hurt him. The probation officer saw no one except her backup officer in the distance and instead of correcting the offender's perception, the probation officer said "Oh! You mean them? They're not after you. They're after me." The offender immediately relaxed and the probation officer was able to get the offender the help that he needed.

Needless to say such techniques when they work are remarkable, but when they do not they can backfire and cause greater problems. The criminal justice counselor is warned to use extreme caution with these techniques.

Having Hidden Agendas for Offenders

Hidden agendas are goals counselors have for offenders, but are not shared with them. Counselors with hidden agendas exert pressures on offenders to do things that are never verbalized or agreed on between them. Frequently, this situation is misunderstood and causes anxiety for the offender. Furthermore hidden agendas represent dishonest ways of dealing with offenders and can result in a suspicious and distrusting counseling relationship. Counselors should always be honest in stating their objectives for offenders to avoid such pitfalls.

Offender Self-Determination

Generally speaking, criminal justice counselors are not ethically bound to counsel offenders who reject counseling, no matter how obvious the need for counseling might be. However, if counseling is directly related to the offender's crime, it can be forced on the offender. An example is if an offender pleaded guilty to an assault on his wife and was placed on probation, the probation officer could insist on marital counseling if the probationer was planning to stay in the marriage (Smith & Berlin, 1981).

Counselors must consider a number of self-determination questions. How much conformity to mainstream values am I going to insist on with offenders? How much should I leave my offenders alone to determine their own futures and destinies? When should I interfere with offenders' lives? There is a great deal of gray area in such questions. With experience, counselors will eventually find their own answers to such questions.

In spite of the above, self-determination is considered to be important and strived for in the criminal justice setting. Most counselors believe in the principle of helping offenders do what they want to do as long as it doesn't break the law. It is also important for counselors to help offenders stay in touch with reality in doing what they want to do. Reality has a stubborn quality to it. It narrows the range of reasonable choices open to us. There are biological, economical, and legal realities that good criminal justice counselors must keep in mind when dealing with offender self-determination issues. For example, if a 55-year-old parolee with brain damage came to his or her parole agent and said that he or she wanted to go to college, should the parole agent discuss the realistic problems with the parolee or not interfere?

Counselors should also be aware that frequently others are affected by the offender's self-determination. Offenders have an unseen audience of parents, spouses, children, friends, and so on who are affected by their decisions. The counselor is in a position to know how much the offender depends on his or her significant others and what affects his or her decision making might have on others. Should a counselor allow others to be victimized by an offender's decision making in counseling? An example is the offender who told the counselor that he or she was tired of all the family problems he or she had and decided that the best thing to do would be to end his or her life. Should the counselor stand by and allow the offender to commit suicide? How would such an act affect the offender's family members? Counselors must learn when it is best to do nothing, and when it is best to interfere with an offender's self-determination.

SUMMARY

At the core of criminal justice counseling philosophy is the protection of society. Rhetoric, supervision, and communication in criminal justice counseling has changed over the years. Criminal justice counseling also carries its own meanings for the terms *rehabilitation, treatment, cure,* and *client.* The terms *counseling* and *therapy* are often used interchangeably by counselors. Criminal justice counselors play many taxing roles with offenders. Some selected roles are cop, friend, confidant, adviser, teacher, moral guider, parent, change agent, crisis intervener, role model, consultant, social influencer, resource broker/advocate, and problem manager. Burnout is a common problem in criminal justice careers. Counselors do not have to be victims of burnout if they know what must be done to handle it. Finally, at all times counselors must be aware of their moral and ethical obligations to offenders and criminal justice organizations.

MATCHING KEY TERMS AND DEFINITIONS
Match each key term with the correct definition.

a. criminal justice counseling
b. protection of society
c. criminal justice client
d. rehabilitation
e. treatment
f. medical model
g. supervision
h. communication

i. criminal justice therapy
j. closure
k. criminal justice counseling roles
l. transference
m. countertransference
n. burnout
o. offender self-determination
p. dual relationship
q. reintegration

___ 1. A transferential reaction toward an offender by a counselor.

___ 2. A term referring to the offender projecting onto the counselor strong early childhood feelings, attitudes, and behaviors frequently directed toward parent figures.

___ 3. The myriad customary functions criminal justice counselors perform.

___ 4. The end or conclusion of the therapeutic process.

___ 5. A process leading to the offender's growth.

___ 6. The act of transmitting thoughts, feelings, opinions, and information to others.

___ 7. The view of the offender as sick and criminality a disease.

___ 8. The act of overseeing the actions of offenders.

___ 9. What the counselor assists in to prevent the offender from recidivating.

___ 10. The restoration of the offender from a law-violating to a law-abiding person.

___ 11. The person the criminal justice counselor works with; often called offenders, parolees, probationers, inmates, residents, and so forth.

___ 12. The core concept at the heart of the criminal justice counseling philosophy.

___ 13. Counseling done in local, state, federal, and private criminal justice organizations.

___ 14. A psychoemotional state or condition characterized by a cynical, hardened, calloused, or numbed attitude toward one's work.

___ 15. The offender's right to determine his or her own destiny.

__ 16. Any relationship between counselor and offender that has the potential to impair the counselor's judgment and increase the risk of offender and/or counselor exploitation.

__ 17. The act of helping the offender readjust smoothly to society by fitting into the community.

DISCUSSION QUESTIONS

1. If a parolee with a heroin addiction relapsed, would he or she be able to approach his or her parole agent for assistance without fear of being locked up? Would a person with a drug problem but not a part of the criminal justice system be able to share relapse behavior with his or her counselor without fear of incarceration?

2. Can a criminal justice counselor successfully treat offenders? What are the arguments for and against this position?

3. How have the criminal justice counseling concepts of protection of society, rhetoric, supervision, and communication changed over the years?

4. How are criminal justice counseling and therapy similar? How are they different?

5. What criminal justice counseling roles have the potential of presenting the counselor and offender with difficult dilemmas? How can the counselor minimize such problems?

6. How can a criminal justice counselor identify transference? How should criminal justice counselors handle transference? What types of problems might criminal justice counselors encounter if transference is not identified?

7. What is criminal justice counselor burnout? How does criminal justice counseling burnout manifest itself? What can the criminal justice counselor do to prevent burnout?

8. What ethical considerations are most troublesome for the criminal justice counselor?

REFERENCES

American College Dictionary, The. (1970). Syracuse, NY: Random House.

Bennett, L. A., Rosenbaum, T. S., & McCullough, W. R. (1978). *Counseling in correctional environments.* New York: Human Sciences.

Egan, G. (1990). *The skilled helper: A systematic approach to effective helping* (4th ed.). Pacific Grove: Brooks/Cole.

Hatcher, H. A. (1978). *Correctional casework and counseling.* Englewood Cliffs, NJ: Prentice Hall.

Ivey, A. E. (1991). *Developmental strategies for helpers: individual, family, and network interventions.* Pacific Grove, CA: Brooks/Cole.

Lehman, P. E. (1975). The medical model of treatment: Historical development of an archaic standard. In E. E. Peoples (Ed.), *Readings in correctional casework and counseling* (pp. 47-60). Pacific Palisades, CA: Goodyear.

Lester, D., & Braswell, M. (1987). *Correctional counseling.* Cincinnati, OH: Anderson.

Monahan, J. (1980). *Who is the client? The ethics of psychological intervention in the criminal justice system.* Washington, DC: American Psychological Association.

Peoples, E. E. (Ed.). (1975). *Readings in correctional casework and counseling.* Pacific Palisades, CA: Goodyear.

Satir, V. (1967). *Conjoint family therapy.* Palo Alto, CA: Science & Behavior.

Sechrest, L., White, S. O., & Brown, E. D. (Eds.). (1979). *The rehabilitation of criminal offenders: Problems and prospects.* Washington, DC: National Academy of Sciences.

Shulman, L. (1979). *The skills of helping individuals and groups.* Itasca, IL: Peacock.

Smith, A. B., & Berlin L. (1981). *Treating the Criminal offender* (2nd ed.). Englewood Cliffs, NJ: Prentice Hall.

Trester, H. B. (1981). *Supervision of the offender.* Englewood Cliffs, NJ: Prentice Hall.

Vinson, J. (1989, September-October). Reflections on dual relationships. *The California Therapist, 1*(2), 15-17.

Counseling and
the Criminal Justice Offender

- Criminal justice counselors must access the moral development of the offenders with whom they work.

- Institutionalized offenders frequently have numerous psychosocial issues to resolve in counseling.

- Counselors must give tough love and develop thick skins to work with offenders addicted to alcohol and other drugs.

- Treatment of addicted offenders starts with the offender's willingness to admit that he or she has a problem that cannot be managed without help.

- Counseling psychotic, neurotic, and sociopathic offenders is difficult and taxing for criminal justice counselors.

- In today's world, many criminal justice counselors feel more secure if they have firearms close at hand, just in case they need to defend themselves against violent offenders.

- Offenders frequently come from poor neighborhoods where violence is a way of life.

- Violence is a salient factor of prison life.

- Criminal justice counselors must protect themselves from violence before they can successfully offer counseling services to offenders.

- Females commit less crime than males.

- Female crime tends to be concentrated in the area of economic crime (e.g., shoplifting and burglary) and not crimes against persons.

- Female offenders find prison painful, mainly because it separates them from their children, family, and friends.

- Counselors working with female offenders must be aware that females express greater emotionality than males.

- Periodically, criminal justice counselors are assigned seriously ill offenders.

- AIDS is an illness that is spreading in the population of addict offenders.

- Sickness narrows the offender's ability to focus on counseling issues that are not directly concerned with survival and health.

- Most sex offenders are male.

- Counselors must put aside their negative stereotypes to counsel sex offenders successfully.

- Most offenders must come to terms with resistance in counseling.

- Counselors must be aware of the ways in which they can be set up and manipulated by inmates.

KEY TERMS

- Adolescence
- Puberty
- Identity crisis
- Institutionalized
- State-raised convict
- Polydrug offender
- Dry drunk
- Postaddiction syndrome
- Tough love
- Psychotic offenders
- Neurotic offenders
- Sociopathic offenders
- Subculture of violence
- Pink-collar job
- Pseudofamily
- AIDS
- HIV positive
- Seropositive offender
- Zidovudine
- Prisonization
- Setup
- Infantalize
- Antabuse
- Methadone
- Naltrexone

INTRODUCTION

Criminal justice offenders come in all shapes and sizes. They are male, female, young, and old. They come from a variety of backgrounds, socioeconomic statuses, and ethnic and racial groups. They have many different problems such as limited income, lack of employment, sporadic job attendance, limited education, lack of vocational training, substance abuse, inadequate problem-solving skills, strained family relationships, unpredictable support from family and friends, poor self-esteem, fears, isolation, feelings of hopelessness, manipulative personalities, violent lives, medical concerns, dependence on welfare and criminal justice systems, and fear and distrust of the criminal justice system and agents of it. Some offenders are psychologically disturbed but most have less extreme emotional and coping problems. Some offenders have problems that stem from being incarcerated. Offenders can be separated into one or more of the following categories for discussion purposes:

Young offenders
Adult offenders
Addicted offenders
Disturbed offenders
Violent offenders
Female offenders
Ill offenders
Sex offenders
Resistant offenders
Incarcerated offenders

Within each of these categories, offenders are likely to have specific problems of which criminal justice counselors should be aware. Counselors must be prepared to deal with every type of offender and offender problem that emerges in counseling. This chapter contains discussions of the different types of offenders criminal justice counselors are likely to be assigned, the typical problems that such offenders have, and what the counselor should be aware of and sensitive to when counseling different types of offenders.

YOUNG OFFENDERS

The majority of offenders who commit common crimes typically are between the ages of 16 and 26. Very young children normally do not have the ability or opportunity to commit serious crime, unless older delinquents and/or adult offenders are using them to avoid punishment. By law, younger offenders cannot be prosecuted for some offenses or, if prosecuted, will get minor punishment compared with what the adult offender would receive. Such youngsters can be easy prey for adult offenders. Generally, it is during the early teenage years that young offenders begin to have the capacity for serious crime. It also appears that the earlier a person gets involved with the justice system as an offender, the greater the likelihood that he or she will continue criminal behavior into adulthood (Masters & Roberson, 1991).

Criminal justice counselors should be aware that there are a number of factors that make it difficult to counsel intelligent younger offenders in the juvenile and criminal justice systems. The first factor that makes it difficult to counsel younger offenders is adolescence, the transition period between puberty (the end of boyhood or girlhood) and adult stages of development. In general, adolescence extends from approximately age 14 to 25 in males and 12 to 21 in females. Young offenders are frequently going through physical and emotional changes brought on by entering puberty and adolescence. Hormone levels are rapidly changing, and young people are learning to become independent adults. Adolescence is a time when young people begin to grow away from their parents and adult influence diminishes. Furthermore, in many young offenders' homes good parenting skills are deficient, and as a result, parents have little, if any, influence on their children.

Adolescence is also a time when young people begin to grapple with identity crises and ask questions such as "Who am I?" "What is my place in the world?" and "What am I going to do with my life?" Normally, young people who are struggling to become independent adults find it difficult to give up control over their lives and take advice and counsel from adults let alone counselors in the justice system. If counseling is to be effective, younger offenders must be willing to admit to themselves that their way of doing things is not working, to accept that they are powerless to help themselves with their problems, and to hand over control of their problems to their counselor. The young offender must emotionally and intellectually accept that he or she is in trouble and doing things wrong. Young people in the process of becoming independent are rarely willing or able to admit they are powerless to control their lives themselves and, therefore, hand over control to the counselor.

The second factor that makes it difficult to counsel young offenders is that the decision to seek help from the counselor is rarely, if ever, made by the young offender on his or her own. It usually takes parents, police, and/or courts to bring the young offender to the attention of the juvenile or criminal justice system. Self-referral by young offenders is virtually nonexistent. Most young offenders perceive the source of referral to the juvenile or criminal justice system as the source of trouble, not themselves.

A third factor that makes it difficult to counsel young offenders is their great difficulty in accepting responsibility for their actions. Most young offenders believe that their behavior had no major role in bringing them to the attention of the justice system. In the young offender's mind, it was the police officer's fault or discrimination and not his or her own behavior that led to arrest and entry into the justice system.

A fourth factor that makes it difficult to counsel younger offenders has to do with their limited life experiences. Young people lack life experiences and maturity to draw on, learn from, and gain perspective and wisdom from. The ability to place oneself in the shoes of another (role take) and to think abstractly develops, for most, between 11 and 15 years of age (Inhelder & Piaget, 1958). Until the youngster learns to think abstractly, he or she will find it difficult to draw appropriate conclusions, generalize, and/or learn from experience and punishment.

A fifth factor that makes it difficult to counsel younger offenders is their tendency to live for the here and now and not to be concerned about the future. Young people tend to live in and for the immediate moment and have a devil-may-care attitude about the future. They are concerned with immediate pleasures and material things. Most young people rarely think about what they would like their lives to be like in 5 years. Young people also tend to see themselves as invincible and immortal and, therefore, will take risks and do things that are daring and dangerous. They have little or no fear. It is this mentality that frequently contributes to their involvement in the justice system.

A sixth factor that makes it difficult to counsel younger offenders is that they tend to be excessively committed to their peers and peer pressure (Sutherland & Cressey, 1974). In many cases, negative peer pressure has contributed to the younger offender's difficulties with the justice system. Counselors must be aware that young offenders whose social worlds are devoid of positive and significant figures are especially vulnerable to negative peer pressure. Young people going through adolescence frequently tend to seek the advice of their peers who are going through similar things. Young offenders feel pressured to dress in certain ways, listen to particular types of music, take drugs, and use alcohol. Boys frequently feel additional pressure to establish and demonstrate their masculinity.

Criminal justice counseling, if effective, must include the young offender's peers. Because adolescence is a time kids learn most readily from their peers, they frequently view information received from their peers as being of greater value than information received from adults. Kids are more likely to listen to peers who tell them that they are self-destructive than adult criminal justice counselors who say the same things. Criminal justice counselors should keep in mind that when working with young offenders, group counseling with peers has great potential in diminishing the young offender's isolation, fear, embarrassment, and shame. Young offenders also learn communication skills in peer counseling groups because such groups encourage openness and public sharing of problems. Counseling approaches that focus on the young offender's peers also deal with life problems from many different points of view so that adolescents can come to terms with their problems emotionally.

Peer counseling groups have other advantages too. They are normally run in nonthreatening, positive ways. They zero in on the young offender's feelings, and frequently self-concepts are enhanced as feelings are expressed. Peers allow each other to examine thoughts, attitudes, and behaviors. Peers are not afraid to take a look at personal drug and alcohol use. Last, peer counseling groups can help young people learn leadership skills.

A seventh factor that makes younger offenders difficult to counsel is that younger offenders tend to see the counselor as being more concerned with and committed to the juvenile or criminal justice agency than to the young offenders' needs. Many times young offenders perceive counselors as too willing to turn them in or incarcerate them when they incur a minor infraction as opposed to working with them in the community.

The final factor that makes younger offenders difficult to counsel is that young offenders normally do not have an investment in counseling. Young offenders are not required to pay for their counseling services as a part of their own contribution to self-help. Most juvenile and criminal justice agencies are public, government agencies and as such do not require that the offender pay for services provided. It is my opinion that effective treatment requires strong involvement and self-investment on the part of the young offender. Perhaps if the offender were required to pay for counseling services, he or she would be less likely to take them for granted. In addition, most younger offenders have little to risk and lose when they commit crime. One reason many young offenders do not perceive themselves as having anything to lose is because they come from abusive families or from families in which parents may care deeply about their children but lack parenting skills to handle them. Also, in most cases, punishments are less severe for juveniles, and the courts look to incarceration as the last resort. Adults fear losing jobs, families, social status, and property. Young offenders, for the most part, do not fear losing things because they have nothing to lose.

Most counselors in juvenile and criminal justice systems consider young offenders extremely difficult to supervise and to counsel. Sometimes it is difficult for counselors to get the attention of the young offender. Here's an illustration of these points.

> I remember a young, out-of-control California Youth Authority parolee I placed in juvenile hall for several days to prevent him from using drugs with his peers. While I was driving him home after release, he promised that he would stay home, keep out of trouble, not associate with his neighborhood delinquent peers who contributed to his juvenile justice problems, and obey his curfew. I watched him enter his house after I dropped him off, and then I drove around the block. Within minutes after professing to me that he had learned his lesson, saw the light, and would never get into trouble again, I observed him walking down the street and entering a delinquent peer's home, a peer he swore he would stay away from. Such experiences for counselors can be disheartening, not to mention frustrating, and can lead to burnout.

Criminal justice counselors should avoid counseling approaches that attempt to scare young offenders into change. From time to time, such approaches become popular; however, there is no strong evidence that shows that scare tactics and physical intimidation produce attitude, value, and behavior changes (Finckenauer, 1982). It takes more than scare tactics to deal with people whose problems stem from lives that have lacked love, respect, and belonging.

Counselors should keep in mind the positive aspects of working with young offenders. As young offenders mature, many outgrow their delinquencies. Delinquents *age out* of delinquency as they begin to take on responsibilities. For example, as young offenders find themselves having children of their own and needing to feed, clothe, and shelter them, there is less time and energy for hanging around peers and those engaging in delinquent behavior. Also, young offenders tend to be less rigid in their thinking than adults and are more willing to give new ideas a try. Counselors who have acted as catalysts or role models for younger offenders' lifestyle changes generally find great satisfaction in their work.

ADULT OFFENDERS

One of the most difficult problems that works against the counseling of any adult offender is that many older offenders have been involved with the criminal justice system for years and, as a result, have become dependent on the criminal justice system as a way of life. When this happens, the offender is said to be *institutionalized.* The more time an offender spends incarcerated, the more likely he or she is to become institutionalized. Another term used to describe institutionalized offenders is *state-raised convict,* referring to those who have been reared by the state and, as a result, have spent more of their lives inside juvenile halls, detention centers, training schools, reformatories, jails, and/or prisons than outside in free society (Abbott, 1981). Frequently, state-raised convicts are angry and easily prone to violence (Johnson, 1987).

Kohlberg (1981) felt that offenders could be best understood by studying their moral development. He postulated that an offender's moral development occurs in six distinct stages and that there are marked differences in each stage in regard to thinking and behavior. The six stages are as follows:

1. Stage 1 is characterized by the belief that doing the right thing means obedience to authority and avoidance of punishment.

2. Stage 2 is characterized by the belief that doing the right thing means taking responsibility for oneself and allowing others to take responsibility for themselves.

3. Stage 3 is characterized by the belief that doing the right thing means having positive motives, having concern for others, being able to role take, and identifying with others.

4. Stage 4 is characterized by the belief that doing the right thing means to support society's rules and the welfare of society.

5. Stage 5 is characterized by the belief that doing the right thing is based on the recognition of the idea that there are two sets of rules that must be reconciled: society's rules and individual rights.

6. Stage 6 is characterized by the belief that doing the right thing is an assumed obligation to universal principles that apply to all human beings.

One of Kohlberg's findings was that offenders, compared with nonoffenders of the same social backgrounds, tend to be classified at Stages 1 and 2, whereas nonoffenders tend to be classified at Stages 3 and 4 (Kohlberg & Turiel, 1973). According to Kohlberg, the growth to higher stages of moral development will generally prevent a person from becoming criminal. Criminal justice counselors must take into account the offender's moral development when working with offenders inside or outside of the institution.

When an offender is institutionalized, he or she learns to deal with life in characteristic and frequently unhealthy ways. Criminal justice counselors must be vigilant observers of unhealthy attitudes, behaviors, and values on the part of offenders. Institutionalized offenders are told when to get up, sleep, eat, and be counted. Such regimentation takes everyday decision making out of the hands of the offender and can lead to infantalizing the offender. When a person becomes infantalized, he or she begins to mistrust his or her abilities to make simple decisions about life. Institutionalized offenders are also suspicious and fearful of free society. Many offenders are convinced that life outside of the institution offers no hope. Offenders who have spent many years behind bars do not have job histories and frequently are at a loss to explain to potential employers what they have been doing for, perhaps, numerous years of their life. Institutionalized offenders also feel the prejudice society holds toward them. Another problem is when an offender is away from society for long time periods, it is difficult for him or her to identify with mainstream society. Criminal justice counselors must be aware of issues related to offender institutionalization and be willing and able to deal with them.

Adult offenders are faced with many problems of which counselors must be aware. Regardless, society makes the assumption with adult offenders that they are responsible for their behavior, are old enough to know what they are doing, and understand the consequences of their behavior. In contrast, society assumes young offenders are not totally responsible for their behavior, are not old enough to know what they are doing, and do not fully understand the consequences of their behavior. Finding and maintaining a job; dealing with relationships and society's scorn; and handling anger, alienation, and stress are but a few obvious problems that many offenders face. Minority offenders may have to deal with issues that stem from race and ethnicity. Some adult offenders have intellectual deficiencies to which counselors must be sensitive. Adult offenders must also learn to get along with probation, parole, criminal justice counselors, and others. These people are in positions to help the offender interface with the criminal justice system, and their alienation can create greater problems for the adult offender.

Another problem for the criminal justice counselor is the older or elderly offender. Street crime is primarily a young person's enterprise, but occasionally criminal justice counselors are assigned older offenders. Older offenders sometimes have specific problems that the counselor must be aware of such as medical concerns, disorientation, fear of incarceration, depression, and other assorted concerns.

ADDICTED OFFENDERS

Many offenders are addicted to either alcohol and/or drugs. Some offenders are addicted to alcohol and more than one drug. Offenders who switch drugs are frequently referred to as *polydrug users*. Although addicted offenders usually have a preferred drug of choice, many addicts are not discriminating and will use whatever is available and convenient. Addiction can happen to anyone from any walk of life, and to date, experts have been unable to isolate a single personality type prone to alcoholism and/or drug addiction. Criminal justice counselors must be aware, however, that after addiction occurs, the addict's personality changes and that active addicts do possess similarities in thinking patterns, personality characteristics, and behavioral traits.

There are good reasons for offering counseling to drug and alcohol addicts in the criminal justice system. Both violent and economic crime is linked to drug and alcohol addiction. A prevalent view in society is that addict crime is becoming more violent, as many addicts engage in muggings, armed robberies, and other crimes against persons. A large portion of today's addicts engaged in criminal behavior before they were using narcotics. After addiction, criminality tends to increase in that criminality frequently becomes the addict's primary means of support. It has been estimated that 55% of all arrests and up to 92% of all arrests for violent crimes are associated with alcohol abuse (Taylor, 1984). Homicide; assault; rape; marital violence; and child abuse, neglect, and molestation are associated with high rates of alcohol consumption, and alcohol can have a role in causing a person to commit a crime (U.S. Department of Health, Education, and Welfare [DHEW], 1978). Many studies show that both offenders and victims were drinking at the time of the offense, and victim-precipitated homicide and stabbings are associated with alcohol consumption (DHEW, 1978). Many prison inmates have drinking problems. The counselor must recognize that almost all addicts will eventually be released to the community again. Without treatment, most will offend again.

Alcohol is considered a liquid drug. Yet most literature separates alcoholics from other substance abusers, because alcohol is not against the law for those who are of the legal drinking age; and for those who use alcohol, there is normally no need to interface with criminal subcultures to obtain it. Nevertheless, the dynamics and process of addiction tend to be similar no matter whether the drug of choice is alcohol, other drugs, or a combination of alcohol and other drugs.

Theorists do not know why people become addicted. People probably become addicted to alcohol and drugs for a number of reasons. There are numerous theories as to the cause of addiction. Some theorists believe that people become addicted because of their inabilities to become attached to others and have intimate relationships (Walsh, 1988). Other theorists believe the causes of addiction are the euphoric qualities of drugs; ignorance of long-term use; relief of pain, depression, and anxiety; escape from reality; and peer pressure to be a part of the in-group. No matter what the cause of addiction, addiction prevents the offender from maturing emotionally, and treatment must teach the offender how to handle all emotions without alcohol and/or drugs. Almost all addicted offenders rationalize, deny, project, manipulate, lie, cheat, and steal to obtain and maintain their supply. Criminal justice counselors must understand the addicted offender and how to break through these behaviors in counseling addicted offenders of any age.

Counseling the addicted offender can be trying and difficult. It involves much more than the addict "just saying no." Most addicted offenders will not admit to having a problem, even when their lives have become totally unmanageable. Many will tell counselors that they can control their addiction, even when there is a lot of evidence to the contrary. Treatment frequently forces addicts into making a choice. They can reject alcohol and/or drugs or reject reality, because they do not want to admit that they have lost control to alcohol and/or drugs. It is the criminal justice counselor's job to keep the offender constantly aware of reality and his or her choices. Even after the offender has been sober, clean, and vigilant for some time, old addictive behavior patterns raise their ugly heads and have to be managed. Alcoholics who are no longer drinking but who display past alcoholic behavior patterns are called *dry drunks.* Drug addicts experience an equivalent to the alcoholic's dry drunk called the *postaddiction syndrome,* in which the recovering addict experiences anxiety, depression, and cravings for drugs even months and years after the last withdrawal (McCarthy & McCarthy, 1984).

Addicted offenders require hard doses of what Alcoholics Anonymous calls "tough love" from criminal justice counselors. Tough love means that the counselor must hold the offender totally and unequivocally responsible for his or her behavior by not cutting the offender any slack whatsoever when it comes to excuse making, alibis, rescuing, and the need to be nice. The criminal justice counselor who uses tough love must be willing and prepared to be rejected and disliked by the offender during the process of counseling. Rejection is frequently difficult for criminal justice counselors, and others who enter the helping professions, because they have a need to be liked and loved by those they serve. In short, criminal justice counselors must develop thick skins and be able to absorb hostility to deal with any addicted person.

Criminal justice counselors must also learn to identify addicted offenders. There are physical and behavioral signs of both alcohol and drug addiction. Arrest records of offenders give counselors clues as to whether the offender has an alcohol and/or drug problem. The offender's physical appearance can also give clues as to whether the offender is addicted to alcohol and/or drugs. For example, heroin addicts who are actively using drugs frequently lose weight; have needle marks on their hands, arms, and legs; wear sunglasses to conceal the pupils of their eyes; and are less concerned with their personal grooming. When I was a parole agent working primarily with heroin addicts, I learned to spot parolees who were using heroin by the monotone, nonemotional quality of their voices. This ability to identify heroin users by the tonal quality of their voices came with repeated experience, and it would be near impossible to teach a novice counselor exactly what to look or listen for. Different drugs produce different physical effects, and criminal justice counselors must learn to recognize how different drugs and alcohol are physically manifested.

Counselors can also obtain clues to help them identify addiction by examining their offenders' behaviors. Offenders addicted to alcohol and drugs do not show up for appointments, miss work, develop alibis designed to convince the counselor that factors other than alcohol and drugs are responsible for their behavior, fail to take responsibility for their actions, blame others for their problems, exhibit irritability and hostility, complain frequently that they do not feel good, and so on. Counselors must confront head on such behaviors on the part of offenders. In addition, counselors must never buy into rationalizations and alibis that are designed to convince counselors that factors other than addiction are responsible for offenders' problems.

Screening tools can also be used to identify alcoholics and drug addicts. One such device frequently used for identifying alcoholism is the Michigan Alcoholism Screening Test. There are numerous pencil-and-paper tests that help counselors identify addiction; however, one problem is that offenders do not necessarily tell the truth on such tests. Criminal justice counselors should not overuse or rely exclusively on pencil-and-paper tests of any sort to diagnose problems when working with offenders.

Treatment for offender addictions rarely results in total success. Occasionally, addicts experience spontaneous recovery without formal treatment, but this situation is rare. Generally, the longer the addict is in formal, residential treatment, the more positive the outcome. It is also important for the addict to get follow-up or aftercare following the residential treatment. For treatment to be successful, the addicted offender must be ready and willing to accept it. Treatment may include interventions and both medical and social types of detoxification and other programs. Unless the criminal justice counselor is assigned to a program that deals with only addiction, most counselors should refer addicted offenders to specialized treatment.

Criminal justice counselors are advised to confine the focus of counseling on the behavior of alcoholics and drug addicts. It is important for criminal justice counselors to identify, understand, and handle addicted offenders with tough love. Not all counselors have to be specialists in the treatment of addiction to do this. Counselors have widespread, free, community-based resources that are accessible to anyone who is addicted. Two of these resources are Alcoholics Anonymous and Narcotics Anonymous. Both Alcoholics Anonymous and Narcotics Anonymous are spiritually based self-help organizations that serve all types of people from all walks of life. Some offenders might need short- or long-term residential programs before beginning an outpatient program. It is frequently up to the criminal justice counselor to make the assessment and refer offenders to specialized treatment programs. Medical approaches to the treatment of alcoholism and drug addiction for offenders usually depend on the referral of the criminal justice counselor. Criminal justice counselors normally are not in a position to prescribe or monitor pharmacological agents such as Antabuse (a drug that causes nausea when an offender takes a drink), methadone (a synthetic, addictive substance that replaces the addiction to heroin and reduces the craving for and severity of withdrawal), naltrexone (a nonaddictive substance that blocks the effects of heroin), and other drugs commonly used in the medical treatment of addiction.

In the last analysis, criminal justice counselors hope that with counseling the offender's alcohol and/or drug consumption will be reduced, the addict will secure and maintain employment, and the addict's interpersonal and physical conditions improve. The greatest barrier the counselor will face when counseling addicts is offender motivation. Counseling addicted offenders is emotionally draining, and counselors must accept that the most effective treatment of addicted populations frequently depends on time and age, factors beyond the counselor's control.

DISTURBED OFFENDERS

It is hoped that offenders with severe mental problems are placed in the care of the mental health system, not the criminal justice system. Nevertheless, some severely disturbed offenders do end up in the criminal justice system and are released to the community, and counselors will have to deal with them. It is important for counselors to recognize the difference between the basic kinds of mental illnesses. Criminal justice counselors must be able to identify psychotics, neurotics, and sociopathic offenders. Psychotic offenders exhibit obvious breaks with reality and their personalities are severely disorganized. They frequently do not know who they are, cannot take care of themselves, and as a result, may pose a threat to themselves and others. The typical criminal justice counselor is not equipped to counsel and treat the specialized problems such offenders have and is advised, when necessary, to make appropriate referrals to mental health agencies. Such offenders often require hospitalization. Criminal justice counselors should always take the necessary steps to protect themselves and the community before attempting to deal with disturbed offenders.

Most neurotic offenders—those with emotional problems but who are in touch with reality, able to function, and take care of themselves—can be advised by criminal justice counselors. Neurotic offenders' personalities are not severely disorganized. In fact, many offenders are neurotic and, generally, pose no severe threat to themselves or others. Neurotic offenders frequently manifest anxiety, obsessive-compulsive behavior, hysteria, phobias, depression, and other disorders.

The criminal justice counselor must also be able to identify sociopaths. Sociopathic offenders are believed to have chronic personality disorders, not mental illnesses, and appear in the population of offenders in excessive numbers (Masters & Roberson, 1990). It is not clear whether offenders start out as sociopaths or if their experiences in the criminal justice system, particularly prisons, contribute to the development of the personality disorder. Sociopathic offenders of all ages and sexes exhibit certain specific characteristics or symptoms. They are egocentric, hostile, impulsive, charming, insensitive to others, asocial, and disloyal; possess poor judgment; blame others for their troubles; are devoid of emotions and inner feelings for what they do to others; do not learn from experience and punishment; are indifferent to others and incapable of deep love for others; and have no distress over their maladjustment (Cleckley, 1941).

Sociopathic offenders are difficult for criminal justice counselors to work with because they are pathological liars, have no conscience, do not learn from experience, are self-absorbed, and as a rule, do not care what they do to others. They have great difficulty in placing themselves in the role of their victims and experiencing the pain of others. They frequently dupe the criminal justice counselor by telling him or her what he or she wants to hear. Sociopathic offenders, on the face, frequently appear to be model counselees, because they can convince the criminal justice counselor that they want to change and will do anything necessary to cooperate with the counseling process. In addition, sociopathic offenders rarely show normal human resistance to the counseling process or the issues that they choose to work with. A clue that the counselor may be dealing with a sociopath is that the offender goes along with the counseling program without experiencing emotions associated with counseling: anxiety, resistance, fear, depression, joy, and so forth. Another factor that should be noted in working with sociopathic offenders is that it takes time to identify the disorder, because the symptoms normally do not leap out at the counselor. In fact, most counselors love to work with offenders who are willing and ready to cooperate.

Criminal justice counselors must keep in mind that sociopathic personality disorders are difficult to treat because little is known about the causes of these disorders. However, some research shows that the sociopathic disorder may go into remission at age 40 or 50, as the brainwaves mature (Bartol, 1980). Counselors must realize that they are powerless to help sociopathic offenders develop consciences, develop inner feelings toward others, or stop the compulsion to lie. Counselors are on safe ground if they concentrate on working with the sociopath to change overt behavior and develop an adult sense of responsibility.

VIOLENT OFFENDERS

Criminal justice counselors are assigned adult and juvenile offenders who can be violent. Offenders frequently come from poor neighborhoods where violence is a way of life. Many grow up in a subculture of violence with drug dealers, gang violence, pimps, prostitution, and other types of criminality (Wolfgang & Ferracuti, 1978). In such neighborhoods, a value system is taught that emphasizes aggression and violence in solving problems. Violence is also a salient factor of prison life. Counselors must keep in mind that offenders who have been incarcerated frequently have had to protect themselves with violence and may be quick to respond with violence when they perceive themselves to be threatened in the community.

> **66***Criminal justice counselors often carry firearms and many agencies require that counselors have the option of protecting themselves with weapons.***99**

Criminal justice counselors must also use care when dealing with offenders who are under the influence of drugs and alcohol. The gentlest offenders when under the influence of alcohol and drugs can be instantly transformed into violent, irrational people. Criminal justice counselors must, first and foremost, protect themselves when dealing with such offenders and must remember that counseling is impossible as long as a person is under the influence of any drug, including alcohol.

Whenever a counselor suspects an offender to be under the influence and/or behaving violently (as frequently occurs when the counselor has to take the offender into custody), he or she should not deal with the offender alone. Counselors should always have backup with them. Today it is popular for criminal justice counselors to carry firearms and many agencies require that counselors have the option of protecting themselves with weapons. (See Chapter 1 for a discussion of the issue of weapons and counseling.) One of the major problems with criminal justice counselors using firearms on offenders is that the weapon can be confiscated by violent offenders and be used against counselors. That notwithstanding, in today's violent world, many counselors feel safer when they enter violence-prone neighborhoods if they have weapons close at hand.

FEMALE OFFENDERS

It is fairly well accepted that women commit less crime than men, but the increase in female crime during the 1960s and 1970s has spurred new interest in female criminals and theories about them. There are fewer female offenders than male offenders; women account for only 16% of all arrests, comprise only 5% of the prison population in the United States, and commit about 10% of all serious violent crimes (McCarthy & McCarthy, 1984). For the most part, women's crime is concentrated in the area of economic crime such as shoplifting, burglary, forgery, and welfare fraud (Pollock-Byrne, 1990). In regard to women prisoners, most are young, minorities, and poor (Glick & Neto, 1977). Nevertheless, female offenders have specific counseling concerns and special problems, of which the criminal justice counselor must be aware.

Almost 50% all female offenders have children. The importance of children to women is one of the differences between incarcerated women and men (Pollock-Byrne, 1990). For women, prison is most painful because it cuts them off from their families and friends. Women, for the most part, bear more physical, financial, and emotional responsibility for their children than do men, and as a result, separation from children during incarceration is considered one of the worst things a female offender has to go through. Dealing with the breakup of the female offender's family is a major part of counseling female offenders, because many offender mothers are single, divorced, and/or separated from the fathers of their children and are raising their children alone. For the pregnant woman who is incarcerated, there are other unique counseling issues that must be addressed: guilt, depression, prenatal care, nutrition, limited time to bond with the newborn, quick separation from the baby, return to prison after giving birth, and perhaps addiction of the newborn.

Another problem facing female offenders is that they have limited job skills and are poorly prepared for work and thus have a difficult time supporting their children financially. Many women are frustrated because when they do find work it is usually considered *pink collar* (a femininely stereotyped job) and, therefore, typically does not pay enough to support their families.

Female offenders are rarely liberated women. Many feel powerless and dependent, play subservient roles to men, do not assume responsibility for their lives, are passive, are devoid of skills, and frequently are under the control and domination of a man, often an offender too. Therefore, it is not surprising that many female offenders are physically battered and psychologically abused by husbands and boyfriends. Some of these women see no way out of pain and danger other than to kill the aggressor (Pollock-Byrne, 1990).

Counseling the female offender must take into account their special problems and concerns. Counseling should focus on helping women take control of their lives and become economically independent by teaching them how to acquire the skills that they need to support their children and by teaching them parenting skills, survival training, personal responsibility, and independence. Besides assisting female offenders economically, counseling must take into account the types of jobs available, the realities of the working world, job discipline, the mechanics of job seeking, résumé preparation, the need to build self-confidence, and myriad other concerns.

Many women offenders prefer the jobs to which females traditionally gravitate; however, generally speaking, the better-paying jobs have been those to which males traditionally gravitate: auto mechanics, welding, truck driving, electrical work, and so on. Such vocations are considered nontraditional for women, and many female offenders reject better-paying vocational opportunities because they view the job as masculine. Counseling may have to focus on the issue of femininity to help women take advantage of vocational training and opportunities that could lead to financial independence.

Incarcerated mothers also have special problems that counselors must take into account. For many mothers, maintaining contact with children and their caregivers may be difficult. When an offender mother is isolated from her children, she frequently is poorly informed about her children's problems. She gets few institutional visits, and many times children are afraid of going to the prison to see their mothers. Even under the best of conditions, the separation that occurs between mother and child may produce emotional barriers for all parties.

The child may learn to see her/his caregivers as parents and the transfer of care back to the biological parent may be difficult and painful for the inmate mother, child, and caregivers. Another problem female offenders face is explaining to their children why they are incarcerated. Still another concern might be the loss of custody of children while incarcerated.

Counseling incarcerated women must also take into account the tendency for females to develop and affiliate with pseudofamilies while incarcerated. Women tend to develop surrogate familial relationships and roles with other incarcerated women to deal with the pains of imprisonment. In addition, counselors must understand the role of female homosexual relationships and deal with the prevalence of homosexuality in women's prisons. The criminal justice counselor must be aware of potential problems women in prison face and be willing to work with them on such issues.

An important factor that criminal justice counselors must take into account in the counseling of women is that women express greater emotionality than men. Incarcerated women are more likely to show their emotions, have mood swings, and develop attachments with other people than incarcerated men (Pollock-Byrne, 1990). Counselors must be prepared to handle emotionality in counseling.

To summarize, female offenders are typically young, minorities, and poor and have a variety of problems and specialized counseling needs. Female offenders have unique problems while incarcerated and a need to control their lives.

ILL OFFENDERS

Periodically criminal justice counselors are assigned seriously ill offenders. Acquired immunodeficiency syndrome (AIDS) is an illness that is spreading in mainstream society as well as in the population of those offenders with substance abuse problems. Counseling efforts must take into account the illness and the offender's feelings about his or her illness. Counselors must be aware of the fact that sick offenders tend to be more self-absorbed than offenders who are healthy. Sickness narrows the offender's ability to focus on counseling issues that are not directly concerned with survival and health. Sick offenders also may be afraid to confront the reality of their situations. If sick offenders are addicts, counselors should be prepared for offenders to use drugs more compellingly than if they were not sick, for addicts are constantly trying to alter their realities.

Counseling offenders who have AIDS or who test positive for human immunodeficiency virus (HIV) requires specialized skill on the part of criminal justice counselors. If the offender is HIV positive or has active AIDS, counselors must do everything possible to educate the offender about the disease and its progression. Making sure the offender has the information to prevent the spread of AIDS should be a counseling priority as well as counseling the offender to get needed medical attention.

The counselor must be well-educated about AIDS and HIV to counsel infected offenders. Criminal justice counselors come in contact with intravenous drug users and others who are likely to be infected with HIV. A total of 27% of the adult and adolescent AIDS cases in the United States have intravenous drug use as a risk factor (Centers for Disease Control, 1989). Counselors may have anxiety about becoming infected with HIV as a result of their employment. It is a myth that AIDS can be gotten by casual contact, the type of contact most counselors have with offenders. There are only three ways in which AIDS can be transmitted: by sexual contact, through contact with infected blood, and perinatally (i.e., from an infected mother to a newborn infant). Counselors should have at their disposal guidelines to follow when they have contact with seropositive offenders—those infected with HIV. Counselors may also counsel rape survivors and other sexually assaulted persons who fear infection as well as homosexuals, bisexuals, and prostitutes. Counseling high-risk offenders may include what many view as radical methods such as teaching drug addicts how to clean their needles and syringes as a way of avoiding infection and its spread, providing condoms, and in some jurisdictions, providing addicts with sterile needles. Knowledge about the disease, the ability to communicate this knowledge, and sensitivity are essential for the counselor to be effective with offenders.

Criminal justice counselors who work in institutional or field settings must be aware that HIV infected offenders are constantly dealing with issues of uncertainty, loss, and isolation. For example, HIV infected offenders are uncertain as to their future. Some HIV infected persons have lived more than 14 years after diagnosis, while others have lived less than 1 year. The medical establishment cannot predict longevity.

Formerly robust offenders frequently find that they have to deal with issues relating to their loss of physical strength, loss of employment, loss of family and friends, and loss of community. Incarcerated inmates fear known HIV infected inmates, making the HIV positive inmate a pariah within a society of pariahs. As a result, support groups within the mainstream prison population are difficult to form, thereby making the criminal justice counselor one of the only persons the infected inmate has to talk with.

According to specialists, some form of communication outlet for the HIV infected offender is critical for well-being (*HIV Infection,* 1993). Criminal justice counselors provide a principal outlet for offenders to talk about their infection and, therefore, should emphasize their availability. Criminal justice counselors must also be aware of the psychological barriers to initiating zidovudine therapy, an antiviral drug (formerly called AZT) active against HIV. Some offenders hold false beliefs that zidovudine is poison, is useless, and/or forced on them by authorities (*HIV Infection,* 1993). It is the counselor's job to provide offenders repeatedly with known facts about the benefits of prophylactic therapies.

Criminal justice counselors must also be aware that the onset of physical symptoms can also cause psychological problems for offenders. There is very little evidence that HIV infection causes mood change or depression in those not already predisposed; however, a second opportunistic infection may be accompanied by thoughts of suicide (*HIV Infection,* 1993). In summary, to provide beneficial counseling services, criminal justice counselors must be aware of the unique problems associated with HIV infected inmates.

SEX OFFENDERS

Sex offenders can be male or female but are usually male. Most criminals themselves hate sex offenders who victimize children. They are considered the lowest form of offender and frequently must be placed in protective custody and/or in special institutions when incarcerated so that other offenders will not harm them.

The general public also holds negative stereotypes about sex offenders. They are frequently viewed as sleazy and inhuman. For the counselor to work successfully with sex offenders, he or she must be able to put aside any negative stereotypes that may exist. It takes a unique person to work with such offenders. Here's an illustration.

A young female parole agent intern was assigned the case of an adult, male child molester. In a counseling class, the intern revealed that the child molester really got to her. Every time she was around him, her skin crawled. She could not get over her image of him as sleazy and sub-human. She had great conflict over her unshakable, negative feelings for the sex offender and her need to be professional and objective with all types of parolees assigned to her. In the counseling class, we tried to get to the root of her feelings and work through them; however, she ultimately was unable to see the child molester as a human being.

If criminal justice counselors cannot work through such biases, then they are in no position to counsel. The offender will feel the disdain the counselor has. Under these circumstances, it is best that criminal justice counselors go to their supervisors, discuss the problems they are having and, if possible, have such cases transferred to counselors who do not harbor such deep-rooted feelings. All parties will benefit from such honesty. To counsel sex offenders, the counselor must be capable of empathy, tough confrontation, and must remember that not all sex offenders are alike.

There are exhibitionists, rapists, child molesters, pedophiles, and so on, and just because the counselor has a problem with one type of sex offender, it does not mean that he or she will have a problem with another type. Counselors must also keep in mind that there are differences between the first-time sex offender and the recidivist. Differences in sex offenders will also affect the counselor's recommendations and counseling strategies.

Criminal justice counseling should focus on how the sex offender defends his or her behavior. Most sex offenders deny, rationalize, and justify their actions in particular ways. Another focus of criminal justice counseling should be getting the offender to take total and unequivocal responsibility for his or her actions. Self-esteem work is also a good counseling strategy, for most sex offenders tend to be powerless and have low self-esteem. Sex is frequently engaged in to make the offender feel powerful and in control. Direct attacks on the offender's dysfunctional thinking are also in order. Group counseling is an excellent tool, because offenders are confronted by other sex offenders who are experts at identifying their fellow sex offenders' thinking patterns.

The treatment of sex offenders is not hopeful. Behavior modification and drug therapies have been used on different types of sex offenders. Neither approach has been fully successful in stopping the sex offender from recidivating. Routine, intermittent criminal justice counseling efforts frequently do not provide enough quantity and consistency in treatment. Most of the time, the treatment of sex offenders requires more than what the criminal justice counselor alone can give the offender. Whether the offender is incarcerated or in the community, criminal justice counselors should tap all available community resources, especially the local mental health departments. The focus of the counselor's efforts should be on identifying and working with behavior patterns that may lead to offending again.

RESISTANT OFFENDERS

Most offenders are resistant to criminal justice counseling to some degree or another, because most have been coerced into the criminal justice system against their will. While some offenders express resistance by kicking and screaming; others express resistance in more subtle ways. Counselors should keep in mind the reasons for resistance by offenders. Some of the reasons are as follows.

1. They see themselves as not having problems and see no reason to be assigned a criminal justice counselor.
2. They resent, distrust, and/or dislike the criminal justice counselor; whenever these feelings are present, offenders will manifest some type of resistance.
3. They feel awkward about anything having to do with counseling and, therefore, do not like to participate in it.
4. They find the counseling process painfully intrusive and resist because they believe their privacy is not respected.
5. They rebel against anything having to do with the criminal justice system. Some offenders believe anyone or anything tied to the criminal justice system is their enemy.
6. They have personality differences with the criminal justice counselor. Some offenders and counselors' personalities do not mesh.

7. They feel that if they work with the counselor, then they must admit weakness and/or inadequacy.
8. They feel that counseling is being forced on them without their permission.
9. They feel the only power they have in the criminal justice system is through resistance.
10. They feel that they have made sufficient changes, but the counselor is encouraging more.
11. They are afraid of what they might find out during the counseling process.

❝The best way to handle offender resistance is to honestly deal with it. ❞

The best way to handle offender resistance to counseling is to deal with it honestly. Criminal justice counselors should keep in mind that whenever offenders perceive themselves as forced to deal with counselors, there will be resistance. In fact, some degree of resistance is normal. The offender and counselor should talk about and express their feelings about resistance. This is the first step toward working through it. Counselors should try to dissolve resistance that prevents offenders from dealing with counseling issues, avoid resistance that is likely to lead no where, and capitalize on and use resistance that can help the offender deal with counseling issues.

INCARCERATED OFFENDERS

The typical incarcerated offender is young, male, poor, and a minority. Incarcerated offenders have different problems and issues to deal with than do offenders who are free and living in the community. When an offender is confined, not only does he or she lose liberty, but he or she is deprived of heterosexual relationships except for conjugal visiting programs and may go through mental and physical duress.

Visits from the outside world are limited, mail is searched, and daily life is regulated and rigid. There are also restrictions on ways inmates and staff are permitted to relate. Many problems incarcerated offenders face cause stress, produced by the nature of confinement. Some problems are separation from family, fear of being forgotten and/or abandoned by family and friends, worry about financial support of their families, adjustment to the community when they are released, communication with the outside world, survival in the institution, institutionalization (see earlier in this chapter), getting along with fellow inmates, and so forth. The counseling of incarcerated offenders must take into account all of these concerns.

Counseling incarcerated offenders has advantages and disadvantages. Some of the advantages are that counselors have easy access to offenders whenever they may need counseling. When in the institution, offenders have round-the-clock supervision and observation. This means the counselor can get objective reports on how offenders may be dealing with issues in daily prison life. Because the offender is in a highly structured environment, quick responses to problems the offender may be having can occur. Some of the disadvantages of counseling incarcerated offenders include the fact that institutional life is not similar to life in the community. Basic offenders' needs such as food, shelter, and work are all taken care of in the institution. The offender does not have to go out and find work, a place to live, and food for himself or herself and others. Some counseling issues may appear to be resolved while incarcerated, but become full-blown problems when the offender is released. Another disadvantage of counseling in prisons is that the offender does not have an opportunity to practice dealing with his or her problems in a real-life environment. The institutional environment also promotes an "us versus them" mentality among inmates, which is laden with distrust and suspicion of all institutional personnel, including counselors. This mentality causes inmates, in an effort to get what they want in prison, to manipulate and play games with counselors.

Another problem that counselors must keep in mind when counseling incarcerated offenders is *prisonization,* or the degree to which offenders adopt the roles, norms, and values of the prison as their own. The more an incarcerated offender comes to accept the subculture of the prison and the inmate code as his or her own, the more difficult it will be for the counselor and offender to work seriously on counseling issues. As male and female inmates become "prisonated," they adopt values that cause them not to share information with counselors, not to respect staff (including counselors), not to portray themselves as weak, and to become generally suspicious of prison personnel (Jensen & Jones, 1976). Inmates who openly accept counseling may be taunted by their peers and lose social standing in the prison culture.

Another problem facing counselors in institutions is the need for inmates to manipulate and control prison personnel. Inmates have sophisticated and subtle control techniques, so subtle that frequently counselors may not be aware of being manipulated until it is too late. Sometimes very subtle comments can create a series of events that could cause great problems for counselors. Therefore, it is important for counselors to be aware of the way they can be set up by inmates and how to identify the characteristics of a setup (Allen & Bosta, 1978).

Counselors frequently deal with an inmate's most private and personal concerns. As a result, the counseling relationship can get heavy with emotions on both parties' parts. This makes the counselor especially vulnerable to manipulation. Therefore, it is best to keep the professional lines drawn. Detailed self-disclosures on the part of the counselor should be avoided. The counselor should treat inmates consistently. It is also important for counselors to deal with counseling issues during designated appointments, not to allow inmates to call them by their first names (to avoid familiarity), not to give inmates knowledge about their own personal problems, and to avoid intimate conversations with inmates that might leave them vulnerable to inmates' manipulation.

In summary, counseling incarcerated offenders is challenging, and counselors learn quickly about game playing and manipulation. Counseling the incarcerated is probably one of the best ways for the criminal justice counselor to learn about offenders in the criminal justice system.

SUMMARY

Criminal justice offenders have many problems such as substance abuse, limited education, lack of employment, sporadic job attendance, lack of vocational training, poor self-esteem, inadequate problem-solving skills, violent lives, manipulative personalities, fears, limited income, and isolation. Counselors in the criminal justice system must be prepared to deal with every type of offender and problem that emerges. Young, adult, addicted, disturbed, violent, female, ill, sex, resistant, and incarcerated offenders are likely to have specific problems that counselors must be aware of.

Young offenders are difficult to counsel because of problems associated with adolescence and identity crises and because of problems in admitting that they are powerless to control their lives. Young offenders do not seek help voluntarily. They have problems in accepting responsibility for their troubles. They have limited life experiences and maturity, and they are not future oriented. Young offenders are subject to peer pressure, have a perception of the counselor as a cop, have no stake or investment in the counseling services, and have poor attention spans.

Adult offenders are difficult to counsel, too. Adult offenders are typically young, minorities, and poor. Adult offenders frequently are state raised and institutionalized, which together cause major problems for them.

Alcohol and drug addicted offenders have unique problems related to addiction. Addiction creates a new personality that can frequently lead to violence and crime. The dynamics and process of addiction tend to be similar no matter whether the addict's drug of choice is alcohol, other drugs, or a combination of alcohol and other drugs. Before accepting treatment for addiction, offenders tend to rationalize, deny, project, manipulate, lie, cheat, and steal to obtain and maintain their supply. Criminal justice counselors must be prepared to be rejected by offenders when they use tough love approaches. For treatment to be successful with addicts, the offender must be ready and willing to accept it. The greatest barrier criminal justice counselors face when counseling addicts is offender motivation. Recognizing sincere motivation as opposed to game playing is important for the criminal justice counselor.

Sometimes criminal justice counselors must provide services for severely disturbed offenders. Typical criminal justice counselors are not equipped to counsel and treat psychotic offenders; however, they frequently find themselves providing services to neurotic and sociopathic offenders. Sociopathic offenders are difficult for counselors to work with, because they dupe the counselor by telling the counselor what he or she wants to hear. Also treatment is not too hopeful;

however, evidence suggests that the sociopathic personality disorder may go into remission at age 40 or 50.

Criminal justice counselors are also assigned offenders who come from neighborhoods in which violence is accepted as a way of solving problems and is also a product of drug and/or alcohol abuse. Counselors frequently have to deal with violence when they have to take an offender into custody and, therefore, should always have backup with them.

Female offenders are typically young, minorities, and poor, with numerous problems and specialized counseling concerns. For female inmates, the most painful aspect of prison is being cut off from children and family. Many women offenders raise their children alone and without help of any kind. Other problems that female offenders face are low-paying pink-collar jobs, limited work skills, lack of education, battered and abused lives, lack of parenting skills, powerlessness, dependency, passivity, domination and control by males, and so forth. The counselor must also take into account the problems that pregnant and incarcerated women have.

Criminal justice counselors must be prepared to deal with the issues that sick offenders have, too. One of the illnesses that is growing in the offender populations is AIDS. Counseling offenders who have AIDS or who test positive for HIV requires specialized skills on the part of criminal justice counselors. Counselors may be called on to educate all types of offenders about how AIDS is transmitted. Counseling may include radical new approaches such as informing high-risk offenders (addicts, homosexuals, prostitutes, etc.) how to clean needles and syringes and passing out sterile needles and condoms. Knowledge about diseases, the ability to communicate this knowledge, and sensitivity are essential for the counselor to be effective with offenders.

Criminal justice counselors are also assigned sex offenders. To counsel sex offenders effectively, counselors must put aside negative stereotypes and biases. If they cannot do this, they should go to their supervisors, discuss the problems that they are having, and try to transfer such cases to other counselors who do not have such feelings.

Almost all offenders are resistant to counseling to some degree. In fact, some degree of resistance in counseling is normal from time to time. There are many reasons why offenders resist counseling services. A few reasons are fear, rebellion, dislike of the counselor, and coercion.

Incarcerated offenders tend to have many problems too. Counselors must deal with problems that emerge from living in the prison and
in the free community.

MATCHING KEY TERMS AND DEFINITIONS
Match each key term with the correct definition.

a. adolescence
b. puberty
c. identity crisis
d. institutionalized
e. state-raised convict
f. polydrug offender
g. dry drunk
h. postaddiction syndrome
i. tough love
j. psychotic offenders
k. neurotic offenders
l. sociopathic offender

m. subculture of violence
n. pink-collar job
o. pseudofamily
p. AIDS
q. HIV positive
r. seropositive offender
s. zidovudine
t. prisonization
u. setup
v. infantalize
w. Antabuse
x. methadone
y. naltrexone

___ 1. The stage of development characterized by boyhood or girlhood.

___ 2. The transition period of development between puberty and adulthood which is manifested by physical and emotional change.

___ 3. A stage of human development that is characterized by asking questions such as "Who am I?"

___ 4. Excessive dependency on institutional life.

___ 5. A manipulation of the criminal justice counselor that an inmate deliberately plans.

___ 6. A reality-based counseling approach that holds the addicted offender totally responsible for his or her behavior and does not allow the counselor to excuse, rescue, or be soft and gentle with the offender.

___ 7. Offenders who exhibit such disorganized personalities that they are divorced from reality.

___ 8. The way women inmates organize and relate to each other in prison, which helps them cope with the pains of imprisonment.

___ 9. A job that is femininely stereotyped and mostly done by women.

___10. An offender whose personality is not disorganized and maintains contact with reality, but has emotional and coping problems.

___11. When an offender accepts the values and culture of the prison as his or her own.

___ 12. A term for a person who has tested positive for HIV.

___ 13. Acquired immunodeficiency syndrome.

___ 14. An offender with a personality disorder manifested by numerous characteristics such as pathological lying, inability to learn from experience and/or punishment, not being able to take the role of another, and so on.

___ 15. An environment that promotes the use of physical and psychological violence in solving problems.

___ 16. An offender who has spent most of his or her life in juvenile halls, training schools, reformatories, jails, and/or prisons.

___ 17. An addicted offender who uses a number of different drugs.

___ 18. The adoption of old alcoholic behavior patterns after the alcoholic has stopped drinking.

___ 19. Depression, anxiety, and craving for drugs after the drug addict has stopped using drugs.

___ 20. A pharmacological agent used to make the offender sick when he or she drinks alcohol.

___ 21. The tendency to treat offenders like infants by doing things for them that they should be doing for themselves.

___ 22. An addictive pharmacological agent that blocks the effects of heroin.

___ 24. A nonaddictive pharmacological agent that blocks the effects of heroin.

___ 25. An antiviral drug active against HIV and formerly called AZT.

DISCUSSION QUESTIONS

1. What factors make young offenders difficult to counsel?

2. What types of problems do adult offenders face?

3. What does the criminal justice counselor have to be aware of in counseling offenders addicted to alcohol and drugs?

4. What are some of the things that criminal justice counselors must keep in mind when assigned psychotic, neurotic, and sociopathic offenders?

5. What must the criminal justice counselor keep in mind when dealing with violent offenders?

6. What are some of the counseling issues that criminal justice counselors must be prepared to deal with when counseling female offenders?

7. What things must the criminal justice counselor keep in mind when counseling sick offenders?

8. What factors must the criminal justice counselor keep in mind when counseling sex offenders?

9. Why are offenders resistant to counseling?

10. What must criminal justice counselors be aware of when counseling incarcerated offenders?

11. In what stage of moral development are the majority of offenders stuck? Explain.

REFERENCES

Abbott, J. H. (1981). *In the belly of the beast.* New York: Vintage.

Allen, B., & Bosta, D. (1978, December). *Anatomy of a set-up* (California Department of Corrections Publication). Norco: California Rehabilitation Center.

Bartol, C. R. (1980). *Criminal behavior: A psychosocial approach.* Englewood Cliffs, NJ: Prentice Hall.

Centers for Disease Control. (1989, August). *HIV/AIDS surveillance.* Washington, DC: U.S. Department of Health and Human Services.

Cleckley, H. M. (1941). *The mask of sanity.* St. Louis: Mosby.

Finckenauer, J. A. (1982). *Scared straight and the panacea phenomenon.* Englewood Cliffs, NJ: Prentice Hall.

Glick R., & Neto, V. (1977). *National study of women's correctional programs.* Washington, DC: Government Printing Office.

HIV infection and tuberculosis in the correctional system: A discussion of professionals in correctional healthcare focusing on HIV/AIDS. (1993). Research Triangle Park, NC: Burroughs Wellcome.

Inhelder, B., & Piaget, J. (1958). *The growth of logical thinking from childhood to adolescence.* New York: Basic.

Jensen, G., & Jones, D. (1976). Perspectives on an inmate culture: A study of women in prison. *Social Forces, 54*(3), 590-603.

Johnson, R. (1987). *Hard time: Understanding and reforming the prison.* Monterey, CA: Brooks/Cole.

Kohlberg, L. (1976). Moral stages and moralization: The cognitive developmental approach. In T. Lickona (Ed.), *Moral development and behavior: Theory, research, and social issues* (pp. 50-51). New York: Holt, Rinehart, & Winston.

Kohlberg, L. (1981). *The philosophy of moral development.* San Francisco: Harper & Row.

Kohlberg, L., & Turiel, E. (Eds.). (1973). *Moralization: The cognitive developmental approach.* New York: Holt, Reinhart & Winston.

Masters, R., & Roberson, C. (1991). *Inside criminology.* Englewood Cliffs, NJ: Prentice Hall.

McCarthy, B. R., & McCarthy, B. J. (1984). *Community-based corrections.* Monterey, CA: Brooks/Cole.

Pollock-Byrne, J. M. (1990). *Women, prison, and crime.* Pacific Grove, CA: Brooks/Cole.

Sutherland, E. H., & Cressey, D. R. (1974). *Criminology* (9th ed.). Philadelphia: Lippincott.

Taylor, L. (1984). *Born to crime.* Westport, CT: Greenwood.

U.S. Department of Health, Education, and Welfare. (1978). "Third special report to the U.S. Congress on alcohol and health." Washington, DC: Government Printing Office.

Walsh, A. (1988). *Understanding, assessing, and counseling the criminal justice client.* Pacific Grove, CA: Brooks/Cole.

Wolfgang, M. E., & Ferracuti, F. (1978). The subculture of violence. In L. D. Savitz & N. Johnson (Eds.), *Crime in society* (pp. 151-162). New York: John Wiley.

Legal Issues in
Criminal Justice Counseling

Ruth Masters
Lester Pincu
Robert F. Perez

CHAPTER HIGHLIGHTS

- Counselors must always be abreast of current legal developments relating to the handling and counseling of offenders in criminal justice settings.

- Laws in each state may differ; therefore, criminal justice counselors must check specific laws of the state in which they work.

- An offender's rights may vary depending on whether the offender is on probation, is on parole, or is incarcerated.

- Criminal justice offenders have two types of rights: due process rights, which protect the offender from unfair procedures, and substantive rights, which give the offender freedom to do something or guarantee the offender freedom from certain conditions.

- Before the 1940s criminal justice offenders had few rights.

- The changes brought about as a result of offenders' legal battles have humanized prison conditions and, at the same time, limited the flexibility of criminal justice professionals.

- Criminal justice counselors must keep these factors in mind and act accordingly to protect the rights of offenders under their supervision.

- The principle of privileged communications is designed to protect the confidential nature of the counselor-counselee relationship.

- In states in which the counselor is a peace officer, confidentiality in counseling becomes secondary to law enforcement responsibilities.

- Criminal justice counselors are not bound to maintain the same type of counselor-client confidentiality that private counselors must maintain.

- The right of privileged communication is granted by the state and applies only to certain licensed professionals.

- According to counseling ethics, counselors must inform offenders at the onset of counseling if they cannot ensure total confidentiality of all information that might emerge in a counseling session.

- Criminal justice counselors are bound to report all instances of unlawful behavior that come to their attention.

- The courts have not held that rehabilitation is required in prisons and such programs have not yet been constitutionally mandated.

- Under certain circumstances an inmate may be treated without his or her consent.

- Criminal justice counselors must have a broad knowledge of HIV infection.

- There is no national AIDS legislation, and many states have few, if any, laws covering AIDS.

- California has taken a leadership role with regard to AIDS issues and has passed comprehensive legislation that spells out the rights and responsibilities of and restrictions on correctional personnel.

- California has held to the principle of confidentiality of HIV test results but has provided for specific exceptions within the criminal justice system.

- In the public health field, the attitude prevails that HIV confidentiality would encourage people to be tested.

- Within the criminal justice field there is a trend toward mandatory HIV testing for some persons and disclosure of the results.

- Criminal justice counselors should understand the dilemmas AIDS poses to the criminal justice field.

- Interest in the field of liability for criminal justice personnel is growing as a result of the increasing number of lawsuits filed against all types of criminal justice personnel.

- Many jurisdictions are providing liability insurance or indemnification to all types of correctional employees.

- Many states have either totally or partially abrogated the doctrine of sovereign immunity by constitutional provision or statute.

- In regard to constitutional rights of the confined, there is presently substantial litigation that can be expected to continue.

Key Terms

- **Due process**
- **Substantive rights**
- *Ruffin v. Commonwealth* **(1871)**
- **Hands-off doctrine**
- *Ex parte Hull* **(1941)**
- *Coffin v. Reichard* **(1944)**
- **Tort lawsuit**
- *Morrissey v. Brewer* **(1972)**
- *Gagnon v. Scarpelli* **(1973)**
- *Estelle v. Gambel* **(1976)**
- **Privileged communications**
- *Tarasoff v. Regents of the University of California* **(1986)**
- *U.S. v. Dawson* **(1973)**
- *Bell v. Wolfish* **(1984)**
- *Hudson v. Palmer* **(1984)**
- *Padgett v. Stein* **(1976)**
- *James v. Wallace* **(1976)**
- *Rouse v. Cameron* **(1966)**
- *Bowring v. Godwin* **(1977)**
- *Whitely v. Albers* **(1986)**
- *Turner v. Safley* **(1987)**
- **HIV Positive**
- **AIDS**
- **Cause of action**
- *Respondeat superior*

- **Doctrine of sovereign immunity**
- *Hudson v. McMillian* **(1992)**
- *Washington v. Harper* **(1990)**

INTRODUCTION

The purpose of this chapter is to give the criminal justice counselor guidance and direction on how to proceed with counseling offenders while minimizing any legal risk. Because the law is continually evolving and changing, counselors must always be abreast of current developments relating to the handling and counseling of offenders in criminal justice settings. This chapter contains a general overview of laws and practices related to counseling offenders, but the reader must be cautioned that laws in each state may differ. It is essential that the specific state laws in the reader's state must be checked. This chapter will answer some common questions counselors have about the legal rights of offenders, counseling confidentiality, offenders' rights to privacy, forced treatment of the offender, the counseling of offenders with AIDS or HIV, and the circumstances by which criminal justice counselors could be held liable by offenders.

RIGHTS AND THE CRIMINAL JUSTICE OFFENDER

Criminal justice offenders' rights can vary depending on whether the offender is on probation, is on parole, or is incarcerated. From a practical and legal standpoint the person on probation has more rights than a parolee who has been awarded conditional release from prison. It also follows that a probationer and parolee in the community have more rights than an inmate confined in a prison. Generally speaking, however, criminal justice offenders have two types of rights: due process, rights which protect the offender from unfair procedures, and substantive rights, which give the offender freedom to do something or guarantee the offender freedom from certain conditions. Offenders have brought before the courts lawsuits dealing with both types of rights.

Before the 1940s, criminal justice offenders had few rights, and for the most part, prisoners had no legal rights. Many states had civil death statutes that applied to prisoners. In fact, prisoners were considered slaves of the state and treated as second-class citizens. *Ruffin v. Commonwealth* (1871) dictated that the loss of certain rights for prisoners was a significant part of punishment. This case led the courts to take a "hands-off" approach to the rights of offenders and to interfering in the business of corrections agencies and institutions.

It was not until the 1940s that the courts began paying attention to the rights of offenders and especially to the rights of prison inmates. The landmark case that signified the end of the hands-off doctrine by the courts was *Ex parte Hull* (1941). This case was the first major case that provided inmates with unrestricted access to federal courts. State prison and jail officials could no longer impair or abridge a prisoner's right to have access to federal courts by determining whether prisoners' petitions were properly prepared. In 1944, another landmark case, *Coffin v. Reichard,* held that prisoners do not lose all their civil rights as a result of confinement. As a result of this case, offenders were able to exercise their rights to sue on the basis of their confinement in prison. Inmates were allowed to take the conditions of their confinement to court. In fact, *Coffin v. Reichard* (1944) started the movement to examine prison conditions and added momentum to the demise of the hands-off doctrine practiced by the courts. Today, most states have abolished civil death statutes for prisoners and prisoners have some limited rights (Hawkins & Alpert, 1989). A typical statute of this type is California's *Penal Code Ann.* § 2600 (West, 1982), which provides that a prisoner may be deprived of only those rights that are necessary to provide for the reasonable security of the institution in which he or she is confined and for the reasonable protection of the public.

There are various avenues available to the criminal justice offender to seek legal redress for alleged wrongs suffered as a result of confinement. First, the offender can engage in state tort lawsuits, which are civil actions against correctional employees for negligence or intentional wrongdoing. Second, the offender can invoke § 1983 of the Federal Civil Rights Act of 1871. If the court finds in favor of the offender, this act can result in injunctions and/or monetary damages (42 U.S.C.A. § 1983 [West, 1981]). In § 1983, actions of monetary damages are rare, but they are a good avenue for class action suits, which have led to injunctions requiring changes in conditions and/or practices. Finally, the offender can invoke the Civil Rights of Institutionalized Persons Act of 1980 (42 U.S.C.A. § 1997-1997j [West,

1981]). Although this act is very complicated, it permits the federal government to bring civil suits for equitable relief (injunctions) against state employees of any state institution; however, it does not allow for monetary damages (Hawkins & Alpert, 1989).

Another possible avenue for an offender to seek legal remedies for alleged wrongs suffered is a *Bivens* cause of action; however, a discussion of *Bivens* is beyond the scope of this text (*Bivens v. Six Unknown Named Agents of the Federal Bureau of Narcotics,* 1971). At one time, writs of habeas corpus were filed in state and federal courts to raise issues relating to conditions of confinement. However, the modern trend is to limit the scope of the writ of habeas corpus to questions relating to the legality of the prisoner's confinement involving legal errors that occurred in the criminal justice process through sentencing.

Offenders have used all of the avenues to gain legal rights and improve conditions of confinement. The changes brought about as a result of offenders' legal battles have, according to some, humanized prison conditions and, according to others, tied the hands of criminal justice professionals to the point of making work in the corrections field more dangerous than ever before.

Some of the general legal rights won by criminal justice offenders that must be kept in mind by criminal justice counselors are a result of the following U.S. Supreme Court decisions.

1. *Morrissey v. Brewer* (1972). This case set the stage for procedural due process rights for parolees. The parolee is entitled to due process protection before parole can be revoked. The parolee is entitled to (a) a written notice of alleged violations, (b) the disclosure of adverse evidence, (c) the opportunity to be heard personally and present documentary evidence and witnesses, (d) the right to confront and cross-examine adverse witnesses, (e) a neutral hearing body, and (f) written statements by fact-finders of evidence and reasons supporting revocation.

2. *Gagnon v. Scarpelli* (1973). This case extended *Morrissey* due process rights to probationers facing revocation. However, *Gagnon* provided probationers with the right to an attorney determined on a case-to-case basis.

3. *Estelle v. Gamble* (1976). This case ruled that deliberate indifference by prison personnel to medical needs of prisoners violated the

prisoner's Eighth Amendment rights to be free from cruel and unusual punishment.

4. *Whitely v. Albers* (1986). This case held that shooting a prisoner is a violation of the Eighth Amendment prohibition against cruel and unusual punishment if the force was not a good faith effort to maintain or restore discipline but rather applied maliciously and sadistically for the very purpose of causing harm.

5. *Hudson v. McMillian* (1992). This case held that the use of excessive physical force against a prisoner by correctional officers may constitute cruel and unusual punishment in violation of the Eighth Amendment, even if the inmate does not suffer serious injury.

The following sections deal with specific legal rights criminal justice offenders have gained over the years. Criminal justice counselors must know how to protect the rights of offenders under their supervision and act accordingly.

CONFIDENTIALITY LAWS AND
THE CRIMINAL JUSTICE COUNSELOR

The principle of *privileged communications* is designed to protect the confidential nature of some special relationships, such as attorney-client, clergy-parishioner, doctor-patient, and in some states, licensed counselor-client. In all states, this privileged communication is considered, in the eyes of the law, confidential and shall not be disclosed unless the client or patient gives explicit permission. According to the California *Evidence Code § 1010,* the term *psychotherapist* is a general term referring to psychiatrists; licensed psychologists; licensed clinical social workers; credentialed school psychologists; licensed marriage, family, child counselors; and assistants and interns who are being supervised by board-certified and licensed professionals. All of the these professionals do counseling and may also be referred to as counselors. In California, sections 1012 and 1014 of the Evidence Code indicate confidential communication between patient and psychotherapist means that the psychotherapist is not permitted to disclose to third persons, except those who are present to further the interest of the patient in the consultation and those to whom disclosure is reasonably necessary for the transmission of the information or the accomplishment of the purpose for which the psychotherapist is consulted. In states where the criminal justice counselor is also a peace officer, the law enforcement responsibility usually comes first, and confidentiality in the counseling role becomes secondary. In most cases the criminal justice counselor is not bound to maintain the same type of counselor-client confidentiality that a private counselor must maintain. The rationale for this difference is that the criminal justice counselor is a peace officer first and a counselor second (*Fare v. Michael C.,* 1979). In addition, privileged communication is granted by the state and applies only to certain licensed professionals. Most criminal justice counselors are not licensed professionals, like counselors employed outside of the criminal justice setting. Even when there is a privileged relationship, there are exceptions to that privilege, and confidentiality might not apply.

There is an ethical duty on the part of the criminal justice counselor to inform the offender at the onset of counseling that he or she cannot ensure total confidentiality of all information that might emerge in a counseling session. This may adversely affect the development of trusting relationships with offenders. It is also important to remember that the counselor's notes, records, case summaries and reports may be subpoenaed and used in open court against an offender.

A major case that deals with the exceptions to confidentiality laws and the concept of privileged communication is *Tarasoff v. Regents of the University of California* (1976). *Tarasoff* is based on the failure of a university doctor to inform a potential victim that his client intended to kill her. The court held that the doctor was aware of the possible future harm to a third person from his patient and, therefore, had a duty to warn her of the threat. Using this rationale, a criminal justice counselor might be found liable if he or she did not warn appropriate third parties of potential threats that arise in counseling situations.

RIGHT TO PRIVACY
AND THE CRIMINAL JUSTICE OFFENDER

As discussed in Chapter 1, criminal justice counseling is different from counseling in other fields in that the criminal justice counselor is normally a peace officer. Consequently, the counselor is bound to report all instances of unlawful behavior that comes to his or her attention.

A number of cases have dealt with the privacy rights of criminal justice offenders. The majority of cases, however, have dealt with the rights of incarcerated offenders. In *U.S. v. Dawson* (1975) the court ruled that prisoners do not enjoy the same rights of privacy as do ordinary citizens in their homes or offices. *Bell v. Wolfish* (1979) and *Hudson v. Palmer* (1984) held that prisoners have few, if any, expectations of privacy when they enter prisons and jails. Such rulings send the message that the security of the prison is paramount. In *Procunier v. Martinez* (1974) the Court held that the prison can censor an inmate's mail to the extent the mail jeopardizes security, order, or rehabilitation, and regulations "must be no greater than is necessary or essential to the protection of the particular governmental interest involved" (p. 413). However, there are some limitations on this broad principle such as attorney mail (*Wolff v. McDonnell,* 1974).

Criminal justice counselors such as probation and parole officers who work with offenders in the community are also peace officers and must act accordingly. Such counselors must disclose to appropriate third parties certain background information about probationers and/or parolees. For example, the probation officer and/or parole agent must tell the offender's employer about the probationer/parolee only if the crime is related to employment—for example, a convicted rapist who is working as a security guard in an apartment complex or an embezzler who is working in a bank as an accountant (Champion, 1990). In addition, the probation and/or parole officer has a duty to warn appropriate third parties and authorities if they are made aware in counseling sessions of any type of child abuse, sexual abuse, potential harm to others, crimes committed, and so on. Failure to warn appropriate third parties may result in a successful lawsuit against probation and parole officers if an offender injures another person.

VOLUNTARY
AND INVOLUNTARY TREATMENT LAWS

Treatment can be defined in different ways. It can mean providing rehabilitation such as education and vocational programs for criminal justice offenders, and it can also mean providing the offender with psychological counseling services. In *Leavitt v. City of Morris* (1908), the court held that the state has the power to "reclaim submerged men overthrown by strong drink, and help them regain self-control" (p. 395). Succinctly, the state has the right to control unacceptable behavior. Although, in *Padgett v. Stein* (1976) the court held that there is no constitutional duty imposed on the state to rehabilitate prisoners.

In regard to rehabilitation programs, the courts, to date, have not held that rehabilitation in prisons is constitutionally mandated (Hawkins & Alpert, 1989). Nonetheless, there are court cases that have required rehabilitation programs for inmates. In *Holt v. Sarver* (1971) the court ordered rehabilitation programs for inmates where the totality of conditions produced deterioration of inmates. In essence, the court considered the lack of meaningful programs in prisons as a major factor in its decision. In 1974, the court held in *Rutherford v. Hutto* that inmates must be enrolled, voluntarily or involuntarily, in educationally oriented rehabilitation programs, and the court upheld the right of prison officials to require an inmate to participate in education and training programs. In *Alberti v. Sheriff of Harris Co., Tex.* (1975), the court ordered county jail officials to provide adequate vocational and educational programs to foster inmates' rehabilitation. And in *James v. Wallace* (1976), the court held that a positive rehabilitation program is not a constitutional right, but states cannot impede the ability of inmates to attempt their own rehabilitation. In regard to juveniles, *Long v. Powell* (1975) held that juveniles who have been judged nonamenable to rehabilitation within programs regularly conducted by the state for that purpose cannot be committed to such programs without provision for greater protection, security, and rehabilitative treatment.

Courts have moved cautiously when there is an attempt to subject inmates to treatment of an intrusive and aversive nature. *Taylor v. Sterrett* (1972) stated that treatment should be a major goal of incarceration. In 1966, *Rouse v. Cameron* held that in the absence of statutes providing for a right to certain kinds of treatment for offenders who are being confined, a right to treatment still exists for psychopaths, juveniles, insane, drug addicts, and/or alcoholics. Although there is some recent authority to the contrary, some courts have held that incarcerated juveniles must be involved in a cohesive treatment strategy that has been professionally designed to meet individual needs to achieve rehabilitation and return to the community. Some courts have held that a juvenile's right to treatment requires that the state employ qualified persons to supervise the rehabilitation of delinquents. These courts reason that if the state assumes a parens patriae attitude toward offenders and incarcerates them on the theory that their confinement is best for society, the state is obligated to provide the promised treatment (*Morales v. Turman,* 1973; *Smith v. Follette,* 1971; *Welsch v. Likins,* 1974).

In *Bowring v. Godwin* (1977) the court held that the state cannot deny a prisoner psychological and psychiatric treatment if (a) the prisoner's symptoms evidence a serious disease or injury, (b) the disease or injury is curable or may be substantially alleviated, and (c) the potential harm to a prisoner by reason of delay or denial of care would be substantial, such as preventing a prisoner from being paroled. Nonetheless, the right to treatment is limited to that which may be provided on a reasonable cost and time basis, and the essential test is medical necessity and not simply that which may be considered merely desirable. In short, the state should not say no to treatment if it is obviously called for and is available in some form. However, the courts have not required the same treatment for all inmates (*Wilson v. Kelley,* 1969). Finally, the courts have permitted forced participation of inmates in rehabilitation programs, unless constitutional issues are raised (*Gilliam v. Martin,* 1984).

In regard to treatment that is considered intrusive and irreversible to offenders, the courts are clear and cautious. There are some prisons that still use drugs, electrical stimulation of the brain by application of electrodes, organic-conditioning techniques, and psychosurgery to change or control institutional behavior, often without the consent of the inmate (Reid, 1981). In fact, in 1976, the National Commission for the Protection of Human Subjects in Biomedical and Behavioral Research recommended that some forms of organic behavior control, such as brain surgery, be permitted to continue with a system of safeguards (Reid, 1981). Law Enforcement Assistance Administration (LEAA) stopped funding grants for behavior modification programs that involved drug treatment, aversion therapy, and/or brain surgery in the early 1970s (Jones, 1974). The California *Penal Code* requires informed consent for organic therapy. Generally speaking, the greatest constitutional protection for inmates is given for procedures that are the most intrusive, irreversible, and least capable of being said no to by inmates (i.e., psychosurgery). Intrusive treatment where only troublesome inmates or those diagnosed as sick are forced into treatment are more likely to run up against constitutional challenges (Hawkins & Alpert, 1989).

In 1990, the U.S. Supreme Court held in *Washington v. Harper* that a seriously mentally ill prisoner may be treated against his or her will provided that certain procedural due process rights are adhered to before the forced treatment. These rights include the right to notice of the intended treatment, a hearing before an independent panel, and the assistance of a lay adviser.[1] Although *Washington v. Harper* establishes a constitutional minimum, some states require more stringent procedural safeguards including judicial approval before nonconsensual treatment can be imposed (California, *Penal Code,* §§ 2670-2680).

THE LAW AND OFFENDERS WHO HAVE AIDS

Criminal justice counselors must be aware of a number of issues and concerns related to counseling HIV positive offenders in institutional and field settings. Counselors must have a knowledge of the virus; its transmission; laws and agency policies related to AIDS, including confidentiality and the duty of the counselor to warn others; the purpose and limits of testing offenders for the AIDS virus; the obligation of the criminal justice system to treat HIV positive and AIDS offenders; the pros and cons of mandatory AIDS testing for criminal justice offenders; management and handling of offenders in prisons who are HIV positive or have AIDS; conjugal visits for AIDS patients; and rights of prisoners with AIDS to refuse treatment. The following discussion is designed to develop counselor sensitivity by raising questions and problems AIDS has created for the criminal justice system, since definitive answers to many problems are not yet available.

AIDS was first identified as a disease in 1979, but not understood until several years later. HIV attacks cells primarily in the immune system and eventually renders the person defenseless against various diseases called *opportunistic infections.* The virus itself is fragile (which can be killed with a 10% solution of bleach and water). It is transmitted through body fluids such as semen and vaginal fluid, via blood by the sharing of intravenous needles by recreational drug users, and from a mother to a fetus during pregnancy.

HIV infection may remain dormant for years and, although often not detectable directly, is diagnosed by tests that identify the presence of antibodies that are produced in response to the infection. The blood is tested by enzyme-linked immunosorbent assay (ELISA), immuno-fluorescent assay (IFA), and the Western blot. Other blood tests can measure the progression of the disease and indicate how compromised the immune system has become as a result of HIV. There are a number of antiviral agents, such as zidovudine (once called azidothymidine, or AZT), which seem to prolong life and delay the onset of symptoms. The counselor should note that the zidovudine is not a cure, as it does not rid the body of the virus but merely retards the onset or progression of the disease.

The Laws

There is much uncertainty, many contradictions, and rapid change regarding AIDS laws with respect to testing, disclosure, confidential-ity, and liability issues. The criminal justice practitioner works in a field that is quickly changing and, as a result, will encounter many uncertainties and conflicts about AIDS and the criminal justice sys-tem's ethical, legal, medical, and management concerns. There is no national legislation at this point, and many states have few, if any, laws covering these issues. Therefore, administrative policies vary widely among the states. California has taken a leadership role in regard to AIDS issues and has passed comprehensive legislation that spells out the rights, responsibilities, and restrictions on correctional personnel. Although no series of laws will meet the needs of all involved, California has made an attempt to address some of the more pressing issues. We do not advocate that other states or the federal government adopt California's approach in its totality, but we present it as an example that may be partially considered as a model.

Confidentiality

Within the medical community, the confidentiality of medical information is a doctrine that is widely accepted, both in practice and in law. This concept of confidentiality and the concept of privacy protect people infected with HIV from the stigma and discrimination associated with an AIDS diagnosis. When HIV antibody testing was first licensed in the United States in 1985, California enacted a law mandating the confidentiality of these test results (Wood, Marks, & Dilley, 1990). California has held to the principle of confidentiality of HIV test results as a general rule, but has provided for specific exceptions within the criminal justice system under exact conditions with deline-ated safeguards. For example, police officers can petition the court to get information about an individual's HIV status if he or she might have been infected and suspects it occurred in the line of duty. Another example is that correctional personnel can request HIV testing when they observe inmates engaging in conduct known to cause transmission of the disease. In addition, the chief medical officer of an institution can request testing of an inmate if he or she observes clinical symp-toms. Last, inmates may request HIV testing of another inmate if they have reason to believe they have come into contact with the bodily fluids of the other inmate (California, *Penal Code,* §§ 7510-7512).

In the public health field, the attitude prevails that HIV confiden-tiality would encourage people to be tested. The California law is representative of those state laws providing broad protection to HIV-related test results, and provides for civil and criminal liability for wrongful disclosure (Wood et al., 1990). Disclosing antibody test results is prohibited by many states, although the level of protection of confi-dentiality of HIV-related medical records varies from state to state. In California, because of the wide scope of need-to-know situations, it is recognized that there is no perfect solution to confidentiality prob-lems in all situations. However, the willful or negligent disclosure of HIV information by criminal justice personnel, including probation and parole officers, is a misdemeanor (California Department of Corrections, 1990). The criminal justice counselor needs to be aware of the laws of the state in which he or she works. In those states with an absence of specific legislation, protection of HIV records may be provided by general medical records, statutes, legal action for inva-sion of privacy, or in the case of a violation of the physician-patient confidence, a lawsuit for malpractice.

Duty to Warn

Because California now has specific legislation dealing with con-fidentiality of HIV, *Tarasoff* (1976) itself does not apply; however, in other jurisdictions that do not have similar statutes, courts may apply

Tarasoff-like principles and may hold individuals liable for failure to warn. (*Tarasoff* was discussed earlier in this chapter.)

❝*Within the criminal justice field there is a trend toward mandatory testing for some persons, and disclosure of the results.* ❞

Disclosure With Mandatory Testing

Within the criminal justice field there is a trend toward mandatory testing for some persons, and disclosure of the results. The U.S. Bureau of Prisons (BOP) initially implemented a policy of screening inmates, which included testing of all inmates every six months. The BOP rescinded that policy and, at this time, tests a sample of inmates about to be released (Jarvis, Closen, Herman, & Leonard, 1990).

Some states, such as Alabama and Ohio, require that all inmates be tested (Jarvis et al., 1990). In other states, such as California, certain groups of prisoners convicted of sex crimes and prostitution are tested. In states where there is mandatory testing or where testing is done upon release from prison, the parole officer might be informed as well as the spouse and/or family (Jarvis et al., 1990). In California, the victim or prosecutor may request that a defendant who is charged with certain sexual crimes be tested (California, *Health and Safety Code*). The victim, jailer, defendant, and Department of Health Services will be notified of the results; however, these results cannot be used as evidence against the defendant in a criminal case. With the conviction of certain sexual crimes, including prostitution, the judge may order testing and the results may be used as evidence (California, *Penal Code*). Should a convicted offender be found to be HIV positive, the information could even be used as an enhancement to sentencing (Jarvis et al., 1990).

Duty to Treat

Although, to date, there are few definitive answers for counselors to rely on, a number of questions must be raised about the duty of the criminal justice system to treat offenders who are HIV positive or who have AIDS. There are a number of questions that are not yet fully answered by the courts but raise important ethical concerns, and the criminal justice counselor should be aware of these. In the medical field, for example, if a person has a disease such as tuberculosis and is incarcerated, the corrections system has a clear-cut duty to treat and would be liable if the patient died as a result of lack of treatment. If there is mandatory testing, and the offender (prisoner) is found to have the virus, does the state have a moral and legal duty to treat? The answer to that question varies according to state law; however, under the Federal Civil Rights Statute of 1983, it is clear that prison officials may not ignore the medical needs of an inmate. The U.S. Supreme Court decision of *Estelle v. Gamble* (1976) held that reckless indifference to serious medical needs of an inmate constitutes cruel and unusual punishment in violation of the Eighth Amendment to the Constitution.

What if the person is not yet symptomatic, but the criminal justice agency has mandated testing and, as a result, it is discovered that an individual has been infected with the virus? Is the system responsible for early intervention protocols and treating the offender, since treatment might retard the onset of the disease and prolong life? For example, the Centers for Disease Control and Prevention (CDC) recommend starting zidovudine when T-cell count drops to a certain level, which is still above what is normally recognized as the level of an AIDS diagnosis. Is the criminal justice agency responsible for treatment and the astronomical costs involved? Note that the treatment of AIDS is costly, and most criminal justice agencies function with limited budgets and, for this reason, might be reluctant to take on this responsibility. Is the agency responsible to see to it the offender gets regular blood work to check on the state of the immune system and possible progression of the disease? There may be liability (due to negligence) if this is not done, because this is the normal and usual medical practice in these cases. Until these issues are tested in the courts, we will not be able to answer such questions definitively.

Criminal Justice Dilemmas and the Offender Who Has AIDS

Other issues are raised in the prison environment if mandatory AIDS testing is enacted. Many of these questions have not yet been resolved by the courts, but criminal justice counselors should understand the dilemmas; thus we pose the questions. If the offender actually had the disease, he or she may be segregated and treated just as any other sick patient would be. What about the offender's right to refuse treatment? The problem arises with respect to infected offenders who have not yet manifested symptoms and are not legally or medically classified as having AIDS. Once the offender has been identified as having HIV, is there now a responsibility to segregate? Is there liability if segregation is not done and the virus is transmitted to other prisoners? If segregation is done, will there be stigma and discrimination and possibly endangerment, because the rest of the population will now be aware of the HIV status of the segregated group? Should the prison distribute condoms to offenders, especially if it is known that they have HIV? It is clear that prisons would be reluctant to do so, because sexual activity between inmates is prohibited. Distribution of sterile needles or bleach for cleaning them would also not be allowed for the same reason. Condoms and sterile needles are distributed in some jurisdictions outside of institutions by private agencies to retard the spread of AIDS. Many states have prohibitions against the use of state funds for these purposes; therefore, this endeavor has often become the responsibility of the private sector.

Should the HIV infected inmate be restricted from conjugal visits? Inmates probably cannot be prevented from such visits in jurisdictions where conjugal visits are authorized as long as the institution has tested the inmate and legally informed and counseled the spouse of the inmate's HIV status. Does the spouse and family have the right to be informed? In California, when a probation or a parole officer learns that a probationer or parolee in his or her custody has not informed his or her spouse, the officer may make sure information is relayed to the spouse only though either the chief medical officer of the institution from which the probationer or parolee was released or the physician/surgeon treating the spouse, probationer, or parolee (California, *Penal Code § 7521*). The probation or parole officer must also ensure that proper counseling accompanies the release of the probationer or parolee's HIV status to the spouse. Again, although this is a clear, allowable exception to the confidentiality principle, it should be noted that there are clear-cut safeguards that limit the exception and provide for counseling.

HIV has presented problems and issues to society, in general, and the criminal justice system, in particular, unlike any that have been seen before. The disease infects ethnic minorities, gay men, and intravenous drug users in numbers that far exceed these groups' representation in society. It carries with it a stigma that goes beyond other illnesses, even those that are sexually transmitted. The detection and treatment of HIV infection has become highly politicized today. The value of confidentiality versus the protection of public health has been decided in many areas, including the criminal justice system, on an emotional, not a rational, basis.

THE LAW AND CRIMINAL JUSTICE COUNSELOR LIABILITY

Interest in the field of liability for criminal justice personnel is growing. This is largely a result of the increasing number of lawsuits filed against all types of criminal justice personnel by probationers, parolees, and jail and prison inmates. In the past, criminal justice professionals were protected from legal actions brought about by those under their supervision. This is not entirely true today.

Although suits are filed for numerous reasons by criminal justice offenders, the majority of suits brought about by prison inmates produce very small, if any, results (Hawkins & Alpert, 1989). Nonetheless, the criminal justice system continues to be assaulted with numerous suits. Many jurisdictions are providing liability insurance or indemnification to all types of correctional employees. Employees with liability insurance are somewhat protected from the financial burdens associated with tort action, because the state will provide financial aid to employees found to violate an inmate's rights when the court awards civil damages. Normally, there is a limit on insurance coverage afforded prison employees, and in most jurisdictions with insurance, the state will not pay punitive damages. Furthermore, the correctional employee may have to pay the offender's attorney fees as provided for in the Civil Rights Attorney's Fees Award Act of 1976 (42 U.S.C.A. § 1988). Consequently, it makes good sense for criminal justice counselors to keep abreast of the changing developments in tort law.

Liability and Tort Law Concepts

The law relating to liability is complex; however, several tort law concepts must be understood if the law is to make sense.

Cause of Action

Cause of action refers to a theory of recovery. When a lawsuit is filed, it is frequently asked under what theory is the suit filed or what causes of action are filed. There are several common causes of action: battery, assault, false imprisonment, negligence, the Federal Civil Rights Statute of 1871, or the Federal Tort Claims Act of 1946.

Respondeat Superior

Respondeat superior is an ancient common law doctrine that means "let the superior respond." Under this doctrine, an employer is liable for the torts of his or her employee, provided those torts are committed in the course and scope of employment. At common law the employee normally had nothing, so suing him or her would yield nothing. Because employers usually had deep pockets, the idea evolved that the employer should respond and pay for the acts of the employee. In fact, today there are frequent legal battles to decide whether an employee commits a tort during the course and scope of employment (e.g., a police officer who commits a rape during working hours or a correctional officer who beats an inmate) (Prosser & Keeton, 1984).

Sovereign Immunity

The doctrine of sovereign immunity started in England and was based on the theory of the divine right of kings. The basis of this theory was that the king was on earth and in charge because it was intended to be so by God. God could do no wrong, and since the king was an agent of God, the king by extension could do no wrong. Also it evolved that anything done in the king's name was not a wrong as a matter of law. Eventually, this doctrine came to the United States, and it is still a strong principle today (*Black's Law Dictionary,* 1990). Under the doctrine, the government cannot be sued for torts, unless the government (state or federal) has waived its immunity by statute or through its constitution to permit this type of lawsuit. At the federal level, the Federal Tort Claims Act (1946) has gone a long way in waiving sovereign immunity in many but not all situations. Thus, even at the federal level, sovereign immunity is still a significant concern for those who wish to sue the federal government. Likewise, under state law, either the state constitution or the state legislature would have to authorize this type of lawsuit against the government for there to be a waiver of sovereign immunity.

> **"The doctrine of sovereign immunity can prevent inmates' lawsuits against prison personnel and offenders' lawsuits against correctional personnel."**

It is almost impossible to talk about state sovereign immunity waivers intelligently, because the laws in the various states are so different that it is impossible to generalize and say that there is sovereign immunity in certain situations and no sovereign immunity in other situations. For example, in California (*Government Code*) there is absolute sovereign immunity in regard to parole decisions in deciding who gets parole and whether to revoke parole. In summary, sovereign immunity is different from state to state and the reader must refer to his or her particular state law. Litigation of the actual cause of action or merits of the case may never occur unless the problem of sovereign immunity is overcome. Many lawsuits end before it is ever determined whether there was in fact negligence, because the court dismisses the case on the grounds of sovereign immunity. Sovereign immunity is the first step in dealing with liability. Whenever the government is sued, it must be shown that the government has waived its sovereign immunity. This is not always easy.

In summary, the doctrine of sovereign immunity can prevent inmates' lawsuits against prison personnel and offenders' lawsuits against correctional personnel. In simple terms, the doctrine assumes that government can do no wrong, and before a lawsuit can occur, the doctrine must be set aside. The doctrine holds that a private citizen may not sue a governmental unit or its agent unless the state has consented to such lawsuits by statute. In a state where there has been no waiver of sovereign immunity for correctional institutions, the state prison system is immune from a private suit for damage, at least under state law. Sovereign immunity protects the state; however, under both state and federal law there is often recognized a qualified immunity that protects governmental employees in tort actions. Under federal tort law a qualified immunity is recognized when an employee's "conduct does not violate clearly established statutory or constitutional rights of which a reasonable person would have known" (Hawkins & Alpert, 1989, p. 369). Many states have either totally or partially abrogated the doctrine of sovereign immunity by constitutional provision or statute.

Liability Focal Points

As was mentioned earlier in this chapter, there are several avenues an offender can take to bring his or her case before the courts. Monetary damages can be awarded offenders against state entities and employees only by using state tort lawsuits and § 1983 of the Federal Civil Rights Act of 1871. Note that under *Bivens* (1971) a cause of action may be initiated against individual federal employees.

The Supreme Court has announced a four-factor *reasonableness test* for determining the validity of a person, regulation, and/or policy. A prison regulation and/or policy is valid if (a) it is reasonably related to a legitimate penalogical interest; (b) alternative means remain open to the prisoner to exercise the right; (c) accommodating the prisoner's right will have an adverse effect on the prison, prisoners, or resources; and (d) no ready alternatives exist (*Turner v. Safley*, 1987). Although the test to be applied to determine the validity of a prison regulation and/or policy is now clear, the application of the test to different factual situations does not lead to clear answers, and substantial litigation can be expected to continue. Although the law is still developing, courts are generally receptive to § 1983 prisoners' claims dealing with denial of court access and racial discrimination.

Today, it appears that criminal justice personnel (including counselors) acting in good faith, reasonably, and with the belief they are complying with the law, cannot be held civilly liable for monetary damages. Under the Federal Civil Rights Act, supervisors may be held liable for conduct committed by persons under their supervision and control, even though they did not commit the act themselves. However, *vicarious liability* is an extremely complicated legal concept, and the topic is beyond the scope of this work.[2]

According to Champion (1990), "where known mentally ill offenders are confined, even for brief periods, there is the chance that sheriffs, jail administrators, and even diagnosing psychiatrists will be liable for physical harm to others through third-party liability actions" (p. 171). Probation officers as well as other correctional officials have a duty to use reasonable care to protect the public from the reasonably foreseeable risk of harm at the hands of a person on probation or parole. If they do not, they may be held liable in some states (*Semler v. Psychiatric Institute,* 1976). However, if probation officers act reasonably, with objective good faith, and are not negligent in ensuring the safety of the community in their supervision of offenders, courts are unlikely to find officers liable in civil lawsuits involving injuries to victims.

SUMMARY

Criminal justice counselors must have direction about how to counsel offenders to minimize the possibility of violating the law and being sued by them. Counselors must keep in mind that state laws may differ, and these laws must be checked.

Generally speaking, probationers have more rights than parolees, and parolees have more rights than prisoners. Lawsuits have been brought before the courts that deal with offenders' due process and substantive rights. In the 1940s, the courts began paying attention to the rights of offenders and especially to the rights of inmates. Inmates won unrestricted access to federal courts and their civil rights, even if they were confined. States eventually began to abolish civil death statutes for prisoners. Today there are conflicting opinions about the changes brought about as a result of offenders' legal battles. Some have the opinion that the changes have humanized prison conditions. Others hold the opinion that the changes have tied the hands of criminal justice professionals.

The concept of privileged communication is a legal one that applies to certain specific relationships, and it protects confidentiality in those relationships. Normally, criminal justice counselors are peace officers who are frequently not licensed professionals. As a result, the doctrine of privileged communication does not apply in its entirety to them. Even when there is a privileged relationship, there are exceptions to that privilege and confidentiality might not apply. Therefore, criminal justice counselors have an ethical duty to inform offenders at the onset of counseling that confidentiality of all information cannot be ensured.

The offender does not enjoy the same rights of privacy that ordinary citizens do in their homes or offices. Therefore, probation and parole officers have a duty under certain circumstances to warn appropriate third parties and authorities as to the statuses of those under their supervision and failure to warn may result in successful law suits if offenders injure others.

The courts have not held that rehabilitation is constitutionally mandated in prison; however, this has not precluded prisons from developing such programs or prisoners from attempting their own rehabilitation. After having been afforded basic procedural due process protections, inmates may be involuntarily subjected to treatment, if such treatment has been determined to be in their best interests. When it comes to intrusive, irreversible psychological procedures, courts have been more conservative and have tended to provide inmates greater protection from such treatment.

Criminal justice counselors must possess a broad knowledge of HIV infection and AIDS, because many offenders they encounter have engaged in conduct that has been linked to the transmission of the disease. In the absence of national AIDS legislation, criminal justice counselors work in a field in which laws related to AIDS are quickly changing, and as a result, they must keep up with laws and administrative policies in their particular states. Confidentiality laws and policies dealing with offenders who have AIDS are complex; states often have a difficult time balancing need-to-know situations with the principle of confidentiality.

There have been increasing numbers of lawsuits filed against all types of criminal justice personnel by offenders. Laws concerning liability are complex and difficult. Criminal justice counselors must remain alert to the fact that they may be held liable for their actions with offenders. Some jurisdictions provide liability insurance or indemnification to correctional employees. This insurance somewhat protects employees from financial burdens resulting from tort action when an employee is found to violate an inmate's rights and when the court awards civil damages.

Matching Key Terms and Definitions

Match each key term with the correct definition.

a. due process
b. substantive rights
c. cause of action
d. *Ruffin v. Commonwealth* (1871)
e. hands-off doctrine
f. *Ex Parte Hull* (1941)
g. *Coffin v. Reichard* (1944)
h. *Respondeat superior*
i. tort lawsuit
j. *Morrissey v. Brewer* (1972)
k. *Gagnon v. Scarpelli* (1973)
l. *Estelle v. Gambel* (1976)
m. privileged communication
n. *Tarasoff v. University of California* (1986)

o. *U.S. v. Dawson* (1975)
p. *Bell v. Wolfish* (1984)
q. *Hudson v. Palmer* (1984)
r. *Padgett v. Stein* (1976)
s. *James v. Wallace* (1976)
t. *Rouse v. Cameron* (1966)
u. *Bowring v. Godwin* (1977)
v. *Whitely v. Albers* (1986)
w. *Turner v. Safley* (1987)
x. HIV positive
y. AIDS
z. doctrine of sovereign immunity
aa. *Hudson v. McMillian* (1992)
bb. *Washington v. Harper* (1990)

___ 1. Rights that give the offender freedom to do something or guarantee the offender freedom from certain conditions.

___ 2. The case that led the courts to take a hands-off approach to the rights of offenders and to interfering in the business of corrections agencies and institutions.

___ 3. The first major case that provided inmates with unrestricted access to federal courts.

___ 4. Rights that protect the offender from sloppy procedures.

___ 5. The theory of recovery used in liability lawsuits.

___ 6. The noninterference in the business of corrections agencies and institutions.

___ 7. A landmark case that held prisoners do not lose their civil rights as a result of confinement.

___ 8. An ancient common law doctrine that means "let the superior respond" and holds an employer responsible for the torts his or her employees commit in the course and scope of employment.

___ 9. Civil actions against correctional employees for gross or wanton negligence or intentional wrongdoing.

__ 10. A case in which the Court extended *Morrissey* due process rights to probationers facing revocation.

__ 11. A case in which the Court held doctors had a duty to warn third parties of a possible future harm from their patients.

__ 12. Two cases in which the Court held prisoners had absolutely no expectation of privacy when they enter prisons and jails.

__ 13. Communications between certain people that are considered by law as confidential.

__ 14. A case in which the Court held prisoners do not enjoy the same rights of privacy as do ordinary citizens in their homes or offices.

__ 15. A case in which the Court held deliberate indifference by prison personnel to medical needs of prisoners violated the prisoner's Eighth Amendment rights.

__ 16. A case in which the Court set the stage for procedural due process for parolees.

__ 17. A case in which the Court held that a positive rehabilitation program is not a constitutional right but states cannot impede the ability of inmates to attempt their own rehabilitation.

__ 18. A case in which the Court held that the state cannot deny a prisoner psychological and psychiatric treatment under certain conditions.

__ 19. A person who has tested positive for the AIDS virus.

__ 20. A principle that can prevent inmates' lawsuits against prison personnel.

__ 21. A case in which the Court announced a four-factor reasonableness test for determining the validity of a person, regulation, and/or policy in a correctional setting.

__ 22. A case in which the Court held, in the absence of statutes providing for a right to certain kinds of treatment for offenders who are being confined, a right to treatment still exists for psychopaths, juveniles, insane, drug addicts, and/or alcoholics.

__ 23. Acquired immunodeficiency syndrome.

__ 24. A case in which the Court held that shooting a prisoner is a violation of the Eighth Amendment prohibition against cruel and unusual punishment if the force was not a good faith effort to maintain or restore discipline but rather was applied maliciously and sadistically for the very purpose of causing harm.

__ 25. A case in which the Court held that there was no constitutional duty imposed on the state to rehabilitate prisoners.

__ 26. A case in which the Court held that the use of excessive physical force against a prisoner by correctional officers may constitute cruel and unusual punishment even if the inmate does not suffer serious injury.

___ 27. A case in which the court held that a seriously mentally ill person may be treated against his or her will, provided that certain procedural due process rights are adhered to before the forced treatment.

Discussion Questions

1. How have offenders' rights changed in the United States since 1940?

2. What are the differences in the concept of privileged communication for counselors within the criminal justice system and those outside of the system?

3. Why do offenders not have the same rights to privacy that ordinary citizens have?

4. What are some of the dilemmas the criminal justice system is facing in regard to offenders who have AIDS?

5. What are some of the ways criminal justice counselors can be held liable by offenders?

NOTES

1. For additional discussion of inmates' rights to refuse mental health treatment and the hands-off doctrine, see Alexander (1991, 1993).

2. For a more detailed discussion of liability law in American policing, see del Carmen (1991).

REFERENCES

Alberti v. Sheriff of Harris Co., Tex., 406 F. Supp. 649 (S.D. Tex. 1975).

Alexander, R., Jr. (1991). The United States Supreme Court and an inmates right to refuse mental health treatment. *Criminal Justice Policy Review, 5*(3), 225-240.

Alexander, R., Jr. (1993). Slamming the federal courthouse door on inmates. *Journal of Criminal Justice, 21,* 103-115.

Bell v. Wolfish, 441 U.S. 520 (1979).

Bivens v. Six Unknown Named Agents of the Federal Bureau of Narcotics, 403 U.S. 388 (1971).

Black's Law Dictionary 1396 (1990). (6th ed.)

Bowring v. Godwin, 551 F.2d 44, 47, 48 (5th Cir. 1977).

California Department of Corrections. (1990, June). *Guidelines for involuntary testing of inmates: Proposition 96 and Senate Bill 1913.* Sacramento: Office of Health Care Services.

California. *Evidence Code,* §§ 1010, 1012, 1014.

California. *Government Code,* § 845.8.

California. *Health and Safety Code,* §§ 199.96-199.97.

California. *Penal Code,* §§ 1202.1, 1202.6, 2600, 2670-2680, 7510-7512, 7521.

Champion, D. J. (1990). *Probation and parole in the United States.* Columbus, OH: Merrill.

Coffin v. Reichard, 143 F.2d 443 (6th Cir. 1944).

del Carmen, R. V. (1991). *Civil liberties in American policing.* Englewood Cliffs, NJ: Prentice Hall.

Estelle v. Gamble, 429 U.S. 97 (1976).

Ex parte Hull, 312 U.S. 546 (1941).

Fare v. Michael C., 442 U.S. 707 (1979).

Federal Civil Rights Statute 42 U.S.C. 1983.

Gagnon v. Scarpelli, 411 U.S. 778 (1973).

Gilliam v. Martin, 589 F. Supp. 680 (W.D. Okla. 1984).

Hawkins, R, & Alpert, G. P. (1989). *American prison systems: Punishment and justice.* Englewood Cliffs, NJ: Prentice Hall.

Holt v. Sarver, 309 F. Supp. 362 (E.D. Ark. 1970, aff'd 442 F.2d 304, 8th. Cir. 1971).

Hudson v. McMillian, 503 U.S. (1992).

Hudson v. Palmer, 468 U.S. 517 (1984).

James v. Wallace, 406 F. Supp. 318 (M.D. Ala. 1976).

Jarvis, R. R., Closen, M. L., Herman, D. H. J., & Leonard, A. S. (1990). *AIDS law in a nutshell.* St. Paul, MN: West.

Jones, R. A. (1974, February 15). Mind control studies will lose funding. *Los Angeles Times,* part 1, p. 10.

Leavitt v. City of Morris, 117 N.W. 393, 395 (S.Ct. Minn. 1908).

Long v. Powell, 388 F. Supp. 422 (N.D. Ga. 1975), jud. va. 423 U.S. 808 (1975).

Morales v. Turman, 364 F. Supp. 166, 175 (E.D. Tex. 1973).

Morrissey v. Brewer, 408 U.S. 471 (1972).

Padgett v. Stein, 406 F. Supp. 287 (M.D. Pa. 1976).

Procunier v. Martinez, 416 U.S. 396 (1974).

Prosser, W. L., & Keeton, W. P. (1984). *Torts* (5th ed.). St. Paul, MN: West.

Reid, S. T. (1981). *The correctional system: An introduction.* New York: Holt, Rinehart, & Winston.

Rouse v. Cameron, 373 F.2d 451 (D.C. Cir. 1966).

Ruffin v. Commonwealth, 62 Va. (21 Gratt.) 790 (1871).

Rutherford v. Hutto, 377 F. Supp. 268 (E.D. Ark. 1974).

Semler v. Psychiatric Institute of Washington, D.C., 538 F.2d 121 (4th Cir. 1976).

Smith v. Follette, 445 F.2d 955 (2d Cir. 1971).

Tarasoff v. Regents of the University of California, 17 C.3d 425, 131 (Calif. Rptr. 14, 551 P.2d 334 1976).

Taylor v. Sterrett, 344 F. Supp. 411 (N.D. Tex. 1972).

Turner v. Safley, 482 U.S. 78 (1987).

United States Code Annotated Title 42 §§ 1983, 1988, 1997-1997j and Title 28 §§ 1346, 1402, 2401, 2402, 2411, 2412, 2671-2680.

U.S. v. Dawson, 516 F.2d 796 (9th Cir. 1975).

Washington v. Harper, 494 U.S. 210 (1990).

Welsch v. Likins, 373 F. Supp. 487 (D. Minn. 1974).

Whitely v. Albers, 475 U.S. 312 (1986).

Wilson v. Kelley, 294 F. Supp. 1005, 1012-1013 (N.D. Ga. 1968, aff'd per curiam 393 U.S. 266 1969).

Wolff v. McDonnell, 418 U.S. 539 (1974).

Wood, G. J., Marks, R., & Dilley, J. W. (1990). *AIDS law for mental health professionals: A handbook for judicious practice.* Berkeley, CA: University of San Francisco.

Criminal Justice Counseling Modalities

CHAPTER HIGHLIGHTS

- There are many criminal justice counseling modalities in use today.

- The adoption of a modality by a criminal justice counselor depends on the counselor's philosophy of how people change.

- Criminal justice counseling style depends on knowledge, training, experience, and personality.

- Counselors embracing all modalities can use any counseling technique.

- The major premise in nondirective criminal justice counseling is that the offender is the only rightful person to determine his or her future.

- Nondirective criminal justice counselors are prohibited from questioning, suggesting, advising, challenging, and confronting offenders.

- Nondirective criminal justice counselors listen, play back to the offender what was said, and enter the offender's world through empathy.

- Nondirective counseling helps offenders find their Selves.

- Directive counseling modalities dominate American corrections.

- Directive criminal justice counselors take charge of and control the counseling process.

- Directive criminal justice counseling permits the counselor to ask leading questions, identify problems, and resolve problems.

- Psychoanalytic/dynamic criminal justice counselors stress the offender's past and insight as central in behavior change.

- Criminal justice counselors find the Freudian concept of defense mechanisms useful in counseling offenders.

- Offenders frequently employ defense mechanisms when they are unable to cope with life's realities.

- Relationship counseling focuses on building a positive relationship with offenders.

- Most corrections agencies discourage the use of relationship counseling with offenders because of its high-risk/low-gain potential.

- Rational-emotive counseling focuses on attacking the offender's illogical thoughts.

- Gestalt counseling approaches emphasize awareness and insight as necessary in problem solving.

- Behavior modification counseling concentrates on immediately changing behavior not on understanding or insight.

- Reality counseling concentrates on making offenders responsible for their behavior.

- Transactional analysis concentrates on the types of interactions offenders have with others.

- Crisis intervention counseling concentrates on helping the offender through immediate stressful situations.

- Eclectic counselors diagnose offenders' needs and use methods and techniques from any modality that might work with offenders.

- In the future, therapeutic communities are likely to be heavily used for counseling incarcerated and non-incarcerated offenders.

- Group counseling in criminal justice settings is likely to be used more frequently in the future because of its advantages over individual counseling.

- Family counseling does not deal with the offender exclusively, but with the offender's whole family.

KEY TERMS

- Modality
- Criminal justice counseling style
- Criminal justice counseling technique
- Nondirective counseling
- Empathy
- Defense mechanisms
- Rationalization
- Intellectualization
- Denial
- Repression
- Regression-sublimation
- Displacement
- Reaction formation
- Projection
- Reaction neutrality
- Relationship counseling
- Gestalt
- Behavior modification
- Reality counseling
- Crisis intervention counseling
- Transactional analysis
- Problem management counseling
- Eclectic counseling
- Therapeutic community
- Group counseling

– **Family counseling**

– **Homeostasis**

INTRODUCTION

This chapter begins with a discussion of what is meant by counseling style. It is followed by a description of the most prevalent counseling modalities used in criminal justice settings. The counseling modalities chosen for discussion are nondirective, directive, psychoanalytic/dynamic, relationship, rational-emotive, Gestalt, behavior modification, reality therapy, transactional analysis, crisis intervention, problem management, and eclectic. Criminal justice counseling fads are not introduced. At the end of the chapter there are discussions of the therapeutic community, group counseling, and family counseling.

Modalities are the models, approaches, prototypes, or orientations used by criminal justice counselors to help offenders adjust to society and, it is hoped, live law-abiding lives. Modalities are important to understand because they depict schools of thought about how offenders should be dealt with by counselors and embody the principles concerning how people change. The objectives of each distinct modality presented in this chapter are indistinguishable. Each modality seeks growth, positive change, and law-abiding behavior for offenders. The modalities differ in the means, methods, and procedures used to achieve these objectives.

As before, the term *counselor* refers to the criminal justice counselor and the terms *offender* and *counselee* refer to the person counseled. Note that the modalities described below are also widely used with counselees outside of the criminal justice system, and the term *counselee* in most cases can be substituted for *offender* without changing the meaning of the text.

CRIMINAL JUSTICE COUNSELING STYLE
AND TECHNIQUE

Criminal justice counseling style can be defined as a distinctive or characteristic mode of expression and action used in working with offenders. It involves the counselor's approach or behavioral orientation to offenders in individual or group settings.

Criminal justice counseling style depends on four elements: knowledge, training, experience, and personality. Knowledge refers to facts, truths, and principles of criminal justice counseling. The counselor must be familiar with the subject of counseling. Academic knowledge provides the theory and foundation for counseling. It allows the counselor to detect, identify, and analyze patterns and trends in offenders' behaviors. Academic knowledge also helps counselors relate the offender's actions to larger issues the offender might experience. Knowledge is important for the criminal justice counselor, but it alone does not constitute counseling style.

Counseling style also depends on training, or practicing of counseling skills, before counseling real offenders. Training is often done in laboratory situations with students and/or criminal justice professionals acting as counselees. The counselor, through drilling and repetition, can develop proficiency.

Experience is another important ingredient on which counseling style depends. Experience is gathered by working with authentic offenders in the field. It involves the process of personally doing and encountering the idiosyncrasies of the counseling process with live offenders in real criminal justice settings. Generally speaking, the more experience a criminal justice counselor has, the more comfortable he or she will be with offenders during the counseling process. The more comfortable a criminal justice counselor is, the more he or she will exude confidence.

Personality is the last factor on which counseling style is based. It is the only factor that cannot be learned by the counselor and, as a result, is the only constant in the development of a criminal justice counseling style. Some psychologists believe that personality is an absolute in that criminal justice counselors are either born with a "counseling personality" or not. Others believe that personality is set in concrete by the age of five or six. Either way, personality factors such as shyness and assertiveness are normally difficult to change, even with years of counseling and/or therapy. This does not mean that quiet, reticent people will not make good counselors and that assertive, loud people will make good counselors or that all good counselors must be charismatic. It means that personality is a factor that we must accept as a given. Some offenders work well with counselors with particular personalities while others recoil from such personalities. The criminal justice counselor must understand that his or her counseling style will not always mesh with the personalities or needs of every offender.

Criminal justice counselors must intuitively feel out the best modality for each offender and, at the same time, must integrate the modality and style that they feel most comfortable using. If the counselor is not comfortable with a modality, it will negatively influence the offender and render counseling ineffective. One of the worst things a counselor can do is to appear phony in the offender's eyes. This will result in a loss of credibility for the counselor.

Counseling style is different from technique. Style is relatively unchanging and may be considered a part of the counselor's professional personality. Technique, on the other hand, is independent of personality and experience. Almost any technique or method can be used by any counselor as long as he or she is properly trained in the technique's use. Techniques are tactics to solve particular problems in counseling individuals and groups, whereas styles are behavioral orientations to individuals and groups. Development of a counseling style is important in selecting and using modalities.

CRIMINAL JUSTICE
COUNSELING MODALITIES

Today's popular thought is "nothing works" in the treatment and correction of offenders' behaviors, attitudes, and values. Criminal justice professionals, politicians, and lay people alike have espoused the "nothing works" rhetoric, although many feel strict punishment and stern discipline work (Martinson, 1974). It is my opinion that dependable modalities do exist that can assist the offender in his or her transition from a law-violating to a law-abiding citizen. We are going to begin by examining nondirective and directive counseling modalities. If we were to place these modalities on a continuum, they would be opposite of each other. Most modalities fall somewhere between directive and nondirective extremes.

Nondirective Counseling

Nondirective counseling is sometimes called client-centered or Rogerian therapy. Each of the terms refer to the modality developed by Rogers, a humanistic psychologist. Nondirective, client-centered, and Rogerian refer to his methodology, which is used to help the counselee. This modality is concerned with a number of human issues:

1. Humanism
2. Individualism
3. Potential of the offender
4. Dignity of the offender
5. Uniqueness of the offender
6. Offender's subjective experience (perceptions)
7. Healthy, nonpathological behavior
8. Love
9. Creativity
10. Spirituality
11. Finding the offender's Self through personal growth
12. Personal values
13. Acceptance
14. Self-actualization

> **❝The offender is the only rightful person to determine his/her future and no one can tell another what is right for him/her.❞**

The major premise in nondirective counseling is that the offender is the only rightful person to determine his or her future and that no one can tell another what is right for him or her (Rogers, 1951). Thus direction in the counseling process emanates solely from the offender. The offender is primary and the counselor plays a less visible, secondary, facilitative role in the counseling relationship. The counselor takes no responsibility for the offender's decisions. The offender diagnoses his or her own problems and has the responsibility to control the counseling process and solve his or her own problems. The nondirective criminal justice counselor does not ask leading questions, suggest, or give advice. Leading questions take the control of the counseling session away from the offender, and advice giving is not in keeping with the philosophy that the offender is the only rightful person to determine his or her future. In addition, nondirective counselors are not experts in solving problems or problem-solving counseling techniques.

The role of the criminal justice counselor is to provide a warm, permissive, nonthreatening, nonjudgmental, and emotional environment in which the offender feels enough trust to open up and freely discuss his or her problems. In this therapeutic atmosphere, rapport is developed, and the offender can begin to accept himself or herself as he or she really is, drop the facades, and begin to explore his or her Self. Once the counselor provides the appropriate conditions whereby positive change occurs, the offender opens up and the criminal justice counselor is supposedly capable of entering the offender's world through accurate empathy. (Empathy refers to understanding what the offender says and feels.) The criminal justice counselor becomes a human projection screen and sounding board for the offender. By actively listening, the counselor plays back to the offender what was said in words, through body language, and by emotional responses. If the counseling procedures are successful, the offender will be able to clarify and gain insight into thoughts, feelings, attitudes, values, and behaviors. The nondirective counselor does not interpret, analyze, or solve the offender's problem(s). In the same spirit, the nondirective counselor does not challenge or confront offenders by pinpointing games, smokescreens, manipulations, avoidance, and so forth. Such confrontation is thought to alienate and scare offenders away from counseling. The nondirective counselor does, however, in a nondirective way challenge offenders to examine, clarify, and find their own answers to their problems. It is believed that offenders will come to see themselves more clearly through nondirective counseling and thus solve their own problems (Rogers, 1961). As a result of this process, offenders develop an increased ability to say no when around those who encourage criminal behavior (Hatcher, 1978).

Nondirective criminal justice counselors normally work with offenders only in the here and now, or present. They also try to act as role models by being honest with offenders.

Over the years, criminal justice students have asked what other things can nondirective counselors do with offenders. There is nothing in nondirective counseling theory that prohibits the counselor from sharing feelings with offenders. For example, if an offender repeatedly makes a counselor tense, it is the counselor's responsibility not to avoid or ignore such behavior but to share it with the offender. If a counselor finds himself or herself repeatedly not liking an offender's behavior, the nondirective counselor must tell the offender. According to nondirective theory, such honesty will give rise to dialogue, clarification, and trust. Nondirective counselors cannot effectively counsel if they stuff their feelings about offenders on their caseloads.

Here are some of the questions nondirective counseling raises:

1. Can nondirective counseling set limits for offenders?
2. How can nondirective counselors reconcile placing offenders in jail or prison?
3. How can nondirective counselors effectively handle offenders without use of the techniques of questioning, challenging, confronting, and advising?

Nondirective counseling has its opponents and supporters in criminal justice settings. Critics believe that the nondirective counselor's role is limited because the techniques do not allow questioning, advising, challenging, and confronting offenders, and critics assert that most offenders need such interventions (Lester & Braswell, 1987). Critics also point out that if the criminal justice counselor relied only on active listening, empathy, and mirroring information to offenders, the counseling process would go on forever and offenders would never resolve problems. Supporters believe that counselors who are good listeners and develop rapport, trust, and empathy with offenders are missing in the criminal justice field today and if counselors used these techniques more offenders could be helped.

Directive Counseling

Directive counseling is the opposite of nondirective counseling. There are many criminal justice modalities that are considered primarily directive in emphasis. The objective of directive counseling is helping the counselee, but directive counselors use a methodology that allows the counselor to take charge and control the direction counseling takes. Directive criminal justice counselors are concerned with the following issues:

1. Helping the offender quickly when time is scarce.
2. Counselor's expertise in helping offenders deal with issues and problems in their lives.
3. Counselor's dominant and assertive role in diagnosing offenders' problems and helping offenders make and carry out decisions.
4. Maximizing the offender's potential by early identification and resolution of problems.
5. Counselor's responsibility for counseling.

The major premise of directive criminal justice counseling is that the offender has failed to solve problems himself or herself and that is why he or she needs help. It is the counselor, not the offender, who is responsible for the counseling process. Therefore, the diagnosis and solution of the offender's problem(s) is left to the counselor. It is the criminal justice counselor, not the offender, who has been educated and trained in problem-solving skills and, therefore, is better prepared to take control of the counseling process. The offender respects the counselor's ability to identify and resolve problems. As offenders experience the counselor's competence, respect and trust develop.

Directive criminal justice counselors take charge of the counseling process. They diagnosis and develop counseling plans for offenders. They come up with solutions to offenders' problems and advise offenders what actions to take. Directive criminal justice counselors ask a lot of leading questions. They challenge and confront offenders for appropriate reasons and make ultimatums. They keep a close and watchful eye on the actions of offenders. In addition, directive criminal justice counselors work with the offender's past, present, and future.

Directive criminal justice modalities dominate American corrections for several reasons. The counselor can get to the heart of problems quickly if the offender is avoiding. Also the counselor is not limited in the type of responses he or she can make. The criminal justice counselor can redirect counseling sessions that appear to be going nowhere. Most criminal justice counselors feel comfortable in directing the counseling, because their jobs make them responsible for protecting the community. Last, directive modalities fit nicely with the philosophy of the American system of criminal justice, which tends to be authoritarian and paternalistic; as a result, it frequently produces reactions such as rebellion and transference by offenders. The criminal justice system gives orders and tells offenders what they must do. Directive counseling modalities allow the criminal justice counselor to do the same.

Some of the questions directive counseling raises concerning counseling offenders are as follows:

1. How can the directive counselor get beyond the cop role?
2. How can directive counselors develop trust with offenders?
3. How can offenders become responsible decision makers if counselors tell them what to do?

The critics of directive criminal justice counseling modalities frequently complain that in practice counselors do not spend enough time listening to offenders and, as a result, are too quick to draw conclusions. They state that directive counselors infantalize offenders by telling them what to do and making decisions for them. Also rapport and trust in the counseling relationship are difficult for directive criminal justice counselors to achieve. Critics indicate that directive counselors often bring out the angry, rebellious side of offenders. Finally, directive criminal justice counseling has been accused of coercing and scaring offenders into immediately changing their behavior, but long-term internal change rarely occurs.

Psychoanalytic/Dynamic Counseling

The terms *psychoanalytic* and *psychodynamic* are frequently used interchangeably; however, *dynamic* refers specifically to understanding the nature of conflict and motivational causes of anxieties (Shore, 1975). The terms identify a therapeutic modality based on Freud's original theories. Freud developed his theories and clinical approach to dealing with behavior during the late 1800s and early 1900s. The modality addresses itself to childhood experiences, unconscious mental life, personality development (id, ego, and superego), stages of human development (oral, anal, phallic, latent, and neophallic), anxieties, psychological conflicts, traumatic events, dreams, and defense mechanisms. In addition, psychoanalysts believe that much of human behavior is predetermined and has its roots in heredity.

A major premise of psychoanalytic/dynamic criminal justice counseling is that only after the offender verbalizes and understands his or her problem can he or she gain insight and change. In addition, insight cannot occur until the offender's unconscious desires are made conscious.

Psychoanalytic/dynamic criminal justice counselors help the offender gain insight by drawing out and interpreting offender's past experiences so that he or she can understand his or her problems. The counselor brings unconscious motives to the offender's consciousness by use of such techniques as free association and analysis of dreams. Counselors also discover the offender's problems by analyzing the elements of personality, stages of development, traumatic events, early childhood experiences, and defense mechanisms.

The counselor develops a case history of the offender. Understanding the offender's past is assumed to be critical to the development of insight. Therefore, a lot of time is spent dealing with things that happened to the offender in early childhood. It is thought that unresolved issues of an offender's past remain and cause problems in the present. (Note that psychoanalytic/dynamic criminal justice counseling emphasizes the offender's past and nondirective criminal justice counseling emphasizes the present.)

Psychoanalytic/dynamic criminal justice counseling can be classified as directive and nondirective. It is nondirective in that the counselor allows the offender to bring up whatever comes to mind. The counselor says little to direct the counseling session, but does take notes that are studied and interpreted after the session. At a future session, the counselor then shares his or her analysis with the offender. In the sense that there is interpretation, analysis, and some questioning, this modality is directive.

This modality in its pure form is seldom used today in criminal justice settings. Some of the reasons are listed below:

1. Most criminal justice counselors are not specialists in psychoanalytic/dynamic theory.

2. Freudian psychology is viewed as interesting but outdated.

3. Criminal justice counselors do not have enough time to allow offenders to free associate.

4. Criminal justice counselors want to help offenders deal with problems in the present not the past.

5. Criminal justice counselors believe that offenders already have too many excuses and rationalizations as to why they behave as they do and the psychoanalytic/dynamic modality gives them more.

6. Criminal justice counselors believe that knowing an offender's unconscious motivation for crime is interesting from an academic standpoint but is not practical.

The psychoanalytic/dynamic approach is concerned with the following questions:

1. How does understanding or insight bring about the offender's behavior change?

2. What are the offender's unconscious desires and thoughts?

3. How did the offender's past influence the present?

The psychoanalytic/dynamic modality has given the counseling field several concepts and techniques. Four major concepts that Freud contributed to psychoanalytic/dynamic counseling are the unconscious, personality structure, stages of development, and defense mechanisms. An understanding of defense mechanisms, ways in which we protect our fragile human egos, is important to the criminal justice counselor. If defense mechanisms can be identified, they can be dealt with therapeutically in the counseling process. The criminal justice counselor must watch for the following defense mechanisms frequently used by offenders (Freud, 1946).

1. *Rationalization.* Rationalization is the offender's tendency to justify or make acceptable unacceptable behavior and thoughts. A subtle alchemy occurs in the offender's mind. It involves making excuses for and explaining unacceptable behavior. For example, an offender who steals from a neighborhood grocery store tells the arresting officer that the grocery owner had it coming because

the owner had been stealing from neighborhood patrons for years by overpricing merchandise.

2. *Intellectualization.* Intellectualization is a specialized form of rationalization. It occurs when offenders are unable to accept their feelings and emotions honestly and directly. So they talk and rationalize in abstractions or speak in the third person. For example, the addict who says "People who use drugs are the victims of an unjust political and economic system." The honest statement would be "I use drugs to escape my pain."

3. *Denial.* Denial occurs when an offender refuses to recognize, acknowledge, and/or believe in the reality or existence of something. It involves refusing to accept the facts of a situation. For example, the offender who has been arrested five times for drunk driving but continues to state that he or she is not an alcoholic. Other examples are the female whose husband beats her repeatedly and still she continues to believe and tell everyone what a wonderful person he is and the wife of a murder victim who believes her husband just went to the corner grocery and will be back shortly.

4. *Repression.* Repression is the process whereby unacceptable impulses are excluded from the offender's consciousness and are left to operate unconsciously. Repression is a more extreme form of denial. In denial, the offender refuses to face the obvious. With repression, the unacceptable impulses are blocked out. For example, an offender has no recollection of pulling the trigger and shooting a convenience store attendant in an armed robbery.

5. *Regression.* Regression is the reversion to behavior patterns that were appropriate at an earlier stage of development or age. For example, an adult prisoner taking a prison class throws a paper airplane at the instructor when he or she is not looking. Note that offenders exhibit childish behavior a great deal of the time.

6. *Sublimation.* Sublimation is the deflection of destructive or unacceptable energies into socially constructive or creative channels. For example, an unmarried woman who chooses a career working with dependent children or nuns who choose to teach sex education.

7. *Displacement.* Displacement is the transfer of an emotion from the object about which it was originally experienced to another object. For example, a prisoner who is mad at a prison guard but who yells at and takes it out on his or her cell mate.

8. *Reaction Formation.* Reaction formation is experiencing an emotion and reacting the opposite way. For example, a preacher who molests a child and then preaches against such behavior.

9. *Projection.* Projection is the tendency to attribute to another person, or to the environment, what is actually within oneself. For example, a parolee tells his or her parole agent that he or she is unfair, cruel, and unyielding. The parolee is actually describing his or her own qualities but is only able to see such qualities in others.

10. *Reaction Neutrality.* Reaction neutrality is not one of Freud's standard defense mechanisms. It involves experiencing an emotion but reacting as if there were no emotion. It is similar to reaction formation. For example, an offender becomes flooded with strong emotion but comes across as if he or she were unaffected and felt nothing.

These defense mechanisms protect the offender's ego from harsh reality. It is normal for people to protect themselves, and defense mechanisms naturally occur in response to data that are hard to process. Defense mechanisms allow people to handle, cope, and process slowly difficult and shocking information. These behaviors are not always intentionally used by offenders to obstruct the counseling process. In time and with help from the counselor, offenders will come to identify the mechanisms that prevent them from getting the help that they need.

Relationship Counseling

Relationship counseling developed from the humanistic school of psychology and centers on the relationship between the criminal justice counselor and the offender. Sullivan (1953) is frequently associated with developmental approaches and modalities such as relationship counseling. The counselor strives to provide a positive, adult relationship for the offender. In addition, counselors strive to work with offenders to develop positive, adult relationships with family and friends. Relationships are built by changing the ways offenders communicate with significant others.

The major premise of this modality is that the offender does not have a good relationship with another human being. If the offender can develop a good, warm, genuine, supportive, trusting relationship, then he or she will be empowered to solve his or her problems outside the counseling setting. It is not the offender himself or herself that is the source of the problem, but the offender's relationships with important people in his or her life.

The role of the counselor is to be available to the offender, develop a friendship with the offender within appropriate professional limits (see Chapter 1 for a discussion of the counselor role of friend), not engage in extensive analysis of the offender's problems, provide structure and limits for the offender, help the offender communicate better, and be sensitive to the offender's needs. One of the problems relationship counseling can produce is confusion in the offender's mind as to the role of the counselor. The counselor may be clear as to his or her professional limitations, but the offender may see the counselor primarily as a friend. If this happens, misunderstandings can develop. Such confusion must be eliminated before the counselor can be helpful to the offender. Note that most corrections agencies frown on relationship counseling because of its high-risk/low-gain possibilities.

Some of the questions relationship counseling raises are as follows:

1. How is trust developed with offenders?
2. Can psychologically sound relationships between counselors and offenders develop in criminal justice settings?
3. How does the offender develop a positive, independent relationship with the counselor?
4. How is it that the experience of a positive, adult relationship can change offenders' attitudes, feelings, behaviors, and values?
5. How can the counselor keep from becoming too emotionally involved with offenders and their families and friends?
6. Can the counselor and offender develop a close relationship without transference and countertransference issues interfering with counseling?

Rational-Emotive Counseling

Rational-emotive therapy and counseling is considered a cognitive therapeutic approach; it was established by Ellis (1973). Cognitive approaches to helping people are concerned with intellect, thinking, logic, and development and use of language. This modality embodies a rational approach by which the counselor makes a direct frontal attack on the offender's illogical thoughts and ideas. Simply speaking, rational-emotive counselors believe that offenders experience situations that produce irrational thoughts, ideas, and beliefs. In turn, irrational thoughts produce strong, negative emotions (hence the term rational-emotive). The object of counseling is to replace irrational thoughts with rational thoughts, thus giving way to more appropriate emotional responses (Ellis, 1977). Theoretically, problem behaviors result from irrational ideas, and if such ideas and resultant emotions are known, then offenders can change those behaviors.

> **❝Rational-emotive criminal justice counselors contend that changing the thoughts of offenders is more expedient than exploring the emotions of offenders.❞**

The major premise of rational-emotive counseling is that offenders will change only when they are ready to perceive things differently. Therefore, rational-emotive criminal justice counselors contend that changing the thoughts of offenders is more expedient than exploring the emotions of offenders. Emotions and feelings play a secondary role in the counseling process.

Rational-emotive counselors are directive and use assertive dialogue. They challenge and confront offenders about their irrational thoughts. They interpret the effects of irrational thinking. Counselors focus on teaching offenders in a persuasive, didactive way how to pinpoint irrational ideas and replace them with rational ones. Counselors also use many counseling techniques available to them. For example, it is not unusual for counselors to give offenders homework assignments or to role play with them. Offenders are encouraged to behave differently as quickly as possible.

Rational-emotive counselors are not concerned with the offender's past, unconscious, transference, empathy, self-determination, relationship building, defense mechanisms, and so forth. They take issue with anything that does not attack the offender's illogical thought processes. In my opinion, this modality is one of the more directive modalities in that the counselor immediately points out to offenders their faulty logic. The counselor then diagnoses and analyzes the illogical ideas. Finally, the counselor tells the offender what to do about them. The session's emphasis is on the counselor's skill, expertise, and professionalism. Sometimes counselors give offenders too much information to digest in a short period of time. It has been estimated that rational-emotive therapy produces change for many in 10 to 20 sessions, although it can take as long as 2 years (Lester & Braswell, 1987).

Some of the questions rational-emotive counseling raises are as follows:

1. Are emotional problems solely a result of faulty thinking and irrational ideas?
2. Are rational thoughts stronger than emotions?
3. Can emotional problems be resolved simply by pointing out the offender's irrational thinking?
4. Can criminal justice counselors be too assertive in attacking the logic of offenders?

Gestalt Counseling

The Gestalt therapeutic approach was introduced to the United States from Europe in the 1940s by Fredrick S. Perls (Simkin & Yontef, 1984). The modality developed as an offshoot of Gestalt psychology. Gestalt stressed the dynamic organization of whole units of behavior not the minute analysis of behavior into stimulus-response bonds as did the behaviorists. Perls's Gestalt therapy emphasizes the following issues:

1. Awareness of problems
2. Whole Self in creative contact with the environment
3. Reshaping one's sensory capacities
4. Importance of the present encounter to make one aware
5. Providing the person with opportunities for self-discovery

In short, Gestalt counseling helps offenders mature and grow by relying less on environmental (outside) support and more on self-support. This is achieved by the offender gaining insight through sensory awareness exercises. The offender is also encouraged to assume responsibility for his or her own behavior. As the offender matures through the process of self-awareness, his or her feelings, thoughts, and behaviors become congruent, and as a result, conflict disappears. When this happens, the offender is said to be integrated and functioning as a whole. It is at this point that the offender is able to cope with problems effectively and with little wasted energy.

The major premise of Gestalt counseling is that as the offender grows and matures, he or she will become more aware and rely more on his or her own instincts and less on the opinions of others. As autonomy develops, conflict (feeling one way and thinking another) will disappear. The healthy offender is in touch with himself or herself and reality (Perls, 1969). When this happens, the offender will be able to cope effectively with any problem that presents itself and to develop more intelligent behavior (Kepner & Brien, 1975).

The role of the counselor in the Gestalt approach is more directive than nondirective. The counselor's role is not to explain or interpret to the offender, but to help offenders achieve insight by perceiving situations differently. Counselors help offenders loosen rigid ways of thinking so that they can perceive things in new ways. Counselors help offenders relive perceptions in the present by encouraging them to verbalize. They also help offenders keep goals reasonable and provide opportunities for self-discovery. Counselors help offenders become more flexible. Confrontation as a technique to achieve self-awareness is encouraged. Counselors also look closely at nonverbal communication. "What" questions, not "why" or "cause" questions, are asked by counselors, because such questions help offenders to avoid intellectualizing (Perls, 1969).

Gestalt has made several contributions to counseling theory. Besides numerous counseling techniques, the understanding of how insight occurs can be traced to Gestalt therapists and counselors.

Insight can be defined as an "aha" experience, or the spontaneous realization of "Why didn't I realize this before." The Gestalt counselor helps the offender achieve insight by reviewing past experiences, arranging for clear observation, searching actively for solutions, and then waiting for new perceptions to replace old ones. The waiting period is known as the *incubation period*. During this time, it feels like nothing new is happening in counseling and like the offender has reached a plateau. Then all of a sudden the offender comes back with a whole new way of attacking problems. Gestalt counselors believe that insight cannot be rushed (Perls, Hefferline, & Goodman, 1951). Gestalt counselors are also advocates of discovery learning, by which the offender comes up with his or her own answers to problems. It is thought that discovery learning leads to long-lasting, irreversible results.

The Gestalt therapeutic approach raises the following questions:

1. Is insight alone enough to produce attitude, behavior, and value changes in offenders?
2. What are the conditions that produce perceptual changes and insight?
3. Does the Gestalt approach contain a complete view of how offenders change?

Gestalt counselors must be well-grounded and trained in Gestalt theory, which is detailed and complicated. Most counselors in criminal justice settings do not understand Gestalt theory well enough to feel comfortable in using the modality (Bennett, Rosenbaum, & McCullough, 1978).

Behavior Modification Counseling

One of the major differences between the behavior modification and Gestalt approaches is that Gestalt emphasizes what the whole human being is doing and the behaviorists emphasize tiny units of stimulus-response behaviors to explain human behavior. In addition, behavior modification counseling approaches use several important concepts. We will examine reinforcements and classical and operant conditioning, and we will look at some of behavior modification's aversive approaches used in criminal justice settings.

There are several premises involved in behavior modification counseling (also called behavior therapy). First, people behave as a result of and are motivated by reinforcements. Second, behavior is learned and, therefore, can be unlearned. Third, the same laws apply to humans and other animals. Fourth, to change behavior, the consequences of behavior (environment) must be changed. Last, once behavior change (external behavior) occurs, how one thinks (internal behavior) also changes.

Behavior modification counseling is directive. Counselors are teachers, directors, experts, and role models, and they are active in diagnosing maladaptive behavior and prescribing procedures. Counselors do not spend much time talking with offenders or developing awareness and insight into problems. They are not concerned with how offenders feel or with their awareness and insight. Counselors care only about seeing behavior change. Since behavior (maladaptive included) is learned, it can be unlearned. Counselors change the consequences of the offender's behavior and this, in turn, changes what the offender does. Once the behavior is changed, how the offender feels about the new behavior also changes. All this can be accomplished with minimum talk or no talk at all. Some have found that the most important variable responsible for behavior change is the counselor's personality (Kratcoski, 1981). If the counselor is perceived in a positive way by the offender, the offender is more likely to want to please the counselor by making changes in behavior.

Contracts

Behavior modification counselors often use contracts with offenders (Ankersmit, 1976). Contracts are quasi-legal, ethical agreements between the counselor and offender and contain clearly stated goals that give the counselor permission to work in specific areas to change behavior. The more clearly defined expected behaviors are, the greater the probability of achieving them (Kratcoski, 1981). Note that behavior modification counseling in criminal justice settings does require the consent of offenders. Offenders must agree to change, and without the contract, the counselor does not have a right to work with the offender on behavior change. The fact that offenders must agree to change distinguishes counseling from brainwashing.

Reinforcements

The concept of reinforcement is central to behavior modification counseling. Reinforcement means that a person can be trained to respond to particular stimuli. There are two types of reinforcements:

positive and negative. Positive reinforcements are frequently viewed as rewards and can be material or nonmaterial. Examples of positive reinforcers are praise, smiles, attention, hugs, money, and privileges. Kratcoski (1981) reported that positive reinforcement is especially important at the beginning of counseling. It is used to develop and maintain new behavior. Examples of negative reinforcers are threats, ostracism, ridicule, corporal and capital punishment, confinement, and withdrawal of rewards. It is thought that the most long-lasting change occurs with positive reinforcement. The fastest change occurs with negative reinforcement; however, it is short lived.

Classical Conditioning

Another concept central to behavior modification counseling is classical conditioning. Classical conditioning is also referred to as Pavlovian Conditioning, named after the Russian physiologist Pavlov. Pavlov found that when we pair an unconditioned stimulus with a conditioned stimulus, we can condition a totally neutral response. He first described his findings with his experiments on dogs (Pavlov, 1927). Pavlov found that when he presented food to dogs (unconditioned stimulus), they salivated (unconditioned response). He then paired the presentation of food (unconditioned stimulus) with a buzzer (conditioned stimulus) and found that his dogs would salivate (unconditioned response). Soon he was able to buzz (conditioned stimulus) without presenting food to the dogs, and the dogs would salivate (conditioned response). The repeated pairing of a conditioned stimulus with an unconditioned stimulus to get a conditioned response is classical or Pavlovian conditioning and is one way humans learn behaviors. Such learning is largely unconscious. It is concerned primarily with the stimulus (what occurs before the response) and finding the correct stimulus to change behavior. Classical conditioning typically works best with reflexive or involuntary behavior, and it provides possible explanations for acquisition of irrational fears and other disruptive emotional responses (Lefrancois, 1972). Classical conditioning is limited in its usefulness, because it cannot be used to change most types of human behavior, but only simple reflex or involuntary behavior.

Several myths have surrounded classical conditioning. First, the offender does not need to be motivated for behavior change to happen.

The truth is that the offender must have motivation to change. Second, once behavior is changed, we do not have to teach new appropriate behavior. The truth is that we must replace old behavior with socially acceptable behavior. Third, by punishing the offender, we can achieve permanent behavior change. The truth is that we get quick and immediate behavior change, but it is not enough to rehabilitate offenders (Lester & Braswell, 1987).

Operant Conditioning

Another major concept in behavior modification counseling is operant conditioning. Operant conditioning is associated with Skinner (1971). It emphasizes human responses, not stimuli, and the judicious use of rewards and punishments. In operant conditioning the counselor waits until the offender makes a desired response or some approximation to a desired response and then reinforces behavior with a suitable reward. Take the example of a noncommunicative offender. The criminal justice counselor will sit and engage in some sort of activity that will encourage mouth movement and talk. When the offender says something, the counselor will show interest and respond in a friendly manner, thus reinforcing the act of speaking. If an offender says nothing, the counselor may initially reinforce any mouth movement by offering the offender a drink of water, gum, candy, cigarette, and so forth.

Some procedures that behavior modification counselors use are satiation, negative practice, implosive therapy, systematic desensitization, and flooding. These procedures are briefly defined, because they are behavioral techniques found in criminal justice settings.

1. *Satiation.* Satiation is a special form of negative reinforcement. For example, a person who is hired to work in a candy store is encouraged to eat all of the candy he or she wants. The idea is that the employee will become satiated with sugar, possibly become sick, and not eat it again.
2. *Negative Practice.* With negative practice, the person is asked to repeat deliberately some undesirable motor habit. The rationale is that repeated voluntary performance of a habit brings it under voluntary control. This technique has been helpful in the elimination of tics, spasms, and stammering.

3. *Implosive Therapy.* For implosive therapy, the offender is asked to verbalize and dwell on things that create anxiety for him or her. By symbolically reproducing anxiety little by little in the counseling setting where the usual negative reinforcement is not allowed to occur, the anxiety is extinguished.

4. *Systematic Desensitization.* Systematic desensitization is used with phobias, neurotic anxieties, interpersonal difficulties, and some types of sexual problems. It involves teaching the offender relaxation techniques. After the offender has a command of relaxation techniques, anxieties are introduced and reintroduced in the counseling setting until desensitization occurs.

5. *Flooding.* In flooding anxiety is introduced to the offender, at full strength, not in small amounts as in implosive therapy. The rationale for flooding is that anxiety at full strength tends to loose its potency to produce fear.

Aversive Techniques

Behavior modification has also given rise to several aversive techniques used in criminal justice counseling. The aversive techniques are the most controversial of the behavior modification counseling tools and are widely used. Some of the most common techniques are discussed.

Chemical Aversion. Chemical aversion involves the administration of drugs to induce nausea and vomiting to deter criminal behavior. Chemical aversion is often used in the treatment of alcoholism. One of the chemicals frequently used is Antabuse. The alcoholic who takes Antabuse will get sick if he or she drinks. The discomfort and odors are thought to be associated with alcohol and eventually the alcoholic stops drinking. Anectine is also used to treat alcoholism; upon ingestion it causes a sensation of suffocation. Two chemicals used in the treatment of heroin addiction are methadone and naltrexone. These drugs do not make the addict sick, instead they are substitutes for heroin. Methadone is an addictive drug that frequently provides the user with a high if the dosage is not regulated.

There are disadvantages to chemical aversion. It is unpleasant and as such may cause the offender to stop treatment early. Many offenders refuse to cooperate. Some offenders build up a tolerance to chemical agents and some agents have negative side effects. Close medical attention is necessary, and it takes a high degree of motivation to complete treatment. Last, there is not enough evidence to indicate that chemical aversion is highly effective.

Electric Shock. Very brief, low-level, electric shock of a nonconvulsive nature is performed under close medical supervision and is used in treatment of self-destructive tendencies, sexual deviations, alcoholism, and aggressive behavior. Supposedly, such shocks cause no tissue damage or lingering pain; however, long-term effects have not been determined. Many jurisdictions do not sanction the use of electric shock in criminal justice settings, only in mental health settings.

Covert Sensitization. Covert sensitization is a verbal aversion method by which unpleasant scenes are paired with scenes of deviant behavior. An example would be the exhibitionist asked to imagine the consequences of getting caught. This is often used in the treatment of sexual deviations. The advantages of this technique are that it is administered on an imaginal level, and it is less unpleasant than chemical or electrical methods. Therefore, it is less likely to be terminated by offenders.

Time-Out. This method involves time out from positive reinforcement and removing the offender to a private area for a short period of time. Young children who are acting negatively are often put on time-outs. They are separated from peers who give them positive reinforcement for their bad behavior. It is thought that if peers cannot give them encouragement, then they will stop behaving badly. An extreme, punitive form of time-out is solitary confinement.

Overcorrection. The use of overcorrection is when the offender is asked to restore his or her environment to the condition it was in before the inappropriate behavior occurred (restitution) and then is told to improve (pay the penalty) the environment and make it better than before. This is often applied to disruptive behavior of juveniles or institutionalized adults. An example would be the incarcerated juvenile who gets into a fight and messes up a classroom. He or she is asked to straighten the room up and then spit shine the floor.

Response Cost. Response cost involves imposing a penalty in the form of a fine or loss of points, privileges, or material goods. Response cost is often used in token economies—environments in which residents are given points that can be exchanged for rewards. Juvenile and adult residential programs frequently have token economies (Ayllon & Azrin, 1968). Normally, token economies work well in a highly controlled environment such as a juvenile hall or prison. Offenders are given points for good behavior and points are taken away for bad behavior. Programs may allow offenders to earn points toward release.

Token economies, however, do have problems. One problem with token economies is that juveniles and adults who become dependent on the institution may behave badly when their release dates are near, because they are afraid to go back to their communities. As a result, they might do stupid and foolish things to sabotage their releases. Another problem with token economies is that most correctional programs assume that every person incarcerated seeks freedom or some other privilege such as more recreation, a trip to the local community, or money. Most programs make assumptions that every offender will be motivated by the same reinforcers. Offenders are motivated by different reinforcers. Some people are motivated to do the right things by freedom. Others are motivated by money. Some are motivated by more recreation. Counselors must keep in mind that every offender is not motivated by the same thing. Offenders have different reinforcers, and correctional programs do a poor job identifying what each offender's specific reinforcers are. The same logic holds true for negative reinforcers. For some, not having extra recreation or being locked in a cell is desired. For token economies to be effective, programs must take time to identify each offender's positive and negative reinforcers and not make gross generalizations about offenders.

In addition, token economies can be demoralizing to residents. Token economies are normally very competitive environments. Residents compete for points and privileges; as a result, they are always in a position to compare themselves with others. This can dishearten those who do not do well in competitive situations.

The last problem with token economies is that most offenders will alter their behavior when they are incarcerated and reinforcements are immediate. Once offenders are released, however, reinforcements are not always immediate or forthcoming. The assumption is that offenders will internalize what was learned while incarcerated and continue to do the correct things in the absence of reinforcements. It would be ideal if behavior modification counseling could continue for the offender outside of the institutional environment. Unfortunately, planned transition between the institution and the offender's natural environment is not usually possible, and hence generalizations to the real world are not always made.

The following questions are raised concerning behavior modification counseling with offenders:

1. Does the counselor have the right to change, direct, or control an offender's behavior without the person's awareness and understanding?
2. Is an offender's freedom and dignity undermined by behavior modification counseling?
3. Is behavior modification a form of counseling or a smokescreen for behavior control?
4. How long will the offender's behavior change last if the counselor uses behavior modification?
5. Does the use of certain behavior modification techniques by counselors violate the offender's constitutional rights?
6. Does behavior modification attack the causes of antisocial behavior or just the symptoms?
7. Are rewards or punishments more effective in changing offenders' behaviors?
8. Does teaching an offender how to respond appropriately in his or her general living situation also change delinquent or criminal behavior?
9. Can behavior modification programs be abusive to offenders?
10. Does behavior modification counseling make human experience mechanical?

Behavior modification counseling in criminal justice settings has been supported and criticized. Supporters argue that it is based on thoroughly researched principles. It is "bull's-eye therapy" as opposed to "shotgun therapy." Its techniques are easily taught and implemented. It can be applied to a number of different populations. It is inexpensive and results are quickly seen (Hatcher, 1978). Critics argue that criminal justice counselors are limited in their abilities to use behavior modification with offenders (Thorne, Tharp, & Wetzel, 1967). Behavior modification normally is successful with offenders in institutions, but not in the real world. Not all offenders are alike and most criminal justice programs assume that they are. Behavior modification counselors must be well-trained for counseling to work. Non-counselors who come in contact with offenders must also be properly taught and willing to apply the principles of behavior modification (Lester & Braswell, 1987). Finally, it is argued by critics that behavior modification is tantamount to mind control.

Reality Counseling

Reality counseling was originated and developed by Glasser, a Los Angeles psychiatrist. This commonsense modality emphasizes that offenders must learn to take responsibility for their behaviors. In fact, psychological health, according to reality counselors, is equated with taking responsibility. To act responsibly, offenders must face reality. Glasser felt the type and severity of an offender's problem(s) depended on how he or she was dealing with reality. To face reality, offenders have to fulfill two basic social needs that all humans must meet: (a) to love and be loved and (b) to feel important, unique, and worthwhile (Glasser, 1965). For offenders to feel worthwhile, a satisfactory standard of behavior must be met and adult interactions with others maintained. Glasser postulated that all human problems resulted from not meeting the above social needs. If offenders cannot meet the above needs through normal social contacts, they will resort to unrealistic and perhaps criminal means to meet them (Wicks, 1975).

The major premise of reality counseling is that offenders' behaviors will change when they feel loved, can give love, and feel worthwhile. Offenders who are not meeting their needs fail to acknowledge the reality of the world. Therefore, this modality encourages the offender to become emotionally involved with others by developing appropriate, reciprocal, and caring relationships. It is assumed when there is no involvement with others, reality is denied and the offender cannot meet his or her needs (Rachin, 1974). As the offender learns responsibility, his or her behavior will change.

Reality counselors follow 14 steps in helping offenders meet their needs and become responsible:

1. The counselor personalizes by becoming involved with offenders.
2. The counselor reveals himself or herself by directly answering offenders' questions.
3. The counselor concentrates on present behavior that can be tested in reality and does not allow the offender to use the past as an excuse.
4. The counselor emphasizes behavior not attitudes or motives.
5. The counselor rarely asks "Why" questions, avoiding counterproductive explanations and excuse making.
6. The counselor helps the offender evaluate his or her behavior to identify irresponsible, unrealistic behavior.
7. The counselor helps the offender develop a better plan for the future.
8. The counselor rejects all excuses.
9. The counselor does not sympathize with offenders.
10. The counselor praises, approves, and only gets involved with responsible, positive, and healthy behavior.
11. The counselor believes that all offenders are capable of changing their behavior and, therefore, has positive expectations.
12. The counselor recognizes the influence of peer pressure and mobilizes it to treat offenders.
13. The counselor does not give up on offenders, even if they show resistance.
14. The counselor does not label offenders as sick or disturbed; behavior is simply responsible or irresponsible (Rachin, 1974).

In summary, the reality counselor becomes appropriately involved with the offender but does not sympathize. He or she accepts no excuses and looks only for results and not causes. The counselor is always frank and outspoken. He or she becomes involved with positive, healthy, and responsible behavior, not negative, irresponsible behavior. The counselor does not allow the offender to blame his or her problems on anyone or anything besides himself or herself. The counselor also provides an example of a responsible role model and teaches the offender how to be responsible.

Reality counseling is currently popular in therapeutic community treatment centers and prisons. It is frequently the modality of choice for alcoholism and drug addiction. Alcoholics Anonymous and Synanon are two examples of programs that use reality counseling. It has also been used at California's Ventura School for Girls (reformatory) and the California Rehabilitation Center, a prison for civilly committed addicts. Note that when reality counseling is used in juvenile halls and prisons, it can become heavily disciplined, punitive, and quasi-military.

The following questions are raised concerning reality counseling with offenders:

1. Are reality counselors too forceful with offenders?
2. In a heterogeneous society, what constitutes moral or responsible behavior?
3. How can the reality counselor become a trustworthy and respectful role model if he or she is constantly engaged in hard confrontation with offenders?
4. Is the counselor in reality therapy prone toward authoritative, paternalistic, and punitive attitudes toward offenders?

An advantage of reality counseling is that it is easy to learn and not as complex as other modalities. Also it is grounded in common sense. It can be used in an individual or group setting, and thus treatment can be economical. It is a no-nonsense approach that leaves the offender without excuses for his or her behavior.

Transactional Analysis Counseling

The counseling modality known as transactional analysis (TA) was originated by Berne (1961) and offers us a practical, conceptual framework to understand how offenders interact with others. Transactional analysis examines basic units of interaction. For the most part, it is assumed that interactions give rise to criminal behavior and that understanding the dynamics of such interactions can go a long way in preventing future criminal behaviors. In the following discussion, we will examine the concept of ego states; how the ego state a person is coming from is determined (behavioral diagnosis); TA's counseling process; how TA differs from the Freudian concepts of id, ego, and superego; TA's concept of psychological health; scripts; structural analysis; transactions; and games. I will be using the term *offender* to explain TA, but note that the terms *offender* and *person* can be interchanged without changing the meaning of Berne's theory.

Ego States

There are three ego states: parent, adult, and child. Ego states are the frames of mind, or psychological orientations, from which the offender is coming at certain moments in time; they give rise to specific types of behavior. Another way of describing ego states is with the phrase *where one's head is at* at any given time. Ego states are not the same as roles, although the two concepts are often confused. In the role of parent, one is often plugged into the adult or child ego states.

The parent ego state (P) is the state of mind that gives rise to behaviors that resemble that of an actual parent. Some parental behaviors are nurturing, protecting, commanding, controlling, demanding, criticizing, judging, moralizing, and domineering. The adult ego state (A) is the state of mind that gives rise to behaviors that resemble that of an actual adult. Some adult behaviors are being objective, factual, insightful, analytical, logical, organized, realistic, and unbiased. I like to think of the adult as the "Mr. Spock" of the ego states; no feelings come from this frame of mind. The child ego state (C) is the one that gives rise to behaviors that resemble that of an actual child. Some child behaviors are asking permission, throwing tantrums, crying, joking, being irresponsible, and being spontaneous. All feelings originate from the child ego state.

Ego states can be broken down more specifically. For example, the child ego state can be divided into three parts: Natural Child, Little Professor, and Adapted Child. The Natural Child is not confused by social learning and expresses real, uninhibited feelings. Frequently spontaneous, unencumbered, honest remarks come from the Natural Child. I often think of a remark my daughter made at age three while we were in a check-out line at the grocery store. The woman in front of us was obese and had an odor. My daughter spontaneously blurted out, "That big, fat woman smells bad!" Anyone of any age can come from the Natural Child ego state and often our social blunders signify we are in this ego state. The Little Professor ego state is the part of the child ego state that often makes intuitive leaps about things. It figures things out without obvious information or data. An example is the young child who knows Mom and Dad are fighting despite the fact that cross words have not been uttered. The Adapted Child ego state is the part of the child ego state that tries to please the parents, usually out of fear. It is also the place where script messages reside (see "Scripts," below). An example of the Adapted Child ego state behavior is manipulation to get one's way or going along with the wishes of others because you feel they won't like you if you don't.

We are capable of moving from one ego state to another. There is nothing inherently good or bad about any of the ego states, and there is no mutually agreed on formula that represents how much time normal, healthy people spend in each ego state. It is normal to move in and out of the parent, adult, and child ego states and the roles we play in life may dictate that we spend greater time in particular ego states. However, Berne (1966) indicates that one or another ego state is predominate in everyone. Excessive time spent in any one of the three ego states can signify possible problems. For example, offenders who impulsively and without warning commit crimes, may spend a preponderance of their time in the child. Sociopathic offenders or professional con artists may spend a preponderance of their time in the adult. Sex offenders may spend a preponderance of their time in the parent.

Behavioral Diagnosis

Behavioral diagnosis along with self- and historical diagnosis helps us determine what ego state the offender (person) is coming from at any given time. Several things are important in behavioral diagnosis. The counselor looks at the offender's demeanor, poise, bearing, and conduct for clues about ego states. For example, a rigid demeanor and pointed finger often signifies the parent. In contrast, a person who avoids eye contact may signify that he or she is in the child. The analysis of the offender's gestures, voice, and vocabulary is also important to help pinpoint ego states. For example, any gesture made out of context normally signifies the child. Monotone voices normally signify the adult. The frequent use of words and/or phrases such as disgusting, naughty, and ridiculous may signify the parent. The behavioral clues along with the offender's own feelings, past experiences, and how he or she gets along with others in the present help to identify accurately ego states at any point in time.

Transactional Analysis Counseling Process

Transactional analysis can be done individually or in groups; however, it frequently takes place in group settings. The counseling process includes

1. No physical violence
2. Development of a contract with goals
3. Counselors (frequently referred to as leaders) working with offenders to find out what ego state is responsible for decision making
4. Counselors/leaders working to make the adult ego state stronger
5. Script analysis
6. Examination of how the parent ego state treats the child ego state
7. Examination of the types of transactions the offender has with others
8. Identification of the games the offender plays with others
9. Identification of what position the offender is coming from.

There are four basic positions that the offender may take: (a) "I'm okay, you're okay" (open and trusting); (b) "I'm okay, you're not okay" (suspicious and mistrusting); (c) "I'm not okay, you're okay" (inferiority); and (d) "I'm not okay, you're not okay" (inferior and suspicious) (Harris, 1969).

Freud's and Berne's Theories of Personality

At first glance, there appears to be a parallel between Freud's dimensions of the personality and Berne's analysis of ego states. However, Berne has dissected and developed Freud's concept of ego, the only part of the personality that is capable of being known, observed, and dealt with (Berne, 1966). The id and superego are unconscious and not capable of being known and observed. The parent, adult, and child are all conscious and can be observed, understood, and dealt with in transactional analysis counseling.

Psychological Health According to Transactional Analysis

Transactional analysis tends to view healthy, nonpathological behavior as behavior in which the adult ego state is in control of the parent and child. When the adult ego state is in control, the offender goes through a rational process of decision making. He or she analyzes, weighs information, and takes a great deal into account before making decisions. If the adult ego state is not in control, the rational decision-making process is circumvented, and there is greater probability that the decisions made will be poor.

Scripts

Transactional analysis defines scripts as blueprints for a life course (Steiner, 1974). They develop early in life and guide and control behavior throughout life. A script develops when inborn expectations of being protected and shielded from life's harsh realities are not met. As pressures force youngsters to cope with their difficulties and modify their expectations, scripts develop. Scripts have prologues, climaxes, and catastrophes. As a rule, scripts are not verbal or rational. They reside at a nonverbal, feeling level and often keep us from changing. Not all scripts are negative, and there are people who are rare exceptions and live script-free lives.

Structural Analysis

Structural analysis is a tool used by transactional analysis counselors to make known what ego state the offender is operating from. It involves diagraming transactions between two or more persons (see Tables 4.1-4.3). Generally parent-adult-child (PAC) charts are used for offenders, and lines are drawn on the chart to indicate which ego state offenders are in during any given transaction.

Transactions

A transaction is an interaction between people. There are five types of transactions: complementary, crossed, indirect, diluted, and ulterior.

Complementary transactions are interactions in which the vectors or arrows in structural analysis are parallel. Communication will

TABLE 4.1. PAC Chart for Structural Analysis

Person A	Person B
P	P
A	A
C	C

TABLE 4.2. Complementary Transaction

Person A	Person B
P	P
A	A
C	C

TABLE 4.3. Crossed Transaction

Person A	Person B
P	P
A	A
C	C

continue as long as the arrows do not cross. Complementary transactions are not necessarily healthy transactions, however.

Crossed transactions are interactions in which the arrows in structural analysis cross. Crossed transactions often cause trouble for us, but they can also be used to redirect the ego state of another to aid communication. Berne believed that if communication between people was broken off, a crossed transaction was the cause.

Indirect transactions are transactions in which something is said to Person A by Person B, but it is intended to influence Person C. Instead of influencing the counselor directly, one offender says to another offender within hearing range of the counselor how unfair the counselor has been with him or her. This is evidence of a poor relationship between the counselor and offender.

Diluted transactions are interactions that involve joking and kidding, which is part hostile and part affectionate. Instead of a counselor confronting an offender with his or her feelings about the offender's rearrest for armed robbery, the counselor says "Next time you want to play *Bonnie and Clyde,* do it in Hollywood." Humor frequently is used with hostile intent. Comics such as Don Rickles have capitalized on this.

Another type of transaction is the ulterior transaction. Games are a series of ulterior transactions. They are dishonest interactions that frequently provide payoffs for those who use them.

Games

A game occurs when an offender is not being honest or when the real message is hidden. People play games to feel that their problems are caused by others, to keep from facing up to fears, to pass the time with others, to get attention, and to prove that they are not okay (McCormick & Campos, 1970). There are innocent and deadly games. Some of the common games played by offenders are See What You Made Me Do; Cops and Robbers; Alcoholic; Addict; Now He Tells Me; If It Weren't for You; Little Old Me; Courtroom; Now I've Got You, You Son of a Bitch; Kick Me; Stupid; Uproar; Let's You and Him Fight; and Psychiatry (Berne, 1964).

The major premise of TA is that offenders will change once they become aware of what part of them makes decisions, face their scripts, and become aware of the games they repeatedly play with others. Another premise of TA is that change is a rational process that is made from the adult ego state.

The role of the counselor is active, directive, and didactic. Counselors explain transactions, games, scripts, and so on. However, TA is predicated on the idea that offenders must also be well versed in the theory. The counselor is not seen as someone who has more knowledge, expertise, and capabilities than the offender in diagnosing ego states, scripts, and so forth. The counselor demystifies the counseling process in that offenders are expected to become expert at TA.

Some of the questions TA raises concerning the counseling of offenders are as follows:

1. Although TA's language is simple, are all offenders intelligent enough to be able to grasp myriad concepts necessary for effective counseling?

2. Does TA overload the offender with too much to learn?
3. Does TA dilute the effectiveness of the counselor as an expert?
4. Is there a danger that counseling can be reduced to an intellectual exercise of simply identifying ego states, scripts, games, and so forth?

Crisis Intervention Counseling

A definition of crisis intervention is "the ability to induce immediate comfort in an otherwise stressful situation by the giving of supportive action such as empathic listening, changing the immediate environment, or building hope" (Bennett et al., 1978, p. 32). The major objective of crisis intervention counseling is to help offenders cope with immediate stressful situations that approach or exceed the limits of their adjusting capacities (Hatcher, 1978). In general, crisis intervention is an intense, immediate form of counseling that is targeted to deal with specific crises rather than designed to deal with overall attitude, behavior, and value change. Some examples of crises are death, termination of employment, attempted suicide, drug abuse, alcohol abuse, rape, emotional states (such as depression, pregnancy, and marital conflict), and medical emergencies. A crisis intervention counselor can be directive and/or nondirective with offenders. However, crisis intervention counseling is seen as different from other modalities in that it is totally focused on managing the crisis.

There are several things counselors must keep in mind when doing crisis intervention counseling with offenders. First, that a crisis is defined by the offender, not the counselor. What is a crisis for an offender may not be a crisis for the counselor. A crisis may occur for offenders at any time and for any reason. The counselor should never minimize or make light of the offender's perceived crisis. If the counselor makes statements such as "Oh! Is that all that's bothering you?" the offender is likely to feel that the counselor does not understand him or her and may feel more isolated than ever. On the other hand, criminal justice counselors should avoid developing a crisis mentality and view most offender problems as crises. By adopting such a mentality, many problems are inaccurately labeled as crises, and counselors are unnecessarily prevented from systematically working with offenders to resolve serious problems (Gambril, 1983). A counselor can create unnecessary problems for offenders when they develop crisis mentalities and view most problems as crises. Some counselors become overempathic with offenders. Counselors should strive for balance in identifying and working with crises.

A second thing that the crisis intervention counselor must keep in mind when working with offenders in crisis is that there is usually one or more stressful events preceding and contributing to the crisis. Offenders are frequently unaware of such precipitating events. Counselors should give offenders a chance to explore feelings and thoughts about the precipitating events leading to the crisis (Smith, 1978). The counselor should ask questions along the lines of "What led up to your feeling this way?"

A third thing that the crisis intervention counselor must keep in mind when working with offenders in crisis is the strong emotional reaction that is experienced by the offender. The offender usually experiences some strong emotion or mixture of emotions that is so powerful that he or she becomes temporarily immobilized or unable to function normally. Offenders are often unable to relate stories factually, logically, or chronologically. They often present stories incoherently. The counselor should recognize this and allow the offender to release his or her emotions without demanding precision and detail. Remember that in crisis intervention counseling, the counselor is not normally looking for information to write a report. It also helps if counselors offer highly emotional offenders a glass of water. The sipping tends to have a calming effect. At this point, counselors should also avoid overempathetic comments such as "How horrible!" or "I don't know how you can go on." Such comments fan the fire of the crisis and keep the emotional reaction going. Note that emotions wax and wane in a crisis. Strong emotional reactions do not go on forever. It is important not to leave offenders in highly emotional states by themselves. They could present a danger to themselves and others.

The last thing that the crisis intervention counselor must keep in mind is the offender's inability to cope. The inability to cope is brought about by the strong emotions. Usually the offender in crisis loses the ability to do simple tasks such as boil water, make coffee, and drive an automobile. Offenders in crisis feel helpless. Counselors should not leave offenders in crisis alone and should always assess the risk of suicide and homicide.

The major premise of crisis intervention counseling is that successfully managing the crisis empowers the offender to tackle other problems and crises. The counselor's primary goal in crisis intervention counseling is to interact with the offender in such a way that tension is reduced so that the offender can use available resources more effectively. It is important for the counselor to be an empathic listener and good communicator who can demonstrate understanding of what the offender is experiencing. It is not necessary for the counselor to say a lot or to concentrate on solving problems, because offenders in crisis are rarely capable of processing information, as they are not rational. Most of the time offenders need and want to talk. They do not want information or a solution to a problem. Offenders in crisis are more amenable to influence because of the pain they may be experiencing, but they should be helped to avoid making major decisions until the crisis is over (Smith & Berlin, 1981). Solving problems should also wait until after the crisis has passed.

Another goal of the counselor in crisis intervention counseling is to provide information about appropriate community referral services. Counselors should write down information about community referrals and securely post referrals on a door, refrigerator, or other obvious place, because offenders in crisis frequently misplace things. Counselors should always follow up with the offender immediately after the crisis is over.

The following questions are raised about crisis intervention counseling with offenders:

1. How does getting an offender through a crisis empower him or her to solve other problems?
2. How much persuasion should a counselor use to influence an offender during a crisis?
3. How much should a counselor commiserate with an offender in crisis to show understanding?

Problem Management Counseling

The problem management counseling modality concentrates on helping offenders resolve their difficulties by teaching them how to identify and resolve problems. This practical model allows the counselor to do something immediately that will help offenders manage their lives more effectively. Egan (1990) is a major proponent of the problem management modality.

The major premise of problem management counseling is that the sooner offenders can resolve problems, even small ones, the more empowered they become to solve other problems. As offenders become empowered and resolve their problems, they begin to feel better about themselves and change their attitudes, feelings, behaviors, and values. The problem management counseling modality takes a three-stage approach to counseling:

Stage I emphasizes the identification and clarification of problems.

Stage II emphasizes developing a preferred scenario regarding problems.

Stage III emphasizes formulating strategies and plans to resolve problems (Egan, 1990).

Problem manager counselors can be directive or nondirective, depending on the problems the offender is experiencing. They use many different viable techniques to help offenders solve problems. Counselors spend a great deal of time teaching the offender how to identify problems and how to develop goals, strategies, and action plans. Counselors focus on assisting offenders in resolving problems as they arise.

Some of the questions raised about problem management counseling with offenders are as follows:

1. Is the counselor too involved in resolving the offender's immediate symptoms to the exclusion of dealing with underlying causes of problems?
2. Is the counselor's job limited solely to solving the offender's problems?

Eclectic Counseling

Eclectic counseling refers to picking and choosing philosophies, methods, and techniques from multiple modalities. There is no one person responsible for the eclectic counseling modality. This modality sprang from a grass-roots, commonsense movement on the part of criminal justice counselors to provide quality counseling to as many offenders as possible. The eclectic counselor is a generalist, not a specialist, who looks at the counselee's needs and then tries to find a modality or mixture of modalities that make sense and have the greatest potential of working. The eclectic counselor is not trained in or loyal to any single modality.

The major premise of eclectic counseling is that offenders have special requirements, and that these requirements dictate what methods will be used in each case. If the offender is to change, the counselor must use the correct mixture of modalities.

The role of the eclectic criminal justice counselor is sometimes directive and at other times nondirective, depending on the needs of the offender. The eclectic counselor is a Jack of all trades, but a master of none. Such a counselor reminds me of someone who reaches into his or her bag of tricks, hoping that he or she will be lucky enough to find something that works. If the trick doesn't work, the counselor chooses another. Sometimes the eclectic counselor emphasizes the intellect and at other times the offender's emotions and feelings. Eclectic counselors make the assumption that all modalities have something to offer and none of the modalities offer everything. The eclectic counselor often counsels by educated guesses and trial and error. Today's burgeoning caseloads and financial restraints often foster eclecticism in the counseling of criminal justice offenders.

The questions raised about eclectic counseling with offenders are as follows:

1. What happens when a counselor is philosophically opposed to a modality that appears to be in the best interest of an offender?
2. What if the counselor misdiagnoses the offender's problem(s) and uses the wrong techniques and modalities?
3. Can an eclectic counselor teach an offender a systematic philosophy of problem solving that can be used in different situations?

OTHER APPROACHES
TO CRIMINAL JUSTICE COUNSELING

In the United States, crime in the 1980s increased dramatically and the national response was to construct more prisons for the large numbers of offenders being sentenced. However, the rapid prison construction rate has not kept up with the increasing prison population, which exceeds 1 million nationwide (Gest, 1990). American prisons are currently operating at 185% capacity, with the rate estimated to be at 245% capacity by 1995 (Travis, 1990). When prisons are over-crowded, programs cannot reach all offenders who need them, and alternatives must be found. Sometimes this results in early release of offenders and/or offenders completing their sentences in the community. It has been estimated that 1 in 75 Americans is now under correctional supervision in the community (Gest, 1990). With so many offenders within the prison system and on the streets, counseling programs and services are likely to mushroom. Community corrections facilities and agencies should also multiply (Hendrickson, 1991). Counseling is likely to play a major role in community corrections. In the future, heavy reliance on therapeutic communities and group counseling is probable. Both are attractive because they are capable of reaching many offenders.

Therapeutic Community

The therapeutic community concept was introduced by Jones (1968) in the UK, where he developed it within a mental hospital setting after World War II, because there was a shortage of trained counselors. The therapeutic community is also sometimes called milieu therapy. The concepts are not new and go back to ancient Greece. It involves creating a total therapeutic milieu within the traditional prison that is meant to create a psychological change within the offender that will make the offender law abiding after release. Therapeutic communities are experiments in social living, in which offenders learn to manage themselves in a law-abiding fashion. The aim of therapeutic communities in criminal justice settings is to create a normal environment within a prison, so that the offender will not be released in a worse condition than he or she was in when incarcerated.

Therapeutic communities have similar principles and objectives, but there is wide variability in how individual communities are run. They all attempt to foster reintegration of the offender. Therapeutic communities are collaborative efforts to modify traditional prison structures and practices in a way that fosters rehabilitation. They try to develop a situation that parallels as closely as possible normal, everyday life for the offender. They are oriented toward productive work and rapid return to the community. Every form of activity in the community is used to help the offender reach a psychological state favorable for early release. All staff members provide therapeutic experiences 24 hours a day, and any situation within the therapeutic community can become a therapeutic example.

An illustration comes to mind of an addict who was part of a therapeutic community. She forgot to replace the role of toilet paper in a bathroom stall. The next offender who went into the stall was then left with the situation of how to get toilet paper. This was the focus of a 3-hour group counseling session. Not replacing the toilet paper became symbolic of the irresponsibility of the offender not only in the bathroom but in other areas of her life.

Therapeutic communities liberally use group dynamics, educational techniques, and group pressure to help the offender. Authority is given to inmates as well as to personnel. Authority is not necessarily based on rank or position, but on the technical competence of the individual. In short, an attitudinal climate exists in which all relationships between staff and offenders contribute toward preparing an inmate for reintegration.

Therapeutic communities can be said to be democratic, unlike traditional prisons, which are authoritarian. Therapeutic communities are supportive and permissive of offenders. Feelings and emotions are freely communicated. The attitudes between staff and offenders are favorable toward rehabilitation. Such communities are treatment oriented, humanistic, and flexible. In contrast, traditional prisons are bureaucratic, custody oriented, oppressive, and rigid. In addition, therapeutic communities involve reshaping the traditional prison social structure to negate the effects of confinement, punitive ideology, inmate social structure, and the pathology of incarceration (Jones, 1973).

Therapeutic communities are more likely to be effective if the institutions are small and allow free movement on the part of offenders within the institution and if work assignments resemble jobs on the outside. Another attractive thing about therapeutic communities is that they can be more economical to construct and operate than traditional prisons. Single cells are not necessary; instead, dormitory housing units are frequently used. Such living conditions facilitate socialization and working things out among offenders themselves. In such communities, the number of staff necessary to supervise offenders is significantly lower, because of the minimum security environment. Therapeutic communities can also incorporate numerous different treatment modalities.

Group Counseling

Group counseling is considered a clinical tool and/or a modality. It involves three or more people who meet to solve personal problems in a group, with the benefit of a group counselor or leader. It differs from individual counseling in that it involves other offenders. During the 1940s and 1950s, group counseling began to be widely used in the criminal justice system as a way to handle offenders more efficiently (Kratcoski, 1981). It is likely to be more widely used in the future both in institutional and field settings because of the following:

1. Group counseling is more economical than individual counseling. Many offenders can receive counseling at the same time. Depending on the size of the group, only one or several group counselors are needed to lead a group counseling session.

2. Group counseling provides the offender with immediate peer pressure, feedback, and information. Offenders' peers become actively involved in the counseling process and confront head on the offender's dysfunctional attitudes and behaviors. It subjects offenders to input from other offenders as well as from counselors, and as a result, it is harder for offenders to deny, rationalize, and dismiss what is being said to them than if only one counselor tells them something.

3. Group counseling serves as a legitimate way offenders can release everyday tension. In so doing offenders can deal with situations that emerge through appropriate communication instead of handling frustration in socially unacceptable ways. In prison settings, it helps prevent disruption of the status quo and is a way of reducing institutional management problems.

4. Group counseling is a way of dealing with and managing offender cliques and gangs, both inside and outside the prison. Offenders associate with other offenders with whom they have common interests. Offenders group themselves racially, religiously, sexually, geographically, and according to offense similarity.

5. Group counseling is also a way to address the influence of the offender subculture.

6. Group counseling is a way offenders and staff are able to legitimately deal with their negative stereotypes about each other.

7. Group counseling can be used on juveniles and adults. It works with all age groups.

8. Group counseling provides for group problem solving. Offenders learn from group problem-solving techniques such as brainstorming and from the experience of others who have faced or are facing similar problems.

9. Group counseling helps the offender reinforce positive values.

10. Group counseling provides a forum for acceptance. It gives offenders the opportunity to see that others can accept them in spite of their past actions. They are able to work through the negative aspects of guilt.

11. Group counseling can be used by lay group leaders with little experience. Almost any correctional professional with appropriate training can counsel in the group setting. Leadership of psychologists or psychiatrists is not necessarily required.

12. All of the modalities discussed in this chapter can be used in a group counseling setting.

Group counseling has been criticized on the following grounds:

1. Offenders use group counseling as a place to play games with other offenders and counselors. Some offenders learn what others want to hear and tell them accordingly, without honesty or genuineness. In prison groups, offenders learn that if they say or do what the counselors want, they may be recommended for early release. Also some offenders use the group setting as a way to manipulate other offenders.

2. Offenders use group counseling as a place to pass the time away and avoid the business of counseling. They bring up and deal with superficial concerns, not substantive issues.

3. Quiet offenders use group counseling as a place to hide or be protected by others.

4. In the institutional setting, group counseling can contribute to the existing pecking order in that the most powerful offenders dominate and control the issues for discussion.

5. Group counseling gives offenders a forum to continue to role play tough attitudes and behaviors.

6. The counselor's time constraints prevent deeper, substantive offender issues from being dealt with thoroughly in group counseling.

Family Counseling

Family counseling deals with the family as a unit, or a whole. Family counseling is based on systems theory. To deal with the acting out person(s), the family as a system must be the starting point, not the individual member(s) of the family. If one family member is delinquent, breaks the law, and/or is exhibiting other troublesome acting out behaviors, then family counseling assumes that such behavior is a symptom of something going on (usually unhealthy and dysfunctional) in the offender's family. It is the job of the family counselor to uncover what is happening in the family, such as the all-pervasive but silent family systemic rules that are frequently believed to be responsible for the members' acting out behavior.

A major premise of family systems theory is that the family is a system and as such strives for balance or homeostasis whenever stress occurs. The family system is thought to have its own needs and a life of its own. The system's survival becomes more important than the happiness of individual family members. In short, the whole becomes greater than the sum of its parts (Bradshaw, 1988).

According to family systems theorists, when dysfunctionality appears in a family, there is normally a fearful, dependent, acting out person who will control the whole system, for example, the delinquent child, alcoholic parent, or hypochondriac mother. Whatever the acting out person does, the whole family will adjust to the stress and disorder caused to achieve balance in the system. It is at this point that the members of the family begin to play identified roles such as the enabler, lost child, scapegoat, hero or saint, and mascot (Bradshaw, 1988).

Dysfunctional families have identifiable characteristics. They can be summarized as follows:

1. *Secrets.* Most dysfunctional families hide things that they do not want those outside of the immediate family members to know. Most of the time these families put on a storybook face for the outside world to see. Some obvious examples of the kinds of secrets that are kept are alcoholism, addiction, incest, abuse, mental illness, etc.

2. *Poor Communication Patterns.* Dysfunctional family members do not know how and/or are not allowed to communicate openly with each other. Frequently family members learn to communicate in destructive ways. Often communication is passive-aggressive, hostile, and/or indirect. Direct, honest communication is absent in dysfunctional families.

3. *Boundary Problems.* Respect for family members' wants, wishes, and desires does not exist in dysfunctional families. Comments like "No," "Stop," "I don't feel comfortable," "Please don't do that," "I don't like that," and "Knock before entering" do not readily occur to members of dysfunctional families as okay to say. When such statements do occur to members, they may be difficult to say.

4. *Enmeshments.* In dysfunctional families, members are entangled or involved in other members' lives to an extreme. Frequently family members take on the feelings of others as though they were their own, living vicariously through them. Family members are excessively involved in other members' concerns.

5. *Stifled Feelings.* In dysfunctional families, members are prevented from expressing how they really feel about things. Expressing how one honestly feels is a taboo and, as a result, family members stiffle their feelings, express their feelings in inappropriate ways, and/or become emotionally numb.

6. *Lack of Freedom and Power.* In dysfunctional families, members are not allowed to speak their own minds, feel their own feelings, hear what they hear, think their own thoughts, see their own images, and want their own wants. The dysfunctional family does not allow its members to have power and freedom to perceive the reality of their family's situation.

7. *System Rules.* Dysfunctional families have potent and often unspoken rules that permeate the family and system rules are "No talking," "No questioning authority," "No defying," "No feeling," and so forth.

8. *Rigid Roles.* Roles are thrust upon dysfunctional family members. They are not freely chosen, but just emerge as ways of adapting to stresses in the family. Typical roles are controller, enabler, lost child, scapegoat, hero or saint, and mascot.

9. *Closed-Off.* Dysfunctional families tend to separate themselves from those who are not family members. The family is not open to non-family members. Others are not brought into the family. Frequently, a "us" versus "them" mentality develops.

10. *Inability to Be Real.* In dysfunctional families, members act in ways to prevent others from getting upset, angry, and so forth. Frequently members try to protect fellow members to the point that they never get to be themselves. As a result, family members do not learn to be authentic and genuine.

11. *Needs Are Not Met.* In dysfunctional families, members' basic life needs (such as security, safety, self-esteem, self-worth, and love and belonging) frequently are not met. As a result, frustration, anxiety, fear, loneliness, pain, and unhappiness are common in dysfunctional families.

Criminal justice counselors help offenders and their families identify the characteristics listed above and assist families through the clinical process of counseling. The process of family counseling involves helping offenders' families recognize the problems and stresses present in the family, bringing problems into the open for all to examine, assisting family members to acknowledge and embrace the feelings they have denied, learning skills to share feelings appropriately with each family member, making decisions to deal constructively with family problems, acceptance, and moving on.

In conclusion, the role of the family counselor is to create an environment in which the family members can take a hard and frequently painful look at themselves and their dysfunctional family systems. The family must identify its systemic rules before such rules can lose their power over the family members' lives. Unless members become aware of their dysfunctional family systems, they tend to stay loyal to them. The counselor is a vigilant monitor of the counseling situation and makes sure that all members are heard and feel safe in expressing their emotions and thoughts. Family counselors also teach and assist members to communicate appropriately with each other, and clarify the roles and functions in the family (Satir, 1967). Therefore, the thrust of counseling is on how the total family functions, communicates, and deals with the members and different situations (Satir, 1967). It is assumed that if families catch on to what is happening in their families and learn to communicate openly, many problems in the family will be resolved.

SUMMARY

There are numerous counseling modalities for criminal justice counselors to consider before a counseling style can be chosen. We have examined nondirective, directive, psychoanalytic/dynamic, relationship, rational-emotive, Gestalt, behavior modification, reality, transactional analysis, crisis intervention, problem management, and eclectic counseling modalities. This list is not exhaustive. Other modalities are found in criminal justice settings; however, some are faddish and trendy or used with less frequency and, as a result, are not examined here. Each of the aforementioned modalities has much to offer, but none offers everything. The counselor must understand the assumptions, premises, strengths, weaknesses, and techniques of as many modalities as possible to be in the best position to help offenders.

Three promising approaches to counseling offenders are therapeutic communities, group counseling, and family counseling. These approaches offer the criminal justice system ways of helping the large number of offenders who are expected to enter the criminal justice system in the future. Family counseling is based on the premise that the family is a system and thus includes the whole family in the offender's treatment.

MATCHING KEY TERMS AND DEFINITIONS

Match each key term with the correct definition.

a. modality
b. criminal justice counseling style
c. criminal justice counseling technique
d. nondirective counseling
e. empathy
f. directive counseling
g. defense mechanisms
h. rationalization
i. intellectualization
j. denial
k. repression
l. regression
m. sublimation
n. displacement

o. reaction formation
p. projection
q. reaction neutrality
r. relationship counseling
s. rational-emotive counseling
t. Gestalt
u. behavior modification
v. reality counseling
w. crisis intervention counseling
x. Transactional Analysis
y. problem management counseling
z. eclectic counseling
aa. therapeutic community
bb. group counseling
cc. family counseling
dd. homeostasis

___ 1. Understanding what a person says and feels.

___ 2. The model or prototype a counselor uses to work with offenders.

___ 3. A criminal justice counseling modality that presumes that the counselee is the only rightful person to determine his or her future.

___ 4. The characteristic mode of expression or action that determines how a criminal justice counselor deals with offenders.

___ 5. Tactics used to solve particular counseling problems.

___ 6. A criminal justice counseling modality that emphasizes the counselor's skill, expertise, and professionalism in solving offenders' problems.

___ 7. According to Freud, the ways in which human beings protect their egos.

___ 8. Feeling strong emotion but reacting without emotion.

___ 9. Being able to see one's own qualities in others, but not oneself.

___ 10. Feeling a particular emotion but reacting with the opposite emotion.

__ 11. The transfer of an emotion from the object about which it was originally experienced to another object.

__ 12. Deflection of destructive or negative energies into acceptable channels.

__ 13. Reversion to behavior patterns that were appropriate at an earlier stage of development.

__ 14. A form of denial whereby unacceptable impulses are blocked out of one's consciousness.

__ 15. Refusal to accept, acknowledge, or face the facts of a situation.

__ 16. Making excuses and explanations for one's behavior in the third person.

__ 17. Making excuses and explanations for one's unacceptable behavior.

__ 18. A modality that focuses on building a positive relationship between the offender and counselor.

__ 19. A modality that focuses on correcting the illogical thoughts of offenders.

__ 20. A modality that focuses on awareness and insight into problems.

__ 21. A modality that uses a mixture of approaches, depending on the needs of offenders.

__ 22. A modality that emphasizes the solving of offenders' problems.

__ 23. A modality that centers on changing behaviors without insight, awareness, or talk.

__ 24. An intense modality that focuses on immediately reducing the offender's tension brought on by stressful events.

__ 25. A modality that focuses on the acceptance of responsibility by offenders.

__ 26. A modality that centers on interactions between the offender and others.

__ 27. A social living approach to the treatment of offenders that heavily relies on group dynamics, total staff involvement in counseling and treatment, and democratic decision making.

__ 28. A counseling approach that involves both the offender's peers and criminal justice counselors.

__ 29. A counseling approach that views the family as a dysfunctional system and the offenders' behavior as a symptom of dysfunction in the home.

__ 30. The concept of balance in family systems.

DISCUSSION QUESTIONS

1. How does criminal justice counseling style differ from technique? Discuss four factors on which criminal justice counseling style depends.

2. How would a nondirective criminal justice counselor handle an offender who told him or her that he or she was planning to commit suicide?

3. What are the positives and negatives of nondirective counseling in criminal justice settings?

4. What are the positives and negatives of directive counseling in a criminal justice setting?

5. What are the basic techniques a psychoanalytic/dynamic criminal counselor would use with offenders?

6. How do relationship, rational-emotive, Gestalt, behavior modification, reality therapy, crisis intervention, problem management, transactional analysis, and eclectic counseling differ in their ideas as to how people change?

7. What makes transactional analysis so attractive as a modality for use with adult and juvenile offenders?

8. What are the advantages and disadvantages of behavior modification counseling in criminal justice settings?

9. Can behavior modification counseling be abused in criminal justice settings? Discuss.

10. Why is reality counseling so attractive with addicted offenders?

11. How does crisis intervention counseling differ from other modalities? Discuss.

12. How successful is eclectic counseling in a criminal justice setting? Discuss.

13. How does behavior modification counseling differ from brainwashing?

14. How is a therapeutic community treatment oriented?

15. How does counseling in a therapeutic community differ from counseling in a prison setting?

16. What are the advantages and disadvantages of group counseling in the criminal justice setting?

17. What is family counseling?

REFERENCES

Ankersmit, E. (1976, June). Setting the contract in probation. *Federal Probation, 40,* 28.

Ayllon, T., & Azrin, N. H. (1968). *The token economy.* New York: Appleton-Century-Crofts.

Bennett, L. A., Rosenbaum, T. S., & McCullough, W. R. (1978). *Counseling in correctional environments.* New York: Human Sciences Press.

Berne, E. (1961). *Transactional analysis in psychotherapy.* New York: Grove.

Berne, E. (1964). *Games people play.* New York: Grove.

Berne, E. (1966). *Principles of group treatment.* New York: Oxford University Press.

Bradshaw, J. (1988). *Bradshaw on the family.* Deerfield Beach, FL: Health Communications.

Egan, G. (1990), *The skilled helper: A systematic approach to effective helping* (4th ed.). Pacific Grove, CA: Brooks/Cole.

Ellis, A. (1973). *Humanistic psychotherapy.* New York: Julian.

Ellis, A. (1977). *Reason and emotion in psychotherapy.* Secaucus, NJ: Citadel Press.

Freud, S. (1946). *The ego and the mechanisms for defense.* New York: International Universities Press.

Gambril, E. (1983). *Casework: A competency-based approach.* Englewood Cliffs, NJ: Prentice Hall.

Gest, T. (1990, February 26). Why more criminals are doing time behind bars. *U.S. News and World Report,* 23-24.

Glasser, W. M. (1965). *Reality therapy: A new approach to psychiatry.* New York: Harper & Row.

Harris, T. (1969), *I'm okay—You're okay: A practical guide to transactional analysis.* New York: Harper & Row.

Hatcher, H. A. (1978). *Correctional casework and counseling.* Englewood Cliffs, NJ: Prentice Hall.

Hendrickson, G. (1991). *Preparing inmates for their return to society— An evaluation of selected release preparation programs within a California prison and a pre-release facility.* M.S. thesis, California State University, Fresno.

Jones, M. (1968). *Beyond the therapeutic community.* New Haven, CT: Yale University Press.

Jones, M. (1973). Therapeutic community principles. In L. Irvine & T. Brelie (Eds.), *Law, psychiatry, and the mentally disturbed offender* (Vol. 2, pp. 102-110). Springfield, IL: Charles C Thomas.

Kepner, E., & Brien, L. (1975). Gestalt therapy: A behavioristic phenomenology. In E. E. Peoples (Ed.), *Correctional casework and counseling* (pp. 317-324). Pacific Palisades, CA: Goodyear.

Kratcoski, P. C. (1981). *Correctional counseling and treatment.* Monterey, CA: Duxbury.

Lefrancois, G. R. (1972). *Psychology for teaching.* Belmont, CA: Wadsworth.

Lester, D., & Braswell, M. (1987). *Correctional counseling.* Cincinnati, OH: Anderson.

Martinson, R. (1974). What works? Questions and answers about prison reform. *The Public Interest, 35,* 22-54.

McCormick, P., & Campos, L. (1970). *Introduce yourself to transactional analysis: A TA handbook.* Stockton: San Joaquin TA Study Group.

Pavlov, I. P. (1927). *Conditioned reflexes.* London: Oxford University Press.

Perls, F. S. (1969). *Gestalt therapy verbatim.* Lafayette, CA: Real People Press.

Perls, F. S., Hefferline, R. F., & Goodman, P. (1951). *Gestalt therapy.* New York: Dell.

Rachin, R. L. (1974, January). Reality therapy: Helping people help themselves. *Crime & Delinquency, 20,* 45-53.

Rogers, C. R. (1951). *Client-centered therapy.* Boston: Houghton-Mifflin.

Rogers, C. R. (1961). *On becoming a person: A client's view of psychology.* Boston: Houghton-Mifflin.

Satir, V. (1967). *Conjoint family therapy.* Palo Alto, CA: Science & Behavior Books.

Shore, M. F. (1975). Psychological theories of the causes of antisocial behavior. In E. E. Peoples (Ed.), *Correctional casework and counseling* (pp. 3-18). Pacific Palisades, CA: Goodyear.

Skinner, B. F. (1971). *Beyond freedom and dignity.* New York: Knopf.

Smith, A. B., & Berlin, L. (1981). *Treating the criminal offender* (2nd ed.). Englewood Cliffs, NJ: Prentice Hall.

Smith, L. L. (1978). A review of crisis intervention theory. *Social Casework, 59,* 396-405.

Steiner, C. (1974). *Scripts people live.* New York: Grove.

Sullivan, H. S. (1953). The meaning of the developmental approach. In H. S. Perry & M. L. Gawel (Eds.), *The interpersonal theory of psychiatry* (pp. 3-12). New York: Norton.

Thorne, G. L., Tharp, R. G., & Wetzel, R. J. (1967, June). Behavior modification techniques: New tools for probation officers. *Federal Probation, 31,* 21-26.

Travis, S. (1990, September). Inmate population explosion: At highest level; no end in sight. *Correction News, 4*(3), 1.

Wicks, R. J. (1975). Reality therapy. In E. E. Peoples (Ed.), *Correctional casework and counseling* (pp. 358-364). Pacific Palisades, CA: Goodyear.

Criminal Justice Counseling Process

- The first contact between the offender and counselor is frequently surrounded with nervousness and anxiety on the part of each.

- During the first stage of counseling, counselors must state counseling rules and expectations of behavior on the part of offenders.

- Criminal justice counselors must be genuine in thought and deed when dealing with offenders.

- During the first contact with offenders, criminal justice counselors must explain their roles.

- Criminal justice offenders are frequently resistant to counseling and resistance is manifested in myriad ways.

- Criminal justice counselors must honestly face their feelings about resistance no matter when in the counseling process it emerges.

- When resistance is identified and dealt with, the offender and counselor are likely to move past it.

- Counseling contracts can be used at any stage of the counseling process.

- Nonverbal communication normally communicates emotional truth.

- Criminal justice counselors must learn to respond to content and feelings expressed by offenders.

- Criminal justice counselors must learn the communication skills of good listening, empathy, genuineness, concreteness, self-disclosure, probing, feedback, summarizing, confrontation, and immediacy.

- Offenders begin to develop trust with the counselor when they tell their problems to the counselor in story form.

- Counselors must learn to identify offenders' problems and blind spots even if offenders do not acknowledge them.

- The identification of blind spots does not mean offenders will automatically see their problems in a new light.

- Counselors must develop the humility to admit to offenders when they make mistakes.

- Diagnosis of the offender's problems is the responsibility of the criminal justice counselor.

- The counselor must be aware of and capitalize on points of leverage that occur during the counseling process.

- The middle of counseling involves offenders developing new scenarios, goal setting, development of agendas, development of contingency plans, making commitments, and taking action.

- Counselors can help offenders develop new scenarios by asking the correct future-oriented questions, helping them find others who have successfully solved similar problems, reviewing better times, and helping them get involved in new experiences.

- Some offenders find goal setting hard and tedious, while others seem to breeze through the process.

- Before offenders can take action toward accomplishing goals, they must make a rational decision to accomplish goals.

- Some offenders never take action to solve problems.

- Endings in counseling should contain reviews, closure, and good-byes.

KEY TERMS

- Johari window
- First contact
- Resistance
- Doorknob communications
- Counseling contract
- Feedback-empathy
- Genuineness
- Concreteness
- Self-disclosure
- Probing
- Feedback
- Confrontation
- MUM effect
- Immediacy
- Diagnosis
- Leverage point
- Barnum effect
- Scenario
- Goal
- Agenda
- Brainstorming
- Contingency plan
- Commitment
- Entropy
- Farewell party syndrome

INTRODUCTION

The focus of this chapter is on what should occur during the criminal justice counseling process. The chapter contains a discussion of what the counselor is expected to do when counseling offenders. In counseling, it is not sufficient for criminal justice counselors only to know, understand, and apply different modalities with offenders. Good counseling involves planning, preparedness, and the application of a system in the counseling of offenders. Knee-jerk approaches do not constitute counseling. Counselors must not only understand the counseling process, but help develop goals for every offender they counsel. The counseling process refers to the systematic series of actions the counselor and offender take that is directed toward an end. Counseling is also an interpersonal process in which the counselor attempts to help the offender develop problem-solving skills. The process should have a beginning, a middle, and an end. It should not be open ended, scattergun, disorganized, or go on indefinitely.

Whether counseling is long term or short term, the process and procedures are similar. Certain events are more likely to occur at the beginning, middle, and end phases of counseling, and criminal justice counselors need to be aware of, expect, and prepare for such things so that they are better able to handle them when they happen. In addition, counselors can prepare offenders for possible spinoffs of counseling, if they are familiar with the process. Last, if counselors are educated about the counseling process, surprises are less likely to catch them off guard and find them unprepared.

Criminal justice offenders are laden with problems. No matter what age, sex, or race, they have everyday life problems to contend with and criminal justice system problems to deal with (see Chapter 2). Counseling criminal justice offenders must include helping offenders manage their problems more effectively. If offenders do not perceive counselors as helping them manage their problems, criminal justice counselors may be in danger of losing credibility. Therefore, problem management must be woven into any modality choice on the part of the counselor. The explanation of the counseling process put forth in this chapter is modeled after Egan's (1990) problem management approach put forth in *The Skilled Helper: A Systematic Approach to Effective Helping.* I have chosen to discuss only what I consider the most important, salient, and useful aspects of the counseling process for the criminal justice counselor, not every nuance of the process.

This chapter is divided into three principal sections: (a) the beginning of counseling, (b) the middle of counseling, and (c) the end of counseling. Please note that the division of the counseling process into three parts is an artificial separation done to aid conceptual understanding. In real life, the phases are not always clear-cut and obvious. What the criminal justice counselor should be working on at each point in the counseling process is discussed in the following sections. Finally, skills that help to strengthen the counseling relationship are also identified.

> **❝Offenders are in precarious positions because they normally do not volunteer to be brought into the criminal justice system.❞**

THE BEGINNING OF COUNSELING

The beginning of counseling can set the tone and pave the way for the type and quality of counseling relationship developed and whether the offender will find successful solutions to his or her problems. Early in the counseling process, foundations are set and expectations are established on the part of the offender and counselor. If beginnings are handled well, offenders may embrace the services the criminal justice counselor can offer. If beginnings are handled badly, offenders may turn away from the services offered.

Counselors must keep in mind that offenders are in precarious positions because they normally do not volunteer to be brought into the criminal justice system. Criminal justice counselors are viewed as authority figures having great power to influence offenders' lives. Offenders also stereotype counselors as agents of the justice system who are out to make life difficult for them. Furthermore, many offenders have had negative past experiences with criminal justice counselors, which they bring to the current counseling relationship. As a result, in the beginning most offenders approach the criminal justice counselor with suspicion, tentativeness, ambivalence, and fear. The hope of receiving help with their problems takes a back seat to their fear. Offenders frequently feel that anything they say or do is being scrutinized and can be used against them by the counselor. In addition, they feel that if they fail to live up to the counselor's expectations, they might be arrested and placed in custody. Therefore, it is not unusual for offenders, in the beginning, to test the waters before taking even the smallest of risks with the counselor.

At the beginning of the counseling relationship, offenders usually have the following questions on their minds:

1. What is going to take place in counseling?
2. What kind of counselor is this?
3. Is the counselor going to be fair with me?
4. What are the counselor's expectations of me?
5. Does the counselor have a hidden agenda?
6. Is the counselor arrest happy?

Criminal justice counselors can and should answer questions 1 and 4 in a direct manner during the first contact; however, the other questions can only be answered for the offender with time. Until the offender gets answers to all these questions, trust is unlikely to develop in the counseling relationship, and the counselor is limited in his or her ability to help.

The Johari window (Table 5.1) is a model that can be used to explain what should ideally happen to the offender during the counseling process (Luft, 1970). The model tells us that at the beginning of the counseling process, offenders are not open with counselors and that they are blind to many things that the counselor and others can see clearly. Offenders also consciously hide a lot from the counselor. For example, offenders may have hidden agendas and sensitivities they choose not to reveal to counselors. Other things are also unknown to both counselor and offender at the beginning of counseling. For example, both counselors and offenders themselves are normally unaware of motives, games, attitudes, values, and certain behavior on the part of offenders. These are learned by offenders and counselors only

TABLE 5.1. Johari Window Diagram of the Counseling Process

	Known to Offender	*Unknown to Offender*
Known to Counselor	Open	Blind
Unknown to Counselor	Hidden	Unaware

after the process of counseling gets under way. Another example of what the offender and counselor are unaware of at the beginning of counseling is how the counseling process will progress. According to the Johari window model, the counseling process not only should help offenders solve problems, but should ultimately help them become more open, expose blind spots, reduce the need to hide things, and make them more aware of things they were never aware of before.

First Contacts

The first contact between the offender and counselor is frequently surrounded with nervousness and anxiety on the part of both parties. The counselor should be aware of his or her body language and tone of voice. Speaking should be natural and nonthreatening. After introductions are made, it is the responsibility of the counselor to clarify the purpose of the session. It is also imperative that the criminal justice counselor go over the rules or conditions of probation, parole, or institutional policy, depending on what agency the counselor represents. The counselor should go over such rules slowly and carefully so that the offender clearly understands and all questions are answered. The counselor must always keep in mind that the first contact is not an interrogation or fact-finding interview, and the offender should be included throughout the process. Whenever offenders ask questions, counselors must respond directly and not beat around the bush. Answering offender questions indirectly will interfere with the newly developing counseling relationship.

The counselor must also explain the counseling process rules and expectations of offender behavior in clear, simple, honest, and direct statements; the counselor should avoid jargon. For example, if the counselor insists on punctuality or that the offender call if he or she cannot make a meeting, this expectation should be unequivocally established during the first contact. In addition, the limits of confidentiality should be reviewed at this time as a part of establishing rules with offenders.

During the first contact, it is also important that the counselor explain his or her role in a genuine and nonphony way. Offenders frequently pose hypothetical or "What if" questions during the first session to see how far the counselor will allow the offender to go. Such questions also help the offender get a feeling for the type of person the counselor is. By clearly describing his or her role, ambiguities are eliminated and limits are set for the offender.

Throughout the first session, counselors should actively include offenders and elicit feedback. Counselors should also keep mental notes

> **"Criminal justice offenders are resistant to counseling, and the counselor must deal with this at the onset of counseling."**

on the offender's interactional style, personal strengths, and weaknesses. Normally intense, in-depth work does not occur during the first few contacts. In general, the counselor should concentrate on (a) developing a workable counseling relationship; (b) developing an accepting, tolerant atmosphere; and (c) empowering the offender by showing confidence in his or her ability to solve problems.

Resistant Offenders

Frequently, from the moment of the first contact, criminal justice offenders are resistant to counseling, and the counselor must deal with this at the onset of counseling. Most offenders do not come into the criminal justice system voluntarily, they are normally court mandated (forced) into the system; therefore, many feel coerced. Generally speaking, anyone who feels coerced into counseling will fight back in the form of resistance. It is wise for counselors to dissolve, avoid, or take advantage of resistance rather than to attempt to whip the offender into submission (Dimond, Havens, & Jones, 1978). Egan (1990) describes the typical resistant counselee as follows:

Resistant clients are likely to present themselves as not needing help, to feel abused, to show no willingness to establish a relationship with the helper, to con helpers whenever possible. They may be resentful, make active attempts to sabotage the helping process, terminate the process at the earliest possible moment, and be either testy or actually abusive and belligerent. (p. 169)

Offenders manifest resistance in a variety of ways and to different degrees. Some are openly hostile and aggressive and let counselors know in no uncertain terms that they want nothing to do with counseling or counselors. Others express resistance in passive ways by being unsure of what they want in counseling, talking about safe issues, being overly cooperative, never accomplishing anything, setting unrealistic and unattainable goals, minimally working at changing behavior, and avoiding responsibility (Egan, 1990). Some offenders express resistance by *doorknob* communications with counselors. These are very significant comments brought up by offenders toward the end of a session as they are leaving or in passing when there is not enough time to deal with them. No matter how resistance is manifested, it presents an obstacle between the counselor and offender and must be dealt with.

All humans respond to resistance on the part of others, and the criminal justice counselor is no exception. At the least, resistance on the part of the offender usually disturbs, bewilders, distracts, and perplexes the counselor. At the worst, resistance can make the counselor angry, and depending on the counselor's temperament, he or she may respond in a controlled way or in a knee-jerk manner. When the counselor's buttons are pushed, it is easy for the counselor to be tempted to turn away from helping the offender.

The first thing that the counselor must do is to face honestly his or her own feelings about the offender's resistance whether resistance is obvious during the first contact or raises its head at any point in the counseling process (Shulman, 1979). Counselors can have any number of emotions about resistant offenders. Irritation, hostility, rejection, hurt, panic, and guilt are only a few feelings that the counselor may experience. If the counselor does not face his or her feelings about what is happening, it can cause the counselor to hold back on offering needed help to the offender. In dealing with the offender, the counselor must also include a discussion of the obstacle that resistance poses to a productive counseling relationship. Egan (1990) also suggests other things that counselors can do: see some resistance as normal, examine their own roles in producing resistance, make resistance a therapeutic issue, be realistic, and deal with the offender's feelings of coercion. Please note that resistance rarely goes away by itself whenever it occurs. However, when it is identified and explored, the offender and counselor are more likely to move past it.

Contracting With Offenders

Counseling contracts, implicit and/or explicit agreements between offenders and criminal justice counselors for the doing or not doing of some definite thing, can be developed and used at any point in the counseling process. They are frequently used in the middle stages of counseling to get offenders to commit to work on specific counseling goals. However, contracts are also used in the beginning of counseling to establish the criminal justice counseling procedures and to define the counselor-offender relationship. Egan (1990) suggests that contracts at the beginning stages of counseling could include an overview of what the counseling process is like, what the counselor-offender relationship is like, the responsibilities of the counselor and offender, what is and is not expected from the offender, and what the counselor will and will not do for the offender during the counseling process. For example, a parole officer might begin the counseling process by explaining to parolees that they will be working on resolving the problems that the parolee is having, that he or she expects that the parolee will be punctual and not miss any meetings, and that he or she will go the extra mile if the parolee is honest.

Communication Skills

Communication is a process that involves our understanding and being able to use certain skills effectively. Criminal justice counselors will not be able to counsel effectively without mastery of basic communication skills. Note that although a discussion of communication skills is included in this section concerning the beginning phase of counseling, skills are used with vigilance throughout the counseling process and at all times. Listening, empathy, genuineness, concreteness, self-disclosure, probes, feedback, summarizing, confrontation, and immediacy are communication skills that criminal justice counselors must master.

Listening

Listening refers to the criminal justice counselor giving his or her undivided attention to the offender for the purpose of hearing what is said. Listening involves concentration, focus, honing, and blocking out extraneous noise. Examples of extraneous noise the counselor must eliminate to develop the skill of listening are ringing phones; interruptions of people, music, and children; preoccupations, and anxieties about one's own personal problems. It is a communication skill that is not simple or easy to do, as one might expect. In fact, sometimes it takes great skill, energy, and concentration to listen and pick up what offenders say both verbally and nonverbally, even though extraneous noises have been eliminated. A number of factors go into the complex job of accurate listening. Some selected factors are discussed below.

Attending. Attending refers to the counselor's physical and psychological presence in counseling or, more simply, giving one's complete attention to the offender. Ideally, attending should communicate the counselor's interest, attentiveness, and undivided attention to the offender. It includes how the counselor physically postures himself or herself and uses gestures, expressions, and mannerisms with the offender. Posture, gestures, mannerisms, and expressions communicate our readiness to respond to the offender's needs and can reflect how well we hear what the offender is saying. For example, as we lean forward toward offenders, face them, and keep eye contact, offenders perceive us as being tuned into their needs and listening. In addition, we become psychologically tuned in to listening better when our gestures, posture, and demeanor are alert. If we lean back, yawn, pick at invisible pieces of dust on our clothing, or repeatedly look at our watches, offenders tend to perceive us as not listening and perhaps even being bored or impatient.

Observing. Observing refers to noticing or perceiving what the offender says or does. It involves the counselor's ability to see the offender's nonverbal behavior such as energy level, grooming, and unstated feelings and emotions. Observation can be superficial and inaccurate when we are hurried or distracted by other things.

Nonverbal Communication. Nonverbal communication includes all of the ways we communicate other than with the spoken word. It includes our behavior, mannerisms, gestures, posture, demeanor, appearance, and voice quality. Counselors will never listen effectively if they ignore the nonverbal communication of offenders. It has been estimated that nonverbal communication accounts for 60% to 70% of the social meaning in interaction (Birdwhistell, 1970). In addition, feelings and emotions are more accurately and honestly conveyed through nonverbal than verbal communication, because nonverbal communication normally is not under our conscious control (Davitz, 1964).

Counselors must be able to understand and read their own and offenders' nonverbal communication throughout the different stages of the counseling process. In the beginning stages of counseling work, tuning into nonverbal communication is important in that it increases the probability of understanding offenders, because they are less likely to be direct with the counselor. Also the counselor should be warned against making inflexible conclusions about the offender's nonverbal communication during the early stages of counseling, since first impressions are likely to change as time goes on. A final point about nonverbal communication is that the counselor must not interpret it independent of its social context. If it is interpreted in isolation, the counselor runs high risk of misinterpreting it.

Understanding. Understanding refers to comprehending what the offender is saying. To comprehend fully what an offender is saying, the criminal justice counselor must understand the experience(s), situation(s), and/or problem(s) the offender describes. The counselor must also understand the problematic behavior the offender exhibits. Last, the counselor must understand the feelings and emotions the offender has. Unless the counselor understands the problems the offender has in terms of experience(s), behavior(s), and feelings, the counselor does not completely understand the problem. Also to understand the offender's problem(s), the counselor must suspend personal judgment, resist distractions, look for themes, and reflect on content (Carkhuff, Pierce, & Cannon, 1977).

Responding. Responding and giving information back to offenders about content and feelings is an important element in good listening and communication. Counselors must learn the appropriate ways to respond to offenders verbally and nonverbally, for if they respond inappropriately, the whole communication process is affected. Counselors should use extreme caution with offenders when responding to them with therapeutic touch, the use of physical contact to communicate that the counselor understands and empathizes with the offender. Some examples of physical contact are hugs, pats on the shoulder, holding hands, and so forth. Although therapeutic touch has a valid and important place in counseling, it is my opinion that novice counselors should avoid its use with offenders because of its potential to be misread and perhaps misunderstood by offenders. One important way counselors must learn to respond to offenders, if they are to become effective communicators, is through empathy.

Empathy

Empathy is a communication skill and can be defined as mentally entering into the feeling or spirit of the offender and communicating that understanding back to the offender. It involves the counselor putting himself or herself into the shoes of the offender and experiencing how the offender sees his or her world. Empathy is different from sympathy or feeling sorrow or pity for offenders. Having sympathy for offenders has limited use in counseling in that it can prevent counselors from doing what needs to be done; thus it should be avoided. When the counselor is able to empathize, he or she begins to understand the offender. When criminal justice counselors are able to communicate such understanding to offenders, trust develops, and the counselor is in a better position to help.

The criminal justice counselor must know how to use empathy with offenders. According to Egan (1990), the counselor must identify the core feelings in the offender's experiences, behaviors, and feelings. Once these core feelings are identified, they must be accurately communicated back to the offender simply and directly. The counselor must communicate empathy to the offender in a genuine way, not in a superficial or ritualistic way. I caution against counselors overusing formulas or patterned types of empathic responses with offenders. One example of such a response would be the statement "You feel . . . because. . . ." The counselor is left to fill in the emotion and the reason for the emotion when responding to the offender. For criminal justice offenders, these responses frequently are perceived as canned, phony, and hard to relate to because they do not show understanding of the offender's reality. Counselors must learn to express empathy with offenders in ways offenders understand. Counselors should never pretend to understand offenders when they do not. Empathy accurately communicated can do wonders to strengthen the counseling relationship, provide support, aid communication, and pave the way for more intense counseling interventions (Egan, 1990).

There are a number of reasons why a criminal justice counselor might find it hard to express empathy with offenders. Some counselors are not in touch with their own feelings; and it is difficult, if not impossible, to get in touch with offenders' feelings if the counselor is not in touch with his or her own. Also criminal justice counselors may have trouble expressing empathy if the offender's problems are similar to problems that touch their own lives. As counselors hear offenders express emotions that they (counselors) are having trouble dealing with, the capacity for empathy may be diminished. When counselors deal with offenders who commit crimes they find horrendous (for example, child abuse and rape), bias frequently occurs, and empathetic responses become blocked. Such blocks sometimes occur at the time when they are needed the most. One thing that seems to be true about empathy is that it is a skill that generally matures with experience.

Genuineness

Genuineness is an important communication skill and refers to a lack of phoniness and role playing and the ability to be nondefensive and freely ourselves (Small, 1989). Being genuine is communicated by what we say, how we act, and how we dress. Counselors must be genuine in thought and deed when dealing with criminal justice offenders. Offenders are frequently astute observers of human nature and can quickly spot a phony. If the offender perceives the counselor as phony, trust is unlikely to develop, severely limiting the counselor's ability to help. Counselors should not make promises they cannot keep. They should not use criminal justice or street jargon unless they fully understand the meaning of the jargon and are comfortable with its use.

Finally, counselors should not dress or emulate their offenders' styles in hopes of establishing rapport, unless the style is honestly their own.

Concreteness

Concreteness is a communication skill used in counseling that involves keeping talk specific and getting to the what, when, where, and how of offender problems (Small, 1989). If counselors ask general questions, they normally get general answers. The more specific the counselor is, the more likely the offender will be specific. To be concrete, the counselor must ask purposeful, open-ended questions that focus on the offender's problems. Concreteness on the part of the counselor leads to concreteness on the part of the offender.

Self-Disclosure

Self-disclosure occurs when the criminal justice counselor shares his or her own feelings, attitudes, and experiences with the offender to help the offender in the counseling process. It can be a powerful communication skill that can hasten trust and rapport in counselor-offender relationships—if used appropriately. All self-disclosures are not appropriate in criminal justice counseling, and the counselor should not share his or her deepest secrets when using self-disclosure. Offenders are not always pure of heart and motive, and the counselor's self-disclosure may not be used by the offender for therapeutic reasons. Here's an example.

A juvenile asked his parole agent if he had used marijuana when he was younger. The parole agent was honest and said he had used it in college and found that it caused him problems. The juvenile then spread this information to almost everyone he encountered. The self-disclosure did not accomplish what the parole agent intended, which was to show the juvenile that he too had difficult choices to make about drug use when he was young. The parole agent failed to predict how the juvenile would use the self-disclosure.

Criminal justice counselors should not use self-disclosure solely for self-disclosure's sake. The counselor should have some idea of how the offender will make use of the disclosure. Any type of self-sharing with offenders must pertain to the context of the offender's problems. Self-disclosures can involve sharing general information such as "I've felt frustration dealing with my children too." Self-disclosures can also involve sharing very specific information such as "I had a nervous breakdown many years ago." With offenders, it is best not to give too much detail in self-disclosure. Unscrupulous offenders can find ways to use information obtained in self-sharing against the counselor or to set up the counselor. Last, the counselor should avoid using self-disclosure for the purpose of venting, confessing, and/or appeasing guilt. As a general rule, the only legitimate self-disclosure in criminal justice settings is when it will assist in the development of the counseling relationship.

Self-sharing is an art that can be developed. To use self-disclosure effectively, the criminal justice counselor must be comfortable with himself or herself, be able to deal with emotions, and understand the purpose of the disclosure.

Probing

Probing is a communication skill that criminal justice counselors use to get more quality information as to the nature of the offender's problem(s). Probing should not be tricky, used to avoid an offender's question(s), or used to put an offender on the spot. Probing involves questioning offenders, and the ways in which counselors probe may facilitate and/or hamper counseling efforts. Probing is especially important for reaching into offender silences; however, too much probing or probing for the wrong information can backfire on the counselor. Information can be obtained verbally from offenders by direct questions and statements or nonverbally by use of eye contact, leaning forward toward the offender, and so on. Egan suggested the following guidelines in the use of probes:

1. Do not assault offenders with a lot of questions.
2. Ask questions that serve a purpose.
3. Ask open-ended questions that get offenders to talk about specific experiences, behaviors, and feelings.
4. Keep the questions focused on the offender (Egan, 1990, pp. 141-144).

There is also a difference between probing and interrogation. Counselors must be sensitive to the fact that offenders have dealt with police and most have probably been interrogated at some point. The information obtained was probably used against them. Such experiences can make offenders leery of counselors who probe.

Feedback

Verbal response to offenders by counselors is known as feedback. Feedback can also involve the counselor giving the offender basic information to help in decision making. Information is normally given to offenders when counselors perceive that time will not permit waiting for the offender to gather information or when information is technical. Note that information sharing is not advice giving. Counselors should avoid responses to offenders that pass the buck, create road-blocks, give advice, put offenders down, judge, admonish, order, threaten, and are not useful; they should refrain from giving amateur psychiatric replies (Neil, 1980). For novice and many experienced counselors alike, giving needed negative feedback is a difficult skill to master. According to Egan (1990), counselors must learn to give feedback that informs offenders when they are on course, gives offenders information they need to have to keep on course, and points out the consequences of not staying on course. Counselors should avoid the temptation not to respond or give feedback to offenders.

Summarizing

Summarizing is a communication skill that can be used at any point and/or stage of the counseling process. Summarizing involves condensing and restating to offenders what they have previously stated in a concise form. Counselors use summaries for different reasons. As noted in Chapter 4, Rogers (1986) used summaries to pull together his client's thoughts and feelings and as a springboard to get the client to explore issues more thoroughly. Summaries can also be used at the beginning of a counseling session to review the past session, to refresh both the counselor's and the offender's memory, and to get the offender prepared to work at the point at which he or she left off. At the end of a session summaries are particularly useful to identify what the offender has learned. They are also helpful with individual and group counseling sessions that are going nowhere. Both the counselor and/or the offender can summarize. The offender or counselor may summarize, and sometimes they may do it together. Summarizing is a skill that is most effective when used at key moments in the counseling process. Note that counselors should not be compelled to use it in every session with offenders.

Confrontation

Confrontation is a frequently misunderstood communication skill that criminal justice counselors must master to be effective. Confrontation has the potential of precipitating crisis in an offender's life. When

> **❝Confrontation is one of the most difficult skills for counselors to use.❞**

used skillfully and carefully, however, confrontation can lead to offender growth. The term *confrontation* has a negative connotation because it conjures up irrational outbursts and perhaps even assaultive behavior. In counseling, the term is used to mean therapeutic confrontation, which is used to bring offenders face to face with reality when engaging in denial, lying, smokescreens, games, negative and/or irresponsible behavior, complacency, and/or inaction, and so on. Counselors must also confront offenders when they perceive discrepancies between what offenders say and their perceptions of what they are experiencing, when offenders make conflicting statements, and when offenders' statements and behaviors conflict. It is hoped that offenders, when confronted, will begin to see their problems differently and, as a result, begin to act differently.

Confrontation is one of the most difficult skills for counselors to use and the use of this skill is directly related to how comfortable the counselor is with confrontation outside the professional setting. It is a risky communication skill as counselors who confront are frequently subjected to unpredictable offender reactions, which can range from minor expressions of displeasure to obvious displays of aggression and hostility. Normally, offenders are shocked and become disorganized when confronted and usually lash out against the bearer of unwanted information, namely the counselor. Most human beings do not seek such reactions from others, and since counselors are people first and professionals second, many criminal justice counselors engage in avoidance when they should be using confrontation on offenders. The tendency on the part of counselors to avoid giving counselees information that is in their best interest to hear is known as the *MUM effect* (Rosen & Tesser, 1970).

There are several characteristic reactions to being confronted. Offenders frequently discredit their counselors, try to persuade counselors to see things differently, devalue the counseling issue, look for others to support their views, and verbally agree with the counselor but never take action (Egan, 1990). The act of agreeing with and supporting the counselor's revelations but never following up on them is a way offenders can get the counselor off of their backs, at least temporarily.

Criminal justice counselors must understand how they feel about and deal with confrontation in their lives outside the counseling environment to use it effectively with offenders. Once counselors are aware of how they feel about and deal with confrontation in everyday life, they can begin to use it in appropriate ways with offenders. Confrontation does not mean unleashing anger on offenders at random. Such behavior is totally unacceptable, misdirected, and should be avoided. Counselors must be aware of the things that are likely to make them react emotionally or, to use counseling jargon, push their buttons and lead to a negative response. Acknowledging that we all have buttons, identifying them, and then learning to control them are the steps the counselor must take to be an effective confronter. Each counselor has a confrontation style that must be examined. If after examination, the style is not working, the counselor must be open to developing a new approach to confrontation. The decision to confront an offender is within control of the counselor and should be done thoughtfully, honestly, caringly, and in a way that has the greatest potential to benefit the offender.

Counselors must use confrontation appropriately and purposely. Counselors must always have a clear idea why they are using it and that its use may result in disorganization and crisis for the offender. If the latter occurs, counselors must keep in mind that confronted offenders may need time to process and accept information that is revealed by the confrontation. As I implied earlier, most confronted offenders react negatively to the counselor because they feel caught and/or exposed. Offenders must learn to deal with such feelings before they can begin to process the counselor's information. My experience with offenders who have been confronted is that some can deal with it on the spot; while others may need several days before they are willing to work on it. Confrontation can be used at any stage of the counseling process; however, the information that accompanies confrontation is less likely to be fought, rejected, and/or dismissed by the offender if trust has already been developed in the counseling relationship.

The last point to be made about confrontation is that criminal justice counselors must also be prepared to be confronted by offenders. Many offenders have been in the criminal justice system for years and have been through numerous treatment programs. As a result, they know the treatment jargon and buzzwords of the trade. Offenders are also astute observers of human nature and intuitively know if counselors are being honest. I have found few offenders who are afraid to confront when they feel they are being yanked around.

Immediacy

Immediacy is a difficult, demanding, powerful communication skill that allows the criminal justice counselor and offender to stay focused in the present (Carkhuff, 1969a, 1969b). It has also been called "direct, mutual communication" (Ivey & Authier, 1978). Immediacy normally does not involve the content of counseling, but what is going on with the relationship between offender and counselor. A counselor uses immediacy when *at the moment* something is noticed, he or she reveals it. Immediacy is more difficult to use than it is to discuss or define. It involves expertise in all communication skills. Counselors must be aware of the difficult moments that happen between the counselor and offender, but have the professional objectivity and distance to catch and react to them at the moment they occur. Immediacy requires more than skill on the part of the counselor, it requires guts, because it entails the same risks as confrontation and frequently results in the same reactions from offenders. Most counseling literature categorizes immediacy as a separate and distinct communication skill from confrontation; however, I tend to view it as a form of confrontation.

Telling the Offender's Story

During the first stage of the counseling process, the criminal justice counselor needs to understand the offender's situation. To do this, the counselor must get the offender to tell his or her story. This means getting the offender to tell the counselor his or her version of the experiences, behaviors, and feelings that contributed to the offender's problem(s). Remember at this point in the counseling process, the counselor is not necessarily looking for factual information such as would be needed for a police report but rather is trying to determine the offender's perceptions of his or her problem(s). This is not to say factual information is not important. It is, but at this stage it is more important for the counselor to get a feel for the offender's problem(s) as the offender sees it (them). As a general rule, the counselor should confront the discrepancies and inaccuracies in the offender's story, only after the counselor develops empathy and trust with the offender. After trust is established the offender will be more likely, over time, to accept the counselor's input.

Offenders can tell their stories in different ways. Some offenders tell long, elaborate, and detailed stories and others tell stories that are short and succinct. Some offenders tell their stories logically and sequentially and others tell their stories illogically and chaotically. For example, offenders in crisis rarely approach their stories in sequential, logical ways. Most of the time the stories of offenders in crisis are fragmented and hard to follow (see Chapter 4). Some stories are emotional and others are matter of fact. Some offenders tell their stories quickly and others take hours or days. The counselor needs to respect the differences in the way offenders approach telling their stories and refrain from trying to mold their storytelling in ways that the counselor prefers (Egan, 1990).

When the offender tells his or her story, listening, attending, observing, nonverbal communication, understanding, responding, empathy, genuineness, concreteness, self-disclosure, probing, feedback, summarizing, confrontation, and immediacy are all important skills for the counselor, because they help the counselor draw out the story. Frequently, offenders will begin telling their stories by raising a general concern expressed in universal or abstract terms. Such statements are first offerings that are often related to specific problem(s). It is up to the counselor to get the offender to elaborate about the specifics (experiences, behaviors, and feelings), and most offenders will not open up until they develop trust with the counselor.

It is also important for counselors to refrain from helping offenders before the whole story is told. This is frequently a problem for novice counselors. If the counselor rushes to help before he or she fully understands the offender's story, the result may not be helpful and can threaten the counseling relationship. Counselors must hold back and not act until they fully understand the offender's story. As the story is being told, counselors should make notes of the main issues that need to be revisited.

The counselor must also prepare for silences when offenders tell their stories. Silences can communicate a number of things, and counselors must realize they are not always negative. Silences can mean the offender is pausing to think; is dealing with difficult, painful emotions; or is ambivalent or tense. It is frequently difficult for counselors to understand what silences mean and handle them appropriately. Counselors must learn to be comfortable with silence in counseling. Rushing in to fill silences often hinders the counseling process and can show disrespect for the offender's work; however, to allow a silence to continue too long may also result in a problem. As offenders tell their stories, counselors must learn to find out what silences mean by asking offenders, after an appropriate silence, what they are thinking about or by attempting to interpret what the silence is about. These techniques tend to draw the offender out.

The themes of offenders' stories frequently deal with issues related to the criminal justice system, family, peers, employment, addiction, transportation, money, housing, relationships, anxiety, depression, and so forth. The offender's problems can fall into several categories. The first is that the culture in which the offender lives does not support the kind of person the offender is. The second is that problems may have to do with feeling inadequate. The third is that problems may have to do with the offender's inability to relate to others successfully. Finally, problems may have to do with personal conflict. As the counselor looks deeper into the stories, offenders' problems frequently are the result of not being able to make appropriate decisions (Dixon & Glover, 1984). Furthermore, problems may be the result of not being able to act to change something they have already decided must be changed (Tyler, 1969). For example, a person may have decided that he or she needs to loose weight; however, the person is unable to start a diet. The counselor must be able to get to the core of the stories that are told by offenders. This sometimes takes a number of sessions.

In telling their stories, offenders begin to open up and understand their problem(s) better. Trust has the potential to develop between the offender and counselor. Finally, telling the story gets the offender's feelings out in the open. Most offenders experience a catharsis and relief in getting their stories out.

Clarifying

Clarifying involves making what the offender says clear and understandable to the counselor so that the counselor can assist the offender in problem solving. One of the primary communication skills at the counselor's disposal in clarifying is the use of probes. Proper use of probes can result in greater understanding of the offender's problems.

A criminal justice counselor will never fully understand an offender's problem(s) unless he or she can understand the problem(s) in terms of the offender's specific experiences (what happened to the offender and how the offender perceives what happened), behaviors (what the offender did or did not do to create, maintain, and/or perpetuate his or her problem), and feelings (how the offender emotionally responds to the problem) (Egan, 1990). A problem will remain vague and unclear until the counselor understands it from each of these three perspectives.

It is particularly difficult for counselors when offenders do not fully understand their feelings and are unable to articulate them. It is also difficult for counselors when offenders hold back their feelings and emotions because they are ashamed of them and are afraid that the counselor will not understand. When these situations occur, empathy can be a valuable communication tool to clarify what is going on emotionally with offenders. The counselor can take a stab at articulating the emotion(s) the offender is experiencing or putting the offender's feelings into words and ask the offender to elaborate on whether the counselor is accurate.

Identifying Problems
and Blind Spots

It is important for the counselor to recognize offenders' problems even if offenders do not acknowledge them. It is hoped that as the counseling process progresses offenders will come to recognize them and see a need to work on them. Counselors are more objective than offenders and are sometimes in a position to see problems behind stated problems. For example, an offender might talk to a counselor about problems with his spouse. With a little probing, the counselor might find that the offender drinks, and his wife is uncomfortable with this. This may mean that the offender has a problem with alcohol that he has not yet recognized. Generally, offenders resent and resist counselors who push them to work on areas that they do not see as a problem. In short, if the counselor forces the offender to work on something he or she does not want, other unforeseen problems emerge, and the counselor runs the risk of destroying the counseling relationship. It is important for the counselor to continue to encourage offenders to explore the areas the counselor sees as problematic, but counselors have to be careful to maintain a balance between encouraging exploration and bulldozing offenders into doing things they are not ready to do.

The counselor must be forever vigilant in identifying offenders' blind spots. However, identifying and pointing out blind spots does not mean that offenders will automatically see their problems in a new light. Frequently, offenders become upset and defensive when counselors point out their blind spots when it comes to denial. Counselors must understand this and continue to work with the offender's denial. An example of how to work with a juvenile's denial that his or her mother is abusive would be to repeatedly confront the juvenile with the obvious facts of broken bones, bruises, burns, hospitalizations, and so forth. When the juvenile makes excuses for the mother's behavior, the counselor must repeatedly confront the juvenile with his or her need to rationalize and make excuses. The counselor must also let the juvenile know that it is natural to love and be loyal to one's mother even if the mother does not do right by her child and that it must hurt deeply to admit that the mother's behavior is harmful; however, this blind spot of not seeing mother's behavior as bad prevents the juvenile from dealing with his or her situation. The counselor must repeatedly state such ideas to the offender until reality sets in.

Diagnosis

Diagnosis, the process of determining by examination the nature and circumstances of an offender's problem(s), occurs during the first stage of the counseling process, frequently after telling the story, clarifying details, and identifying problems. Diagnosis is normally made by the criminal justice counselor, and its accuracy depends on the counselor's expertise, training, and the background information available on the offender. Diagnosis in criminal justice settings is not as precise as diagnosis in medical settings. The diagnosis often is crude and amounts to an educated guess on the part of the counselor as to the nature and extent of the offender's problem(s).

There are a number of clues that help the criminal justice counselor diagnose the offender's problems. The first clue is the counselor's spontaneous reaction(s) and/or first impression(s) of the offender. A word of caution: Not all first impressions are accurate. First impressions usually result from instinct and intuition, not fact; however, they must not be totally dismissed. Instinct and intuition are not measurable, but they nonetheless are a valuable source of information. For example, if the counselor becomes tense or nervous around an offender, he or she must explore the reasons. The counselor must be able to evaluate his or her spontaneous reactions.

A second clue to diagnosing the offender's problem(s) is the offender's reaction(s) to the counselor. In the criminal justice system, the reaction to the counselor often begins before the offender ever meets the counselor. News about the counselor travels by the powerful offender grapevine. Offenders talk to each other about criminal justice professionals. An offender's negative experience with a counselor is shared with other offenders and can affect the reputation of the counselor even with offenders they have not met. Offenders' reactions can tell the counselor whether there is a problem behind what is stated as the problem.

Criminal justice counselors must be careful not to make diagnoses that are universally valid or apply to almost everyone, such as astrology readings and horoscopes do. The tendency on the part of counselors to devise global or general diagnostic statements is known as the

Barnum effect (Meehl, 1956). A universally valid diagnosis that has applicability to most people is meaningless because it does not tell us specific information about the offender. Such general statements do not discriminate between offender problems and, as a result, make problems difficult to work with. Diagnoses should clearly differentiate between different offenders' problems and should particularize our generalizations about offenders.

The counselor must realize that diagnoses of offenders' problems may not always be accurate and are subject to change. Counselors are only human and sometimes make mistakes. Whenever mistakes are made, counselors must be humble enough to admit it freely to themselves and offenders.

Identifying Leverage Points

During the first stage of counseling, counselors must also look for the offender's leverage points. Leverage points are power and/or advantage points in the counseling process at which the counselor's influence and pressure has the greatest likelihood to create change for the offender; thus the payoff for the offender and the client is greatest. Leverage points also offer counselors guidelines to choose what offender problems should be worked on first. Egan (1990) describes a number of principles of leverage that the counselor must be keenly aware of when working with offenders. Egan's principles of leverage are meant to apply to any type of helping relationship; however, the focus here is the criminal justice counseling relationship.

1. If there is a crisis, first help the offender manage the crisis.
2. Begin with issues the offender sees as important.
3. Begin with the problem that seems to be causing the greatest pain for the offender.
4. Focus on a problem, regardless of importance, that the offender is willing to work on.
5. Begin with some manageable subproblem of a larger problem.
6. Begin with a problem that can be managed relatively easy.
7. Begin with a problem that will lead to improvement in the offender's condition, if worked on.

8. When possible, move from less intense to more intense problems.
9. Focus on problems for which benefits to offenders will be greater than costs.

In short, knowing the principles of leverage will help counselors wisely choose what offender problems to work on first and help counselors know when their influence has the greatest probability of resulting in change for the offender.

THE MIDDLE OF COUNSELING

At the beginning of the second phase of counseling, the offender's problems are usually already defined to some degree. During the middle phase of counseling, offenders develop ideas about what they want their lives to be like. Goals are developed and examined. Choices and commitments are made. The middle phase of counseling involves hard work on the part of both the counselor and offender. During this phase, counselors must be forever vigilant about not putting the offender in a dependent position by taking on the task of handling the offender's problems themselves. Offenders are infantalized and made to feel helpless by such misdirected, but well-intentioned, actions by counselors. Such behavior on the part of counselors frequently brings on more problems for the offender.

The second phase of counseling generally includes the development of new scenarios, goal setting, development of workable agendas, development of contingency plans, making commitments and choices, and taking action. Note that some of the enterprises that are undertaken during this phase also occur during the last phase.

Development of New Scenarios

A scenario can be defined as a picture the offender carries in his or her mind about his or her problems. Most adults are capable of envisioning a future with problems that are successfully resolved (Markus & Nurius, 1968). The scenario includes an estimate of the problem's seriousness and whether the problem is capable of being solved. Scenarios can be so overwhelming that they can immobilize offenders and prevent them from solving problems. Much about the offender's current scenario is revealed when the story is told, during the first phase of counseling. During the second phase of the counseling process, a new, more hopeful picture of the offender's problems should develop. The new scenario is a mental picture of where the offender wants to be in relation to his or her problem(s). The new scenario must be realistic. For example, an unmarried, pregnant 14-year-old with no money, no family support, and no prospects for marriage cannot be allowed to develop a new scenario in which her family and the baby's father come to her rescue; however, a scenario in which she does not try to change others, but takes total responsibility for herself and child can be developed. The new scenario is frequently the basis on which goals are set.

Counselors can help offenders develop new scenarios by asking the correct future-oriented questions, helping them to find others who have successfully solved similar problems, reviewing better times, and helping them to get involved in new experiences (Egan, 1990). Once a new and realistic scenario is established, the offender can begin to set goals.

Goal Setting

Goals are specific statements of what the offender needs to do to handle problems (Egan, 1990). They include what offenders hope to accomplish and are developed in conjunction with counselors. Goals have to be identified, defined, and operationalized, which includes developing steps (agendas) that outline how the offender will accomplish them. If goals are not identified and defined and methods for attaining goals are not delineated, offenders may encounter an interesting experience in counseling, but they normally cannot move forward or articulate what they have gained from the process.

Offender's goals can be categorized in several specific areas: knowledge acquisition, behavior change, personal growth, and/or professional growth. Sometimes offenders need to become educated about a situation or increase their knowledge bank, for example, become literate, learn another language, or learn the principles of good parenting. Sometimes offenders need to change certain behaviors such as not use drugs and/or alcohol, go to work, not be tardy, be polite, be organized, and not fly off the handle. Sometimes offenders need to become more open minded and tolerant of people different from them. Sometimes they need to be more assertive and overcome lack of self-confidence or feelings of inferiority. Sometimes offenders need to change jobs or gain another type of work experience.

Egan (1990) indicated that goals are more likely to be workable, and thus met, if they meet the following requirements:

1. Goals must be stated as accomplishments.
2. Goals must be clear and specific.
3. Goals must be measurable or verifiable.
4. Goals must be realistic.
5. Goals must have substance.
6. Goals must be in keeping with the offender's values.
7. Goals must be set in a reasonable time frame.

Counselors are in the best position to make sure offenders keep these in mind during the goal-setting process, because they are professional, objective, and not blinded by the offender's problems. Until offenders learn how to set goals, they are not in a position to develop and operationalize goals by themselves. Therefore, it is essential that the counselor take an active and directive role in helping offenders set goals. The counselor must be alert to the fact that some offenders find goal setting hard and tedious, while others seem to breeze through the process. There is a lot of variability in how offenders approach this task with the counselor. Counselors must always remain flexible in helping offenders develop goals. Goals should be modified and changed, as needed. Some offenders may have only one goal, while others may have many goals. The number of goals offenders have frequently depends on the nature of the problems they have. Counselors must also realize that they should focus on working with offenders' goals that have the likelihood of being successfully met, for offenders become empowered by accomplishing even small goals.

Developing Workable Agendas

Once the counselor and offender set goals, it is important to develop an outline or list of the steps (things needed to be done) necessary to accomplish goals. This is known as developing a workable agenda or, in lay terms, a plan used to reach a goal. If an offender's goal is to stop using drugs, then he or she might need to do some or all of the following things:

1. Find a place to detoxify from drugs.
2. Enter a facility to detoxify from drugs.
3. Not associate with others who use drugs.
4. Join Narcotics Anonymous.
5. Go to Narcotics Anonymous meetings three or more times per week.
6. Secure a Narcotics Anonymous sponsor.
7. Read the Narcotics Anonymous literature.

This agenda is not exhaustive, and it does not necessarily represent the order in which the offender should take the steps. It merely illustrates the difference between a goal and an agenda.

How a counselor goes about formulating these plans with offenders can lead to workable agendas. Egan suggested that the counselor use creativity and the principles of brainstorming with counselees when developing a plan to reach goals. Brainstorming is a creative technique used to develop new ideas. During the brainstorming process with offenders, counselors must use certain principles. Both the counselor and offender must suspend judgment, come up with as many ideas and plans as possible, use a developed idea to develop another, express wild or extreme ideas (even though they may never be used), and clarify the things to be done (Osborn, 1963).

After agendas are outlined and before the offender commits to taking action, the counselor and offender should extensively talk about each step identified in the agenda. During these talks, the offender must weigh the pros and cons of taking each step and talk about potential problems that might arise. Some steps may be particularly difficult for offenders and result in outcomes they were not prepared for. By talking about the possibilities beforehand, the offender is better prepared to deal with situations that might arise.

Developing Contingency Plans

The development of contingency plans are extremely important during this phase of the counseling process. Since neither the counselor nor the offender can be sure that the offender can carry out his or her agenda, it is good to develop contingency plans for offenders to fall back on in the event that they cannot accomplish certain steps in their agendas. For example, in the case of the offender whose goal was to stop using drugs, he or she might not be able to check himself or herself into a detoxification facility, but could go to Narcotics Anonymous community meetings regularly. An offender is less likely to give up on his or her goal, if criminal justice counselors have the foresight to develop contingency plans for the offender to fall back on.

Commitment

Before offenders can take action toward accomplishing counseling goals, they must make a rational decision to accomplish goals. Commitment involves pledging oneself to the accomplishment of the goal(s). Unless commitments to the accomplishment of goals are made rationally and freely by the offender, goals are not likely to be reached. If the counselor forces the offender to give lip service to commitment or if the offender merely tells the counselor what the counselor wants to hear, any attempt to reach goals is doomed to failure. The counselor is also in for a great deal of frustration and disappointment. Note that criminal justice counselors cannot control offenders.

Incentives and inducements help offenders commit to accomplishing goals. The knowledge that life would be more manageable if the offender had stable employment or marital discord would be reduced if the offender stopped drinking are examples of incentives that help offenders commit to accomplishing goals. In addition, the use of contracts by counselors can be useful in helping offenders commit to accomplishing goals.

Taking Action

Taking action to resolve problems for some offenders is easy and for others is difficult. For some, as they tell their stories during the first phase of counseling, they are empowered to act and do so immediately without the help of the counselor. For others, action comes later in the counseling process and some never act. The tendency for offenders to be reluctant to act is natural. It may be hard to get started and sometimes frightening for offenders to accomplish goals that lead to the resolution of problems.

Action involves movement on the part of offenders to accomplish their goals. There are different types of action. Some types of offender action can be observed and measured. Many times action is not observable, for example, when offenders begin to perceive their problems differently. Frequently, such internal action leads to external, measurable types of action.

An enemy to accomplishing goals is the tendency to give up action that has been started. The tendency for counselees to give up what they start is known as *entropy* in the counseling literature. Offenders typically need support to act and sustain action. The counselor, family members, employers, and friends may be significant sources of support for the offender. In addition to support, sound plans help offenders act and sustain action.

Counselors in the criminal justice system, not offenders, should be the strategists who guide the counseling process. They are responsible for leading the offender to action and ultimately helping the offender resolve problems.

THE END OF COUNSELING

Like the beginning and middle phases of the counseling process, the end of counseling has its own specifications that the counselor must be aware of. The final phase of counseling is important because, if approached positively by the criminal justice counselor, it gives the offender a chance to review the progress made, gain closure over unresolved issues, and say thanks and good-bye to the counselor.

The proper termination of counseling is also important for the criminal justice counselor in that the counselor can review the offender's progress during the counseling process, tie up loose ends with the offender, and gain perspective on the role he or she played in helping the offender solve problems and grow. For the counselor, such experiences help provide evidence that he or she has made a difference in the lives of offenders, not to mention that it makes the counselor feel good about his or her work and prevents burnout. Counselors should avoid abruptly or matter-of-factly ending counseling relationships and, whenever possible, bring the ending to the offender's attention early enough to establish the ending process and provide time to handle the last minute concerns of the offender. For some offenders, ending can bring with it a sense of necessity to work on more difficult issues that were avoided early on. Sometimes the most significant and important work occurs at the end of the counseling process.

In the criminal justice system, the proper termination of counseling seldom occurs, unless the counselor has the foresight to prepare for it. The fact that the criminal justice offender is usually given a sentence for a specific length of time, and thus does not remain in the system long enough for counseling to be completed, works against appropriate endings. In addition, determinate sentence laws passed in many U.S. jurisdictions no longer allow corrections systems to incarcerate offenders for indefinite terms or until counseling (treatment) is considered completed by treatment staff. In summary, there is a great deal of premature termination of offenders in criminal justice counseling. Proper endings both in individual and group counseling should include review, closure, and termination.

Review

During the final counseling session(s), it is a good idea to review the progress made by the offender. This is an appropriate practice in cases for which the counseling process is brief or long term. Of course, in long-term cases, there is greater likelihood of strong bonds existing between offender and counselor and, therefore, greater likelihood that the review process can bring about strong feelings and emotions on the part of both offender and counselor. Such feelings and emotions must be acknowledged and dealt with.

The review of the offender's problem(s) and contract (if any), how the offender handled the problem(s), how the offender felt about the progress made in counseling, and the identification of major learnings are in order at this time. Such discussions will put the counseling work in perspective and reinforce advances the offender has made. Also, it is at this time that the offender's questions are answered and decisions about future counseling are made (Wicks, 1977).

Closure

Closure, or the act of bringing counseling to an end or a conclusion, involves a number of things. At this time, both the offender and counselor must deal with their feelings of ambivalence about the counseling process drawing to a close. Other feelings that must be dealt with during closure by both the offender and the counselor are regret for what was not said or done (both positive and negative); pain over the loss of an ongoing, formal, and significant relationship; and guilt for what both the offender and the counselor did not do in counseling. In addition to dealing with feelings, the closure phase should include dealing with all unfinished business on the part of the counselor and offender. Counselors should also specifically evaluate the work the offender did in counseling. Counselors should not withhold negative feedback and should put personal feelings and recollections of the counseling process out for discussion. It is important that the content of closure be substantive and honest.

Schwartz (1971) outlined the dynamics involved in the termination phase of counseling. The wise criminal justice counselor must be alert to the fact that offenders may go through certain phases that typify counseling coming to a close. The phases are outlined below.

1. *Denial.* As offenders realize counseling is coming to a close, they may have difficulty in facing their feelings about it. Some common denial behaviors include refusing to talk about termination and not bringing up important issues. Counselors should put denial and avoidance on the table with offenders.

2. *Anger.* As denial comes to a close, many offenders get angry. Anger may be directed toward the counselor. Sometimes counseling comes to a close not as a result of the sentence being finished, but because counselors resign, are transferred, leave the criminal justice agency, retire, and so on. No matter what the reasons for counseling coming to an end, anger is usually present. Anger can be manifested by the offender directly confronting the counselor or indirectly by the offender being antagonistic, sarcastic, and picking fights over minor issues. Counselors should confront such behaviors on the part of offenders and invite offenders to discuss their anger.

3. *Mourning.* Sadness often underlies the feelings of anger. Counselors should attempt to draw out such feelings and express their own feelings about the termination of counseling. Mourning may be manifested behaviorally by offenders through lethargy, depression, and withdrawal. Counselors should invite offenders to discuss and deal with their feelings of loss over a meaningful relationship coming to a close.

4. *Trying It on for Size.* Trying it on for size is manifested by the offender showing his or her independence and learnings by resolving tough problems themselves and then reporting their accomplishments to counselors. This phase frequently takes on a see-I-can-do-it-without-you quality. Counselors should give credit to offenders for their positive work.

5. *Farewell Party Syndrome.* The farewell party syndrome refers to the tendency to concentrate during ending sessions only on the positive aspects of counseling. Counselors should identify, point out, discuss, and reach past this syndrome with offenders in both individual and group counseling.

Good-Byes

Termination refers to bringing the formal relationship to a close. In the criminal justice system, counseling termination usually is decided on by law or the time limits of the offender's sentence not by the offender himself or herself or by mutual agreement between the offender and counselor.

Note that short counseling relationships normally do not result in bonding between the offender and counselor. Long counseling relationships generally involve bonding between offender and counselor and should be acknowledged and dealt with before terminating the formal relationship. No matter whether the counseling relationship resulted in strong bonding or not, the offender and counselor must say their thank-yous, farewells, and good-byes.

Criminal justice counselors sometimes find themselves in the position where offenders voluntarily return to the counselor after they are formally released from parole and probation. This occurrence is rare, but normally indicates that the offender is in need of help. Technically, once the offender is no longer a part of the criminal justice system, the counselor need not follow-up or provide services to the offender; however, from a moral, human, and societal perspective, the counselor is obligated to provide needed services and follow-up himself or herself or refer to other agencies.

SUMMARY

This chapter discussed what should occur during the criminal justice counseling process and what the criminal justice counselor is expected to do with the offender during counseling. Criminal justice counseling should be a planned and systematic process, as counselors should always know what they are working on and how to get from one point to another with offenders.

The criminal justice counseling process should have a beginning, middle, and an end. The beginning of counseling can set the tone and pave the way for the type and quality of counseling relationship developed. Offenders are normally gun shy at the beginning of counseling and especially during the first contact. Offenders are also frequently resistant in the beginning. Counselors must be masters in the use of contracting and communication skills such as listening, empathy, genuineness, concreteness, self-disclosure, probes, feedback, summarizing, confrontation, and immediacy. During the first phase of counseling, counselors should get offenders to tell their stories, clarify, identify blind spots, diagnose, and determine leverage points.

During the middle phase of counseling, offenders develop a mental picture (scenario) of what they want their lives to be like and develop goals and agendas to resolve their problems. Offenders also make commitments to work on their goals and develop contingency plans in case selected agendas do not work out. Action is a theme of this counseling phase.

The last phase of counseling involves termination and ending the counseling process. During this phase, counselors help offenders review the whole counseling process, get closure on unfinished business, and say good-bye. Note that during the entire counseling process, communication skills are used by counselors and that action on the part of offenders can occur. There is nothing carved in granite about the beginning, middle, and end phases of counseling. There is no requirement that certain things discussed in this chapter must happen exclusively in one phase or another. Therefore, criminal justice counselors must always be prepared, flexible, and adaptable.

MATCHING KEY TERMS AND DEFINITIONS
Match each key term with the correct definition.

a. Johari window
b. first contact
c. resistance
d. doorknob communications
e. counseling contract
f. empathy
g. genuineness
h. concreteness
i. self-disclosure
j. probing
k. feedback
l. confrontation

m. MUM effect
n. immediacy
o. diagnosis
p. leverage point
q. Barnum effect
r. scenario
s. goal
t. agenda
u. brainstorming
v. contingency plan
w. commitment
x. entropy
y. farewell party syndrome

___ 1. The first meeting between the criminal justice counselor and offender.

___ 2. A model that can be used to view how the offender is supposed to change in the counseling process.

___ 3. Implicit and explicit agreements between offender and counselor to do or not do some specific thing.

___ 4. A way that offenders fight back in counseling.

___ 5. The counselor's ability to get to the specifics of a problem.

___ 6. The counselor's ability to get into the shoes of the offender and communicate this understanding back to the offender.

___ 7. The counselor's qualities of authenticity and not being phony.

___ 8. The counselor's response to the offender's information sharing and feelings.

___ 9. Sharing of Self on the part of counselors and offenders.

___10. The tendency not to give the offender negative or confrontive feedback.

___11. Asking questions or making statements to draw out information about an offender's problems.

___12. Direct mutual talk that keeps the focus on the counseling relationship in the present.

___13. A communication technique that brings the offender face to face with reality when he or she is in denial, lying, engaging in smokescreens, games, negative and/or irresponsible behavior, complacency, and/or inaction.

___ 14. The process of determining by examination the nature and circumstances of an offender's problems.

___ 15. A point in the counseling process at which the counselor's power and influence has a greater chance of being accepted by the offender.

___ 16. Significant comments made by the offender to the counselor, usually at the end of the counseling session, when there is not enough time to deal with them.

___ 17. The counselor's tendency to make diagnostic statements that are valid for most people.

___ 18. The tendency to concentrate during ending sessions only on the positive aspects of counseling.

___ 19. The picture the offender carries in his or her mind about his or her problems.

___ 20. Tendency for offenders to give up what they start in counseling.

___ 21. Specific statement of what the offender needs to do to handle problems.

___ 22. Pledging oneself to the accomplishment of goals.

___ 23. Things needed to be done or a plan to reach goals.

___ 24. A plan to fall back on in case offenders cannot accomplish their agendas.

___ 25. A creative technique used to develop new ideas.

DISCUSSION QUESTIONS

1. What are the problems that emerge during the first contact between the criminal justice counselor and offender?

2. Why are criminal justice offenders so resistant to counseling?

3. How should the criminal justice counselor deal with resistant offenders?

4. What factors influence good listening?

5. Why must the criminal justice counselor gain mastery over communication skills?

6. Why is it important for the offender to tell his or her story to the counselor?

7. What counseling events are more likely to occur during the middle of counseling?

8. What should the counselor concentrate on during the final phase of counseling?

9. Should the criminal justice counselor avoid encouraging offenders to take action during the beginning of counseling and during the ending of counseling? Explain your answer.

REFERENCES

Birdwhistell, R. L. (1970). *Kinesic and context.* Philadelphia: University of Pennsylvania Press.

Carkhuff, R. R. (1969a). *Helping and human relations. Vol. 1, Selection and training.* New York: Holt, Rinehart, & Winston.

Carkhuff, R. R. (1969b) *Helping and human relations. Vol. 2, Practice and research.* New York: Holt, Rinehart, & Winston.

Carkhuff, R. R., Pierce, R. M., & Cannon, J. R. (1977). The art of helping III. Amherst, MA: Human Resource Development.

Davitz, J. R. (1964). *The communication of emotional meaning.* New York: McGraw-Hill.

Dimond, R. E., Havens, R. A., & Jones, A. C. (1978). A conceptual framework for the practice of prescriptive eclecticism in psychotherapy. *American Psychologist, 33,* 245.

Dixon, D. N., & Glover, J. A. (1984). *Counseling a problem-solving approach.* New York: Wiley.

Egan, G. (1990). *The skilled helper: A systematic approach to effective helping.* Pacific Grove, CA: Brooks/Cole.

Ivey, A. E., & Authier, J. (1978). *Microcounseling* (2nd ed.). Springfield, IL: Charles C Thomas.

Luft, J. (1970). The Johari window: A graphic model of awareness in interpersonal relations. In J. Luft, *Group processes: An introduction to group dynamics* (pp. 11-20). Palo Alto, CA: National Press Books.

Markus, H., & Nurius, P. (1968). Possible selves. *American Psychologist, 41,* 954-969.

Meehl, P. E. (1956). Wanted—A good cookbook. *American Psychologist, 11*(6), 226.

Neil, T. C. (1980). *Interpersonal communications for criminal justice personnel.* Boston: Allyn & Bacon, Inc.

Osborn, A. F. (1963). *Applied imagination: Principles and procedures of creative problem solving* (3rd ed.). New York: Scribner's.

Rogers, C. R. (1986). Reflection of feelings. *Person-Centered Review, 2,* 375-377.

Rosen, S., & Tesser, A. (1970). On the reluctance to communicate undesirable information: The MUM effect. *Sociometry, 33,* 253-263.

Schwartz, W. (1971). On the use of groups in social work practice. In W. Schwartz & S. Zalba (Eds.), *The practice of group work* (pp. 3-24). New York: Columbia University Press.

Shulman, L. (1979). *The skills of helping: Individuals and groups.* Itasca, IL: Peacock.

Small, J. (1989). *Becoming naturally therapeutic: A return to the true essence of helping.* New York: Bantam.

Tyler, L. E. (1969). *The work of the counselor* (3rd ed.). New York: Appleton-Century-Crofts.

Wicks, R. J. (1977). *Counseling strategies and intervention techniques for the human services.* Philadelphia: Lippincott.

Effectiveness of
Criminal Justice Counseling

CHAPTER HIGHLIGHTS

- There is no agreement among criminal justice professionals as to what constitutes counseling effectiveness.

- Studies have measured counseling effectiveness in many different ways.

- There is evidence to support the idea that criminal justice counseling is both effective and ineffective.

- There is evidence suggesting that to force counseling on offenders who are not amenable to it can do them harm.

KEY TERMS

- Counseling effectiveness
- Cambridge-Somerville Youth Study
- PICO Project
- Highfields program
- Youth Center Research Project
- California Community Treatment Project

INTRODUCTION

Does criminal justice counseling work? In an attempt to answer this frequently debated question, this chapter examines a number of selected studies dealing with counseling in different criminal justice settings. It should be noted, however, experts have reported that most research conclusions concerning counseling effectiveness in criminal justice settings are problematic. Most conclusions are formulated in terms of what we do not know, research methodology is painfully inadequate, and only a few studies ensure unequivocal interpretations (Sechrest, White, & Brown, 1979).

STUDIES OF CRIMINAL JUSTICE
COUNSELING EFFECTIVENESS

There is no single agreed on definition among criminal justice professionals as to what constitutes counseling effectiveness. The phrase *counseling effectiveness* has many different meanings, as does the term *recidivism*. Some professionals believe counseling to be effective if a prison runs smoothly and the status quo of the institution is not disturbed. Effective counseling is also seen as providing economical counseling services to as many offenders as possible. Effective counseling to some can mean simply providing programs to assist offenders in emotional well-being. Finally, counseling is seen to be effective only if it results in lower recidivism rates (Lester & Braswell, 1978). Some criminal justice professionals believe that counseling is not effective unless it meets all of the above requirements. This contributes to the confusion surrounding the definition of counseling effectiveness.

Criminal justice professionals are also confused about whether or not counseling proves effective for offenders. This heated argument among criminal justice professionals has been ongoing for at least 40 years. Criminal justice professionals stack up on both sides of the debate, because evidence and studies are available that conclude counseling can be effective and ineffective at times. Much depends on a counselor's beliefs as to what evidence and arguments he or she supports. Also contributing to the confusion is that all evaluative measures of counseling effectiveness are imperfect. Some of the approaches taken to evaluate counseling effectiveness include long-term posttreatment

> **❝There is no single agreed on definition among criminal justice professionals as to what constitutes counseling effectiveness.❞**

follow-up, case studies, psychological testing to measure personality change, and recidivism rates before and after counseling (Lester & Braswell, 1978). Each approach to research has its strengths and weaknesses. There are some experts who are of the opinion that the counseling techniques are good but have been delivered in a weakened form; therefore, contaminating conclusions about counseling effectiveness (Sechrest et al., 1979).

Egan (1990) makes some commonsense points about the effectiveness of counseling debate. He feels that there is too much positive evidence that helping (counseling) works, especially if certain conditions are met. He states:

> Like most practitioners, I side with those who, after reviewing the evidence, say that helping can be helpful. Empirical studies aside, my own experience, together with the experience of colleagues I trust, makes it quite clear to me that helping can help. (Egan, 1990, p. 10)

The conditions that must be met if counseling is to be effective are that (a) the counselee and counselor both have to do their parts and

(b) helpers (counselors) must be competent. Egan (1990) believes that helpers who are *exemplars* are effective, and poor helping (counseling) can do harm to counselees. The studies presented below have all attempted to evaluate the effectiveness of criminal justice counseling with adult and/or juvenile offenders. It is left up to the reader, after reviewing them, to judge the effectiveness of counseling in the criminal justice system.

Cambridge-Somerville Youth Study

The Cambridge-Somerville Youth Study was conceived by Richard C. Cabot of the Harvard Medical School and took place between 1935 and 1945. This was a carefully organized study to determine whether early and intensive counseling could prevent delinquency in Cambridge, Massachusetts. During the heyday of the project, it had 10 employed counselors, and each had a caseload of approximately 33 boys. Local teachers and police and a committee of experts identified and selected 650 predelinquent boys between the ages of 9 and 11 to participate in the study. The boys were then randomly divided into a treatment group of 325 boys who received one-to-one counseling and a control group of 325 boys who did not receive counseling. The group that received treatment was given counseling for a median of 5 years. Then rates of court appearances, institutional commitments, and estimates of the seriousness of the delinquencies were used as indices to evaluate the effectiveness of counseling.

The study found that in every year the boys were studied—except for boys aged 17—the number of counseled boys charged with offenses progressively exceeded the number of uncounseled boys charged with offenses. By the time the boys were 20 years old, the ratio was two to one in favor of the uncounseled boys. By the boys' 21st birthdays, there were no reports of uncounseled boys appearing in court. When the researchers looked at the total number of all types of offenses committed by the boys and seriousness, the counseled boys committed more offenses than the uncounseled boys.

To evaluate the seriousness of offenses, Powers and Witmer (1951) devised a scale of seriousness. In consultation with law enforcement agencies the researchers were able to rank offenses according to seriousness. They found that the counseled boys committed more offenses and the number of uncounseled boys committing the most serious offenses slightly exceeded that of the counseled boys. The counselors who were interviewed did not believe that inadequate counseling contributed to counseled boys committing more offenses than the uncounseled boys. Powers and Witmer (1951) concluded that the main advantages of counseling for the counseled boys were that it tended to reduce the incidence of serious offenses associated with psychopathology and that it was not particularly effective with typical, goal-directed criminality. In summary, there were no statistically significant differences between the counseled and uncounseled boys as far as seriousness of offenses, but counseled boys got into trouble much more often.

In the mid-1950s, McCord and McCord (1959) reevaluated the Cambridge-Somerville Youth Study to see if counseling affected the boys' behaviors when they were older. They found that both the counseled and uncounseled boys tended to become less involved in crime as they got older. For the most part, the researchers failed to find any significant differences between the counseled and uncounseled boys 10 years after the original study, except they noted that boys who received intensive counseling appeared to be less involved in criminality as adults.

To summarize, the results of the research on the Cambridge-Sommerville Youth Study are confusing and unclear. Cabot's original work found no significant differences between counseled boys and boys who were not counseled. On the other hand, Powers and Witmer's analysis revealed some evidence that counseling may have prevented boys from engaging in the most serious offenses. Last, McCord and McCord's research contradicted the original results as they found that counseling was beneficial. Such diverse results make it difficult to say with certainty just what role counseling has in preventing crime and delinquency.

PICO Project

Adams's (1961) PICO Project was a very detailed study of counseling effectiveness with institutionalized older delinquents. It took place at Deuel Vocational Institution, a California Department of Corrections institution in 1961.

A total of 1,600 male inmates took part in the study. Staff identified the offenders they felt would be most disposed to or amenable to counseling and those least disposed to or nonamenable to individual and group counseling. Once this was done, the researchers divided the amenables into those who got counseling and those who did not get counseling. They did the same thing with the nonamenables. This made four groups: untreated amenables, treated amenables, untreated non-amenables, and treated nonamenables. The researchers then evaluated all the inmates being studied as to institutional and postinstitutional measures of adjustment: some of which were parole success, length of time spent in return to custody after parole failure, and time spent in lock-up.

It was found that the counseled amenables fared significantly better than did the uncounseled amenables, counseled nonamenables,

“Do we do more harm than good when we force counseling on those who are not predisposed to it?”

and uncounseled nonamenables. They also found that the uncounseled amenables and the uncounseled nonamenables fared about the same. However, the counseled nonamenables fared worse than the uncounseled nonamenables. These results raise the question of whether we do more harm than good when we force counseling on those who are not predisposed to it.

Kassebaum, Ward, and Wilmer's Study of Adult Male Prisoners

Kassebaum, Ward, and Wilmer's (1971) study took place at the California Men's Colony in San Luis Obispo. At the time, California Men's Colony was one of the newest California Department of Corrections prisons with a security level classification of medium.

Approximately 1,000 adult male offenders (they were at least 18 years old) took part in the study for 6 months to 2 years. Upon release from prison, those who took part in the study under went follow-up for 36 months. The researchers were interested in finding out whether group counseling would reduce the number of institutional disciplinary problems and improve postinstitutional adjustment.

The study group was divided into four groups. The first group volunteered for group counseling. The second group was given mandatory intensive counseling by specialized counselors. The third group was given small- and large-group counseling as a part of a community living situation. The fourth group was the control group. These inmates had a regular institutional program without group counseling.

The study found that there were no differences in the institutional adjustment of inmates in any of the four groups. Approximately half of each group studied managed to remain free of disciplinary problems. In regard to postinstitutional adjustment, there were no significant differences between the groups after 36 months of follow-up.

Highfields Program

The Highfields Program, a New Jersey project, was started in 1950 and involved 237 male offenders between 16 and 18 years old who had never been incarcerated before. Boys volunteered to be sent to Highfields instead of being given traditional incarceration or probation. The program involved milieu therapy and "guided group interaction" counseling in a noncustodial, residential setting. The program's length was approximately 2 to 6 months. Freeman and Weeks (1956) compared the boys who went through Highfields for 6 months with boys who went through a traditional institution. They found that 63% of the Highfields boys but only 43% of the boys from a traditional institution did not recidivate. Other criteria Weeks (1958) examined were the boys' attitude and personality changes. There were no significant differences except with the criterion of recidivism. This fact coupled with the knowledge that both Highfields and the traditional institution cost about the same to operate made Highfields more cost-effective than the traditional institution.

Lamar Empey

Empey (1967) started a program in which he hoped to determine the effectiveness of counseling with offenders. This program was known as the Provo experiment and involved group counseling in a residential environment. A total of 200 juveniles between 15 and 17 years old received counseling for approximately 7 months. These juveniles were then compared with juveniles who received probation and those who received incarceration. Results of the study showed that more juveniles who had completed the treatment program were arrest free during the follow-up period than those on probation, and both those in the program and on probation did significantly better than those who were incarcerated.

Youth Center Research Project

The Youth Center Research Project took place at two California Youth Authority institutions for males near Stockton. Two treatment modalities were studied—behavior modification and transactional analysis—in an attempt to discover their effectiveness. In one institution, the modality behavior modification was used and in the other transactional analysis. Staff in both youth authority institutions were trained in the modalities they would be using. It was assumed that transactional analysis would be more effective with more mature offenders and behavior modification with less mature offenders. It was also assumed that both modalities would be more effective than a traditional program of individual and group counseling. Eventually, 130 male youth between the ages of 16 and 20 were randomly assigned to the two institutions. The results of the study did not show that one modality was more successful than the other, but the study concluded that counseling can help reduce recidivism if the whole institution is committed to counseling. Also mature offenders respond more favorably to counseling than immature offenders. The rate of failure on parole as measured by revocation was approximately 32% for boys counseled in both modalities; however, the rate of parole failure for boys counseled in both modalities was significantly less than boys released from other California Youth Authority institutions (Jesness, De Risi, McCormick, & Wedge, 1972).

A critique of this project is that it compared two experimental groups (those in behavior modification and those in transactional analysis) to those in traditional institutions. Such a comparison is problematic because it compares apples and oranges. There was no real control group, since the experimental institutionalized youth got more and perhaps better counseling than the control group. It may be that the added attention was the significant factor, rather than the modality used.

California Community Treatment Project

The California Community Treatment Project (CTP), a two-part research study spanning 12 years, began in 1961 under the direction of the California Youth Authority and was sponsored in part by the National Institute of Mental Health with Palmer (1975) as the principal investigator. This study was also known as the Grant and Grant study and the Interpersonal Maturity Study. The CTP accepted first commitment male and female delinquents who were not violent and could be handled in the community. Only those who had been sent to the California Youth Authority for armed robbery, assault with a deadly weapon, or forcible rape were deemed ineligible to participate. If a county was included in the study, any delinquent who met the requirements was eligible to participate. The project randomly assigned youth to either experimental or control groups. A total of 802 boys and 212 girls took part in the first phase of the experiment. The youth assigned to control groups stayed in institutions and got traditional counseling and treatment. Those assigned to experimental groups were released into the community and placed in intensive community treatment units, matched to parole agents according to their interpersonal maturity level (I-level) scores, and received intensive parole supervision and counseling. Parole caseloads were limited to no more than 12 youths.

CTP studied male and female youth according to their I-level scores. According to I-level theory, there are seven interpersonal maturity levels and delinquents are usually classified between the second and fourth level, depending on their behavioral responses and perceptions of the world.

Delinquents who were in the experimental group were matched with parole agents according to I-level scores, had intensive parole intervention in all areas of their lives, and had extensive counseling (Beker & Heyman, 1972).

For approximately 11 years, Beker and Heyman (1972) evaluated this research. They found that the reliability was not good and the construct development was lacking. It was concluded that many youth could be handled in community programs as opposed to incarceration for less money and with similar success. Some differences were found between the experimental and control groups, but because of research biases, inadequate controls, different types of follow-up practices, and unclear conclusions, it was difficult to determine what parts of the counseling/treatment program made a significant difference for offenders (Smith & Berlin, 1981).

SUMMARY

It is not possible to state with absolute certainty whether counseling in criminal justice settings is effective or not. All of the research

> **"***It is not possible to state with absolute certainty whether counseling in criminal justice settings is effective or not.***"**

presented was laden with methodological difficulties, not to mention evaluation problems.

Criminal justice counseling is a difficult job to say the least. The large, continually increasing size of the offender population, burnout of criminal justice professionals, offender codes and value systems, and lack of desire for change on the part of offenders are only a few of the factors that work against effective counseling in criminal justice settings.

The Cambridge-Somerville Youth Study concluded that the uncounseled boys in the study were charged with fewer offenses but committed the most serious offenses. At the end of the study, no significant differences emerged between those counseled and those not counseled. The PICO Project concluded that offenders who are amenable to counseling and get it do significantly better than those who do not receive it. However, for those offenders who are nonamenable to it but received it did the worst. Kassebaum, Ward, and Wilmer's (1971) study of adult male prisoners found those who received various forms of counseling in prison did no better than their control group. Highfields Program compared male youth who received milieu therapy with male youth who received traditional sentences. The researchers found that the Highfields Program's boys had less recidivism. Empey (1967) found that youngsters who completed a program that offered heavy doses of counseling did better during the follow-up period than those getting traditional sentences. The Youth Center Research Project failed to show that transactional analysis or behavior modification was clearly a more effective modality. However, boys released from the two institutions using the modalities had better rates of parole success than those released from other California Youth Authority institutions. The California Community Treatment Program research failed to reveal significant differences between those in the program and those not in the program, because of research bias, inadequate controls, and inconsistent follow-up practices.

MATCHING KEY TERMS AND DEFINITIONS
Match each key term with the correct definition.

a. counseling effectiveness
b. Cambridge-Somerville Youth Study
c. PICO Project
d. Highfields Program
e. Youth Center Research Project
f. California Community Treatment Project

___ 1. A phrase that refers to the counseling process producing the intended or expected results; namely, lower recidivism rates, offender emotional well-being, satisfactory prison adjustment, and/or economical counseling programs.

___ 2. The results of this study showed that milieu therapy and guided group interaction counseling were effective in reducing the recidivism rate of boys involved in the study.

___ 3. A California Department of Corrections study of older incarcerated delinquents that concluded that there was no difference between the institutional or postinstitutional adjustment of those who got counseling and therapy and those who did not.

___ 4. A study focusing on how counseling impacts juveniles. It was found that those who received counseling had higher recidivism rates than those who did not.

___ 5. A California research project that attempted to match parole agents and delinquents according to I-level scores and concluded that delinquents could be handled in the community for less money than incarceration with about the same results.

___ 6. A California Youth Authority study that attempted to compare the effectiveness of the behavior modification and Transactional Analysis modalities.

DISCUSSION QUESTIONS

1. Why is criminal justice counseling effectiveness so difficult to measure?

2. Can counseling, when forced on those who are not disposed to it, do harm?

3. What conclusions emerge from counseling effectiveness studies?

REFERENCES

Adams, S. (1961). *Interaction between individual interview therapy and treatment amenability in older youth authority wards* (California Board of Corrections No. 29). Sacramento: California Board of Corrections.

Beker, J., & Heyman, D. S. (1972). A critical appraisal of the California differential treatment typology of adolescent offenders. *Criminology, 10*(1), 3-59.

Egan, G. (1990). *The skilled helper: A systematic approach to effective helping* (4th ed.). Pacific Grove, CA: Brooks/Cole.

Empey, L. (1967). *Alternative to incarceration* (U.S. Department of Health, Education, and Welfare Publication No. 9001). Washington, DC: Department of Health, Education, and Welfare.

Freeman, H. E., & Weeks, H. A. (1956). Analysis of a program of treatment of delinquent boys. *American Journal of Sociology, 62,* 56-61.

Jesness, C. F., DeRisi, W. J., McCormick, P. M., & Wedge, R. F. (1972). *Youth center research project.* Sacramento, CA: American Justice Institute.

Kassebaum, G. G., Ward, D. A., & Wilmer, H. M. (1971). *Prison treatment and parole survival.* New York: Wiley.

Lester, D., & Braswell, M. (1978). *Correctional counseling.* Cincinnati, OH: Anderson.

McCord, W., & McCord, J. (1959). *Origins of crime: A new evaluation of the Cambridge-Somerville Youth Study.* New York: Columbia University Press.

Palmer, T. (1975). The youth authority's community treatment project. In E. Peoples (Ed.), *Readings in casework and counseling* (pp. 136-157). Pacific Palisades, CA: Goodyear.

Powers, E., & Witmer, H. (1951). *An experiment in the prevention of delinquency: The Cambridge-Somerville Youth Study.* New York: Columbia University Press.

Sechrest, L., White, S. O., & Brown, E. D. (Eds.). (1979). *The rehabilitation of criminal offenders: Problems and prospects.* Washington, DC: National Academy of Sciences.

Smith, A. B., & Berlin, L. (1981). *Treating the criminal offender* (2nd ed.). Engelwood Cliffs, NJ: Prentice Hall.

Weeks, H. A. (1958). *Youthful offenders at Highfields: An evaluation of the effects of short-term treatment of delinquent boys.* Ann Arbor: University of Michigan Press.

Glossary

Adolescence. The transition period of development between puberty and adulthood, which is manifested by physical and emotional change.

Agenda. Things needed to be done or plan to reach goals.

AIDS. Acquired immunodeficiency syndrome.

Antabuse. A pharmacological agent used to make the offender sick when he or she drinks alcohol.

Barnum Effect. The counselor's tendency to make diagnostic statements that are valid for most people.

Behavior Modification. A modality that centers on changing behaviors without insight, awareness, or talk.

Bell v. Wolfish. A case in which the Court held that prisoners had absolutely no expectation of privacy when they enter prisons and jails.

Bowring v. Godwin. A case in which the court held that the state cannot deny a prisoner psychological and psychiatric treatment under certain conditions.

Brainstorming. A creative technique used to develop new ideas.

Burnout. A psychoemotional state or condition characterized by a cynical, hardened, calloused, or numbed attitude toward one's work.

California Community Treatment Project. A California research project that attempted to match parole agents and delinquents according to I-level scores and concluded that delinquents could be handled in the community for less money than incarceration with about the same results.

Cambridge-Somerville Youth Study. A study focusing on how counseling impacts juveniles. It was found that those who received counseling had higher recidivism rates than those who did not.

Cause of Action. The theory of recovery used in liability lawsuits.

Closure. The end or conclusion of the therapeutic process.

Coffin v. Reichard. A landmark case that held prisoners do not lose their civil rights as a result of confinement.

Commitment. Pledging oneself to the accomplishment of goals.

Communication. The act of transmitting thoughts, feelings, opinions, and information to others.

Concreteness. The counselor's ability to get to the specifics of a problem.

Confrontation. A communication technique that brings the offender face-to-face with reality when he or she is in denial, lying, engaging in smokescreens, games, negative and/or irresponsible behavior, complacency, and/or nonaction.

Contingency Plan. A plan to fall back on in case offenders cannot accomplish their agendas.

Counseling Contract. Implicit and explicit agreements between offender and counselor to do or not do some specific thing.

Counseling Effectiveness. A phrase that refers to the counseling process producing the intended or expected result(s), namely lower recidivism rates, offender emotional well-being, satisfactory prison adjustment, and/or economical counseling programs.

Countertransference. A transferential reaction toward an offender by a counselor.

Criminal Justice Client. The person the criminal justice counselor works with; often called offender, parolee, probationer, inmate, resident, and so forth.

Criminal Justice Counseling. Counseling done in local, state, federal, and private criminal justice organizations.

Criminal Justice Counseling Roles. The myriad customary functions criminal justice counselors routinely perform.

Criminal Justice Counseling Style. The characteristic mode of expression or action that determines how a criminal justice counselor deals with offenders.

Criminal Justice Counseling Technique. Tactics used to solve particular counseling problems.

Criminal Justice Therapy. A process leading to the offender's growth, development, improved problem-solving abilities, and in some cases, personality change.

Crisis Intervention Counseling. An intense modality that focuses on immediately reducing the offender's tension brought on by stressful events.

Defense Mechanisms. According to Freud, the ways in which human beings protect their egos.

Denial. Refusal to accept, acknowledge, or face the facts of a situation.

Diagnosis. The process of determining by examination the nature and circumstances of an offender's problems.

Directive Counseling. A criminal justice counseling modality that emphasizes the counselor's skill, expertise, and professionalism in solving offenders' problems.

Displacement. The transfer of an emotion from the object about which it was originally experienced to another object.

Doctrine of Sovereign Immunity. The principle that may prevent inmates' lawsuits against prison personnel.

Doorknob Communications. Significant comments made by the offender to the counselor, usually at the end of the counseling session, when there is not enough time to deal with them.

Dry Drunk. The adoption of old alcoholic behavior patterns after the alcoholic has stopped drinking.

Dual Relationship. Any relationship between the counselor and counselee that has potential to impair the primary counseling relationship.

Due Process. Rights that protect the offender from unfair procedures.

Eclectic Counseling. A modality that uses a mixture of approaches, depending on the needs of offenders.

Empathy. Understanding what a person is feeling by placing oneself into the role of another and then being able to communicate such understanding.

Entropy. Tendency for offenders to give up what they start in counseling.

Estelle v. Gambel. A case in which the Court held that deliberate indifference by prison personnel to medical needs of prisoners violated the prisoner's Eighth Amendment rights.

Ex Parte Hull. The first major case that provided inmates with unrestricted access to federal courts.

Farewell Party Syndrome. The tendency to concentrate only on the positive aspects of counseling at the end of the counseling process.

Feedback. The counselor's response to the offender's information sharing and feelings.

First Contact. The first meeting between the criminal justice counselor and offender.

Gagnon v. Scarpelli. A case in which the Court extended *Morrissey* due process rights to probationers facing revocation.

Genuineness. The counselor qualities of nonphoniness and authenticity.

Gestalt. A modality that focuses on awareness and insight into problems.

Goal. Specific statement of what the offender needs to do to handle problems.

Group Counseling. A counseling approach that involves both the offender's peers and criminal justice counselors.

Hands-Off Doctrine. The noninterference in the business of corrections agencies and institutions.

Highfields Program. The results of this study showed that milieu therapy and guided group interaction counseling were effective in reducing the recidivism rate of boys involved in the study.

HIV Positive. A person who has tested positive for HIV.

Homeostasis. The concept of balance in family systems theory.

Hudson v. Palmer. A case in which the Court held that prisoners had absolutely no expectation of privacy when they enter prisons and jails.

Identity Crisis. A stage of human development that is characterized by asking questions such as "Who am I?"

Immediacy. Direct mutual talk that keeps the focus on the counseling relationship in present.

Infantalize. The tendency to treat offenders like infants by doing things for them that they should be doing for themselves.

Intellectualization. Making explanations for things while speaking in the third person and not owning one's own feelings. For example, "Spanking children is an appropriate form of discipline" really means "*I* believe that spanking is an appropriate form of discipline for children."

Institutionalized. Excessive dependency on institutional life.

James v. Wallace. A case in which the court held that a positive rehabilitation program is not a constitutional right, but states cannot impede the ability of inmates to attempt their own rehabilitation.

Johari Window. A model that can be used to view how the offender is supposed to change in the counseling process.

Leverage Point. A point in the counseling process at which the counselor's power and influence has a greater chance of being accepted by the offender.

Medical Model. The criminological perspective of the offender as sick and criminality a disease.

Methadone. An addictive pharmacological agent that blocks the effects of heroin.

Modality. The model or prototype a counselor adopts to work with offenders.

Moral Development. The process by which a person learns the distinction between right and wrong.

Morrisey v. Brewer. A case in which the Court set the stage for procedural due process for parolees.

MUM Effect. The tendency not to give the offender negative or confrontive feedback.

Naltrexone. A nonaddictive pharmacological agent that blocks the effects of heroin.

Neurotic Offenders. An offender whose personality is not disorganized and who maintains contact with reality, but he or she has emotional and coping problems.

Nondirective Counseling. A criminal justice counseling modality that presumes that the counselee is the only rightful person to determine his or her future.

Offender Self-Determination. The offender's right to determine his or her own future destiny.

Padgett v. Stein. A case in which the court held that there was no constitutional duty imposed on the state to rehabilitate prisoners.

PICO Project. A California Youth Authority study of older incarcerated delinquents that concluded that there was no difference between the institutional or postinstitutional adjustment of those who got counseling and therapy and those who did not.

Pink-Collar Job. A job that is femininely stereotyped and mostly done by women.

Polydrug Offender. An addicted offender who uses a number of different drugs.

Postaddiction Syndrome. Depression, anxiety, and craving for drugs after the drug addict has stopped using drugs.

Prisonization. When an offender totally accepts the values and culture of the prison as his or her own.

Privileged Communication. Communications between certain people that are considered by law as confidential.

Probing. Asking questions or making statements to draw out information about an offender's problems.

Problem Management Counseling. A modality that emphasizes the solving of offenders' problems.

Projection. Being able to see one's own qualities in others but not in oneself.

Protection of Society. The concept at the heart of the criminal justice counseling philosophy.

Pseudofamily. The way women inmates organize and relate to each other in prison that helps them cope with the pains of imprisonment.

Psychotic Offenders. Offenders who exhibit such disorganized personalities that they are divorced from reality.

Puberty. The stage of development characterized by boyhood or girlhood.

Rationalization. Making excuses and explanations for one's unacceptable behavior.

Reaction Formation. Feeling a particular emotion, but reacting with the opposite emotion.

Reaction Neutrality. Feeling strong emotion, but reacting without emotion.

Reality Counseling. A modality that focuses on the acceptance of responsibility by offenders.

Regression. Reversion to behavior patterns that were appropriate at an earlier stage of development.

Rehabilitation. The restoration of the offender from a law-violating to a law-abiding person.

Relationship Counseling. A modality that focuses on building a positive relationship between the offender and counselor.

Repression. A form of denial whereby unacceptable impulses are blocked out of one's consciousness.

Resistance. A way that offenders fight back in counseling.

Respondeat Superior. An ancient common law doctrine that means "Let the superior respond" and holds an employer responsible for the torts his or her employees commit in the course and scope of employment.

Rouse v. Cameron. A case in which the court held that in the absence of statutes providing for a right to certain kinds of treatment for offenders who are being confined, a right to treatment still exists for psychopaths, juveniles, insane, drug addicts, and/or alcoholics.

Ruffin v. Commonwealth. The case that led the courts to take a hands-off approach to the rights of offenders and to interfering in the business of corrections agencies and institutions.

Scenario. The picture the offender carries in his or her mind about his or her problems.

Self-Disclosure. Sharing of Self on the part of counselors and offenders.

Seropositive Offender. A person who has tested positive for HIV.

Set Up. A manipulation of the criminal justice counselor that an inmate deliberately plans.

Sociopathic Offenders. An offender with a personality disorder manifested by numerous characteristics such as pathological lying, not learning from experience and/or punishment, not being able to take the role of other's, and so forth.

State-Raised Convict. An offender who has spent most of his or her life in juvenile halls, training schools, reformatories, jails, and/or prisons.

Subculture of Violence. An environment that promotes the use of physical and psychological violence in solving problems.

Sublimation. Deflection of destructive or negative energies into acceptable channels.

Substantive Rights. Rights that give the offender freedom to do something or guarantee the offender freedom from certain conditions.

Supervision. The act of overseeing the actions of offenders.

Tarasoff v. University of California. A case in which the court held doctors had a duty to warn third parties of a possible future harm from their patients.

Therapeutic Community. A social living approach to the treatment of offenders that heavily relies on group dynamics, total staff involvement in counseling and treatment, and democratic decision making.

Tort Lawsuit. Civil actions against correctional employees for gross or wanton negligence or intentional wrongdoing.

Tough Love. A reality-based counseling approach that holds the addicted offender totally responsible for his or her behavior and does not allow the counselor to excuse, rescue, and be soft and gentle with the offender.

Transactional Analysis. A modality that centers on interactions between the offender and others.

Transference. A term referring to the offender projecting onto the counselor strong early childhood feelings toward authority figures, especially parents.

Treatment. The therapeutic interventions the counselor takes to prevent the offender from recidivating.

Turner v. Safley. A case in which the U.S. Supreme Court announced a four-factor reasonableness test for determining the validity of a person, regulation, and/or policy.

U.S. v. Dawson. A case in which the court held that prisoners do not enjoy the same rights of privacy as do ordinary citizens in their homes or offices.

Whitely v. Albers. A case that held shooting a prisoner is a violation of the Eighth Amendment prohibition against cruel and unusual punishment if the force was not a good faith effort to maintain or restore discipline but rather was applied maliciously and sadistically for the very purpose of causing harm.

Youth Center Research Project. A California Youth Authority study that attempted to compare the effectiveness of the behavior modification and transactional analysis modalities with youthful offenders.

Zidovudine. An antiviral drug active against HIV infection. It was formerly called AZT.

Bibliography

Abbott, J. H. (1981). *In the belly of the beast.* New York: Vintage.

Adams, S. (1961). *Interaction between individual interview therapy and treatment amenability in older youth authority wards* (California Board of Corrections No. 29). Sacramento: California Board of Corrections.

Alexander, R., Jr. (1991a). The United States Supreme Court and an inmate's right to refuse mental health treatment. *Criminal Justice Policy Review, 5*(3), 225-240.

Alexander, R., Jr. (1991b). Slamming the federal courthouse door on inmates. *Journal of Criminal Justice, 21,* 103-115.

Allen, B., & Bosta, D. (1978). *Anatomy of a set-up* (California Department of Corrections Publication). Norco: California Rehabilitation Center.

Ankersmit, E. (1976). Setting the contract in probation. *Federal Probation, 40,* 28.

Ayllon, T., & Azrin, N. H. (1968). *The token economy.* New York: Appleton-Century-Crofts.

Bartol, C. R. (1980). *Criminal behavior: A psychosocial approach.* Englewood Cliffs, NJ: Prentice Hall.

Beker, J., & Heyman, D. S. (1972, May). A critical appraisal of the California differential treatment typology of adolescent offenders. *Criminology, 10*(1).

Bennett, L. A., Rosenbaum, T. S., & McCullough, W. R. (1978). *Counseling in correctional environments.* New York: Human Sciences.

Berne, E. (1962). *Transactional analysis in psychotherapy.* New York: Grove.

Berne, E. (1964). *Games people play.* New York: Grove.

Berne, E. (1966). *Principles of group treatment.* New York: Oxford University Press.

Birdwhistell, R. L. (1970). *Kinesic and context.* Philadelphia: University of Pennsylvania Press.

Black's Law Dictionary 1396 (6th ed., 1990).

Bradshaw, J. (1988). *Bradshaw on the family.* Deerfield Beach, FL: Health Communications.

Burgess, A. (1963). *Clockwork orange.* New York: Norton.

California Evidence Code. (1993). St. Paul, MN: West.

California Government Code. (1993). St. Paul, MN: West.

California Health and Safety Code. (1993). St. Paul, MN: West.

California Penal Code. (1993). St. Paul, MN: West.

California Department of Corrections. (1990, June). *Guidelines for involuntary testing of inmates: Proposition 96 and Senate Bill 1913.* Sacramento: Office of Health Care Services.

Carkhuff, R. R., Pierce, R. M., & Cannon, J. R. (1977). *The art of helping III.* Amherst, MA: Human Resource Development Press.

Centers for Disease Control. (1989, August). *HIV/AIDS surveillance.* Washington, DC: U.S. Department of Health and Human Services.

Cleckley, H. M. (1941). *The mask of sanity.* St. Louis: Mosby.

Champion, D. J. (1990). *Probation and parole in the United States.* Columbus, OH: Merrill.

Davitz, J. R. (1964). *The communication of emotional meaning.* New York: McGraw-Hill.

del Carmen, R. V. (1991). *Civil liberties in American policing.* Englewood Cliffs, NJ: Prentice Hall.

Dixon, D. N., & Glover, J. A. (1984). *Counseling a problem-solving approach.* New York: Wiley.

Egan, G. (1990). *The skilled helper: A systematic approach to effective helping* (4th ed.). Pacific Grove, CA: Brooks/Cole.

Ellis, A. (1973). *Humanistic psychotherapy.* New York: Julian.

Ellis, A. (1977). *Reason and emotion in psychotherapy.* Secaucus, NJ: Citadel.

Empey, L. (1967). *Alternative to incarceration* (U.S. Department of Health, Education, and Welfare Publication No. 9001). Washington, DC: Department of Health, Education, and Welfare.

Finckenauer, J. A. (1982). *Scared straight and the panacea phenomenon.* Englewood Cliffs, NJ: Prentice Hall.

Fischer, C. T., & Brodsky, S. L. (1978). *Client participation in human services: The Prometheus principle.* New Brunswick, NJ: Transaction Books.

Freeman, H. E., & Weeks, H. A. (1956). Analysis of a program of treatment of delinquent boys. *American Journal of Sociology, 62,* 56-61.

Freud, S. (1946). *The ego and the mechanisms for defense.* New York: International Universities Press.

Gambril, E. (1983). *Casework: A competency-based approach.* Englewood Cliffs, NJ: Prentice Hall.

Gest, T. (1990, February 26). Why more criminals are doing time behind bars. *U.S. News and World Report*, 23-24.

Glasser, W. (1965). *Reality therapy: A new approach to psychiatry*. New York: Harper & Row.

Glick, R., & Neto. V. (1977). *National study of women's correctional programs*. Washington, DC: U.S. Government Printing Office.

Hatcher, H. A. (1978). *Correctional casework and counseling*. Englewood Cliffs, NJ: Prentice Hall.

Harris, T. (1969). *I'm OK—You're OK: A practical guide to transactional analysis*. New York: Harper & Row.

Hawkins, R., & Alpert, G. P. (1989). *American prison systems: Punishment and justice*. Englewood Cliffs, NJ: Prentice Hall.

Hendrickson, G. (1991). *Preparing inmates for their return to society—An evaluation of selected release preparation programs within a California prison and a pre-release facility*. M.S. thesis, California State University, Fresno.

HIV infection and tuberculosis in the correctional system: A discussion of professionals in correctional healthcare. (1993). Burroughs Wellcome.

Inhelder, B., & Piaget, J. (1958). *The growth of logical thinking from childhood to adolescence*. New York: Basic Books.

Ivey, A. E. (1991). *Developmental strategies for helpers: Individual, family, and network interventions*. Pacific Grove, CA: Brooks/Cole.

Jarvis, R. R., Closen, M. L., Herman, D. H. A., & Leonard, A. S. (1990). *AIDS law in a nutshell*. St. Paul, MN: West.

Jensen, G., & Jones, D. (1976). Perspectives on an inmate culture: A study of women in prison. *Social Forces 54*(3), 590-603.

Jesness, C. F. (1975, July). The impact of behavior modification and transactional analysis on institutional social climate. *Journal of Research in Crime and Delinquency, 12*(2), 79-91.

Jesness, C. F., De Risi, W. J., McCormick, P. M., & Wedge, R. F. (1972). *Youth center project*. Sacramento, CA: American Justice Institute.

Johnson, R. (1987). *Hard time: Understanding and reforming the prison*. Monterey, CA: Brooks/Cole.

Jones, M. (1968). *Beyond the therapeutic community*. New Haven, CT: Yale University Press.

Jones, M. (1973). Therapeutic community principles. In L. Irvine & T. Brelie (Eds.), *Law, psychiatry, and the mentally disturbed offender, 2* (pp. 102-110). Springfield, IL: Charles C Thomas.

Kassebaum, G. G., Ward, D. A., & Wilner, D. M. (1971). *Prison treatment and parole survival*. New York: Wiley.

Kepner, E., & Brien, L. (1975). Gestalt therapy: A behavioristic phenomenology. In E. Peoples (Ed.), *Readings in correctional casework and counseling* (pp. 317-324). Pacific Palisades, CA: Goodyear.

Kohlberg, L. (1969). Stage and sequence: The cognitive development approach to socialization. In D. A. Goslin (Ed.), *Handbook of socialization theory and research* (pp. 347-480). Chicago: Rand McNally.

Kohlberg, L. (1976). Moral stages and moralization: The cognitive developmental approach. In T. Lickona (Ed.), *Moral development and behavior: Theory, research, and social issues* (pp. 31-53). New York: Holt, Rinehart, & Winston.

Kohlberg, L. (1981). *The philosophy of moral development.* San Francisco: Harper & Row.

Kohlberg, L., & Kramer, R. (1969). Continuities and discontinuities in child and adult moral development. *Human Development, 12,* 93-120.

Kratcoski, P. C. (1981). *Correctional counseling and treatment.* Monterey, CA: Duxbury.

Lefrancois, G. R. (1972). *Psychology for teaching.* Belmont, CA: Wadsworth.

Lehman, P. E. (1987). The medical model of treatment: Historical development of an archaic standard. In E. Peoples (Ed.), *Readings in correctional casework and counseling* (pp. 47-57). Pacific Palisades, CA: Goodyear.

Lesser, D., & Braswell, M. (1987). *Correctional counseling.* Cincinnati, OH: Anderson.

Luft, J. (1970). The Johari window: A graphic model of awareness in interpersonal relations. In J. Luft, *Group processes: An introduction to group dynamics* (pp. 11-20). Palo Alto, CA: National Press Books.

Mannheim, H., & Wilkins, L. T. (1955). *Prediction methods in relation to Borstal training.* London: Her Majesty's Stationery Office.

Martinson, R. (1974). What works? Questions and answers about prison reform. *The Public Interest, 35,* 22.

Masters, R., & Roberson, C. (1991). *Inside criminology.* Englewood Cliffs, NJ: Prentice Hall.

McCarthy, B. R., & McCarthy, B. J. (1984). *Community-based corrections.* Monterey, CA: Brooks/Cole.

McCord, W., & McCord, J. (1969). *Origins of crime: A new evaluation of the Cambridge-Somerville Youth Study.* New York: Columbia University Press.

McCormick, P., & Campos, L. (1970). *Introduce yourself to transactional analysis: A TA handbook.* Stockton, CA: San Joaquin TA Study Group.

Meehl, P. E. (1956). Wanted—A good cookbook. *American Psychologist, 11*(6), 226.

Monahan, J. (1980). *Who is the client? The ethics of psychological intervention in the criminal justice system.* Washington, DC: American Psychological Association.

Neil, T. C. (1980). *Interpersonal communications for criminal justice personnel.* Boston: Allyn & Bacon.

Palmer, T. B. (1971). California's community treatment program for delinquent adolescents. *Journal of Research in Crime and Delinquency, 8*(1), 74-94.

Palmer, T. B. (1975). Marinson revisited. *Journal of Research in Crime and Delinquency, 12,* 133-152.

Pavlov, I. P. (1927). *Conditioned reflexes.* London: Oxford University Press.

Peoples, E. E. (Ed.). (1975). *Readings in correctional casework and counseling.* Pacific Palisades, CA: Goodyear.

Perls, F. S. (1969). *Gestalt therapy verbatim.* Lafayette, CA: Real People Press.

Perls, F. S., Hefferline, R. F., & Goodman, P. (1951).*Gestalt therapy.* New York: Dell.

Pollock-Byrne, J. M. (1990). *Women, prison, and crime.* Pacific Grove, CA: Brooks/Cole.

Powers, E., & Witmer, H. (1951). *An experiment in the prevention of delinquency: The Cambridge-Somerville Youth Study.* New York: Columbia University Press.

Prosser, W. L., & Keeton, W. P. (1984). *Torts* (5th ed.). St. Paul, MN: West.

Rachin, R. L. (1974, January). Reality therapy: Helping people help themselves. *Crime & Delinquency, 20,* 45-53.

Reid, S. T. (1981). *The correctional system: An introduction.* New York: Holt, Rinehart, and Winston.

Rogers, C. R. (1951). *Client-centered therapy.* Boston: Houghton-Mifflin.

Rogers, C. R. (1961). *On becoming a person: A client's view of psychology.* Boston: Houghton-Mifflin.

Rosen, S., & Tesser, A. (1970). On the reluctance to communicate undesirable information: The MUM effect. *Sociometry, 33,* 253-263.

Satir, V. (1967). *Conjoint family therapy.* Palo Alto, CA: Science & Behavior.

Schwartz, W. (1971). On the use of groups in social work practice. In W. Schwartz & S. Zalba (Eds.), *The practice of group work* (pp. 3-24). New York: Columbia University Press.

Sechrest, L., White, S. O., & Brown, E. D. (Eds.). (1979). *The rehabilitation of criminal offenders: Problems and prospects.* Washington, DC: National Academy of Sciences.

Shah, S. A. (1969). Privileged communications. *Professional Psychology, 1,* 56-69.

Shah, S. A. (1977, February). Tarasoff and its implications: A broader perspective. *APA Monitor, 8*(2), 2.

Shore, M. F. (1975). Psychological theories of the causes of antisocial behavior. In E. E. Peoples (Ed.), *Correctional casework and counseling* (pp. 3-18). Pacific Palisades, CA: Goodyear

Shulman, L. (1979). *The skills of helping individuals and groups.* Itasca, IL: Peacock.

Siegel, M. (1976). Confidentiality. *The Clinical Psychologist, 30,* 1-23.

Simkin, J. S., & Yontef, G. M. (1984). Gestalt therapy. In R. J. Corsini (Ed.), *Current psychotherapies* (pp. 279-319). Ithasca, IL: F. E. Peacock.

Skinner, B. F. (1971). *Beyond freedom and dignity.* New York: Knopf.

Slovenko, R. (1973). *Psychiatry and law.* Boston: Little, Brown.

Small, J. (1989). *Becoming naturally therapeutic: A return to the true essence of helping.* New York: Bantam.

Smith, A. B., & Berlin, L. (1981). *Treating the criminal offender* (2nd ed.). Englewood Cliffs, NJ: Prentice Hall.

Smith, L. L. (1978). A review of crisis intervention theory. *Social Casework,* *59,* 396-405.

Steiner, C. (1974). *Scripts people live.* New York: Grove.

Sullivan, H. S. (1953). The meaning of the developmental approach. In H. S. Perry & M. L. Gawel (Eds.), *The interpersonal theory of psychiatry* (pp. 3-12). New York: Norton.

Sutherland, E. H., & Cressey, D. R. (1974). *Criminology* (9th ed.). Philadelphia: Lippincott.

Taylor, L. (1984). *Born to crime.* Westport, CT: Greenwood.

Thorne, G. L., Tharp, R. G., & Wetzel, R. J. (1967, June). Behavior modification techniques: New tools for probation officers. *Federal Probation,* 21-26.

Travis, S. (1990, September). Inmate population explosion: At highest level; no end in sight. *Correction News,* 1.

Trester, H. B. (1981). *Supervision of the offender.* Englewood Cliffs, NJ: Prentice Hall.

Tyler, L. E. (1969). *The work of the counselor* (3rd ed.). New York: Appleton-Century-Crofts.

United States Code Annotated Title 42 §§ 1983, 1988, 1997-1997j and Title 28 §§ 1346, 1402, 2401, 2402, 2411, 2412, 2617-2680.

U.S. Department of Health, Education, and Welfare. (1978). *Third Special Report to the U.S. Congress on Alcohol and Health.* Washington, DC: U.S. Government Printing Office.

Vinson, J. (1989, September-October). Reflections on dual relationships. *The California Therapist, 1*(2), 15-17.

Walsh, A. (1988). *Understanding, assessing, and counseling the criminal justice client.* Pacific Grove, CA: Brooks/Cole.

Weeks, H. A. (1958). *Youthful offenders at Highfields: An evaluation of the effects of short-term treatment of delinquent boys.* Ann Arbor: University of Michigan Press.

Wicks, R. J. (1974). *Correctional psychology.* San Francisco: Canfield.

Wicks, R. J. (1975). Reality therapy. In E. E. Peoples (Ed.), *Readings in correctional counseling and casework* (pp. 358-364). Pacific Palisades, CA: Goodyear.

Wicks, R. J. (1977). *Counseling strategies and intervention techniques for the human services.* Philadelphia: Lippincott.

Wolfgang, M. E., & Ferracuti, F. (1978). The subculture of violence. In L. D. Savitz & N. Johnson (Eds.), *Crime in society* (pp. 151-162). New York: Wiley.

Wood, G. J., Marks, R., & Dilley, J. W. (1990). *AIDS law for mental health professionals: A handbook for judicious practice.* Berkeley, CA: University of San Francisco.

Cases Cited

Alberti v. Sheriff of Harris Co., Tex., 406 F. Supp. 649 (S.D. Tex. 1975).
Bell v. Wolfish, 441 U.S. 520 (1979).
Bowring v. Godwin, 551 F.2d 44, 47, 48 (5th Cir. 1977).
Coffin v. Reichard, 143 F.2d 443 (6th Cir. 1944).
Estelle v. Gamble, 429 U.S. 97 (1976).
Ex parte Hull, 312 U.S. 546 (1941).
Fare v. Michael C., 442 U.S. 707 (1979).
Gagnon v. Scarpelli, 411 U.S. 778 (1973).
Gilliam v. Martin, 589 F. Supp. 680 (W.D. Okla. 1984).
Holt v. Sarver, 309 F. Supp. 362 (E.D. Ark. 1970, aff'd 442 F.2d 304, 8th.
    Cir. 1971).
Hudson v. McMillian, 503 U.S. (1992).
Hudson v. Palmer, 468 U.S. 517 (1984).
James v. Wallace, 406 F. Supp. 318 (M.D. Ala. 1976).
Leavitt v. City of Morris, 117 N.W. 393, 395 (S.Ct. Minn. 1908).
Long v. Powell, 388 F. Supp. 422 (N.D. Ga. 1975), jud. va. 423 U.S. 808
    (1975).
Morales v. Turman, 364 F. Supp. 166, 175 (E.D. Tex. 1973).
Morrissey v. Brewer, 408 U.S. 471 (1972).
Padgett v. Stein, 406 F. Supp. 287 (M.D. Pa. 1976).
Procunier v. Martinez, 416 U.S. 396 (1974).
Rouse v. Cameron, 373 F.2d 451 (D.C. Cir. 1966).
Ruffin v. Commonwealth, 62 Va. (21 Gratt.) 790 (1871).
Rutherford v. Hutto, 377 F. Supp. 268 (E.D. Ark. 1974).
Semler v. Psychiatric Institute of Washington, D.C., 538 F.2d 121 (4th Cir.
    1976).

Smith v. Follette, 445 F.2d 955 (2d Cir. 1971).

Tarasoff v. Regents of the University of California, 17 C.3d 425, 131 (Calif. Rptr. 14, 551 P.2d 334 1976).

Taylor v. Sterrett, 344 F. Supp. 411 (N.D. Tex. 1972).

Turner v. Safley, 482 U.S. 78 (1987).

U.S. v. Dawson, 516 F.2d 796 (9th Cir. 1975).

Washington v. Harper, 494 U.S. 210 (1990).

Welsch v. Likins, 373 F. Supp. 487 (D. Minn. 1974).

Whitely v. Albers, 475 U.S. 312 (1986).

Wilson v. Kelley, 294 F. Supp. 1005, 1012-1013 (N.D. Ga. 1968, aff'd per curiam 393 U.S. 266 1969).

Wolff v. McDonnell, 418 U.S. 539 (1974).

Index

About the Authors

Ruth E. Masters, Professor of Criminology at California State University, has been teaching criminal justice counseling courses since 1970. In addition, she has had hands-on, practical counseling experience in both adults and juvenile criminal justice systems. She has worked as a parole agent for the California Department of Corrections and the California Youth Authority. Her research can be described as a unique blending of theoretical and practical and includes work in both corrections and law enforcement. She is a member of American Society of Criminology; Academy of Criminal Justice Sciences; Western Society of Criminology; Women's Criminal Justice Association; California Probation, Parole, and Correctional Association; and California State Juvenile Officers' Association. She received her doctorate in higher education from the University of Southern California, her master's degree in criminology from California State University at Fresno, and her bachelor's degree in sociology from the University of California at Berkeley.

Robert F. Perez, Professor of Criminology at California State University at Fresno, has taught law-related courses for 13 years. He is an attorney who was admitted to practice law in California in 1972. He has extensive experience in civil and criminal litigation. He is also admitted to practice law in the Federal District Court for the Eastern

District of California as well as the U.S. Court of Appeals for the Ninth Circuit. He received his law degree from the University of the Pacific—McGeorge School of Law and his bachelor's degree in social sciences from California State University at Chico.

Lester Pincu has been employed as a Professor of Criminology at California State University at Fresno since 1970. He also has experience in the criminal justice system as a probation officer for Contra Costa County in California. He received his bachelor's degree in psychology from Tufts University and his master's degree in counseling psychology and his doctorate in criminology from the University of California at Berkeley. He is a state of California licensed Marriage, Family, and Child Counselor. He has published and has had extensive experience in counseling and the training of practitioners, students, and volunteers in the area of HIV infection and AIDS.